Ready or not, here comes the future. Richard Carlson and Bruce Goldman take aim at a shifting target—the world, and America's place within it—over the next thirty years: the reunification of Europe into a powerhouse whose boundaries exceed even those of the Roman Empire. Simmering regional conflicts fed by fire sales of Cold War weaponry. Within the United States, radically realigned political coalitions. A torrent of immigrants. Scientific advances that will give us undreamed-of power over our environment, our bodies, and even our heredity. Sprawl. The rise of environmentalism as a quasi-religion. From these disparate trends, *2020 Visions* distills a coherent world view.

The Portable Stanford Book Series

Published by the
Stanford Alumni Association

Long View of a Changing World

RICHARD CARLSON and BRUCE GOLDMAN

THE PORTABLE STANFORD is a book series sponsored by the Stanford Alumni Association. The series is designed to bring the widest possible sampling of Stanford's intellectual resources into the homes of alumni. It includes books based on current research as well as books that deal with philosophical issues, which by their nature reflect to a greater degree the personal views of their authors.

THE PORTABLE STANFORD BOOK SERIES
Stanford Alumni Association
Bowman Alumni House
Stanford, California 94305-4005

Library of Congress Catalog Card
Number: 90-71563
ISBN: 0-916318-44-3

10 9 8 7 6 5 4 3 2 1

To Chris and Allegra, who will build this future, Pat, who will share it with me, and my parents, who kept the flame of freedom, hope, and love alive to pass along to the next generation.

R.C.

To Lois, who put up with my obsession for a whole year, and little Eva, who decided three days was quite enough.

B.G.

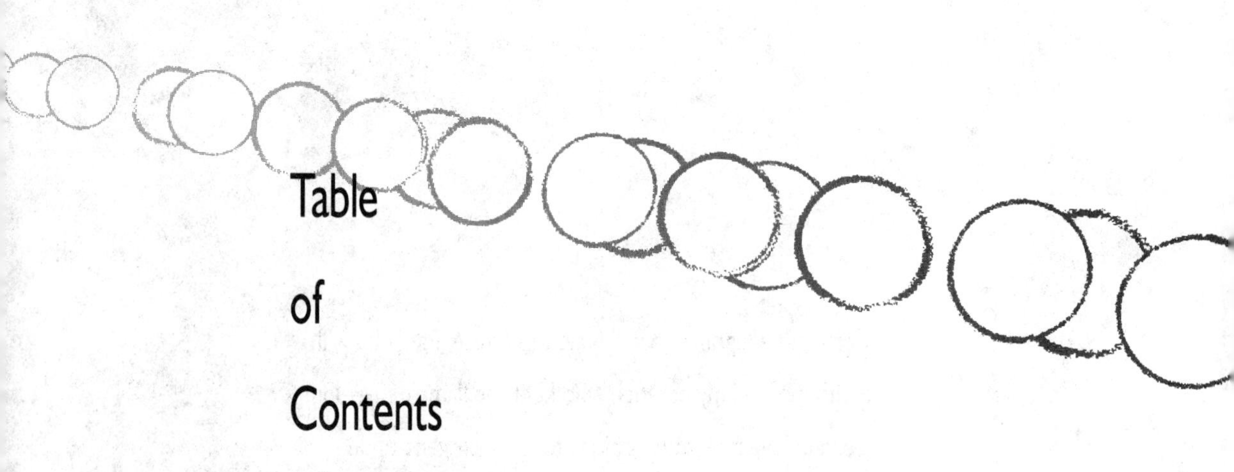

Table of Contents

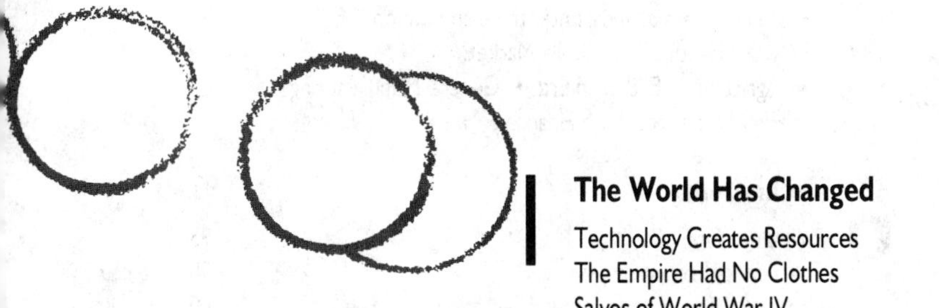

CHAPTER

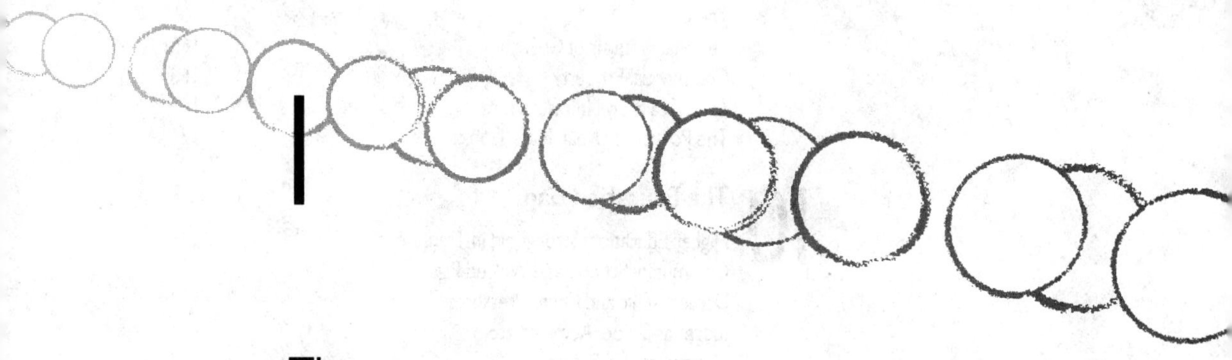

1

The World Has Changed

Ah, that golden decade of futuristic speculation, the 1950s. As the dust cleared from World War II, the enemy cities in ruins, America dreamed about the future. Fantasies of space travel reached an all-time peak. Automobiles, mocking Darwin, grew tail fins and evolved into dinosaurs. In 1954 Atomic Energy Commission chairman Lewis L. Strauss bragged that within a generation nuclear energy would make electrical energy "too cheap to meter." At drugstore cosmetic counters, you could even pick up a brand of lipstick called "Futurama."

If the picture looked rosy here at home, a darker image glowered at us from overseas: The Cold War was on. Totalitarianism, vanquished in Germany and its hostage nations, still controlled the vast Soviet empire—or, to the American ear, simply "the Russians." In 1949 China, a nation with a third of the world's people, became "Red China"; within a few years, our soldiers and theirs were facing off in a bloody conflict in Korea. Hot War was very much a live option.

Popular culture duly recorded the American angst. In science-fiction movies with names like *Invasion of the Body Snatchers,* aliens turned free Americans into mindless robots. Flash Gordon's antagonist, "Ming the Merciless," bore facial features and an accent suggesting the common American stereotype of an Asiatic warlord.

Small school children learned to sing a sweet little ditty called "Duck and Cover" as they dived under their wooden desks to practice for the nuclear attack that could come at any time, on any fine day.

While the kids were ducking and covering, some of their hard-working parents flirted with communism; others experienced a nagging suspicion that, communism or no communism, total regimentation was the wave of the future. For collectivism seemed to be wrapping its tentacles around the post-war American body politic. Those who remember the 1950s and early 1960s also remember the "Man in the Gray Flannel Suit," "the organization man," the proclamation that "what's good for General Motors is good for the U.S.A." Bigger was better. Computers would keep track of everything, the argument went, and we were all going to be working for IBM or General Motors; so why not just let the government, which at least might be fairer and—who knows—possibly even more efficient, run the whole show?

Economist-philosopher Karl Marx's most powerful idea was that the economic and social organization of a nation is fundamentally driven by its technology. When Marx looked around in 19th-century England he saw dark, Satanic mills; hosts of disciplined laborers executing routine, repetitive functions on cue; and a financial structure that seemed unable to maintain production.

Capitalism, Marx claimed, could not handle the political impact of its own new industrial technology, that of mass production; for purely financial reasons, productive forces were tied down rather than released by the capitalist economy. Collective rather than private ownership of the means of production would liberate these forces, he predicted. Communism would provide the new governmental and cultural superstructure to better fit modern production technology. Until then, surplus productivity would periodically be squandered in orgies of war among competing capitalist entities.

To an extent, Marx was right: Technology did drive economic and political change. But, while the peak of the old technology was marked by big heavy industry, massive computers, and a regimented work force, since the 1970s technology has been driving us down a new road Marx couldn't have foreseen.

The triumph of this new technology is that nearly all the key resources of the modern world are embodied in free, educated people—not hidden in the ground. Possessing resource-rich colonies like those of the 16th to 19th centuries is no longer necessary, and can be counterproductive. The great sea-based empires of Spain, Britain, the Netherlands, and France have long since dissolved. The land-based Soviet Union, the largest and last-surviving empire in the world, is disintegrating. Tiny, independent countries, swallowed up by expansionist regimes, are being spit out whole. In these countries, the Western model of capitalism, democracy, and civil rights has gained critical mass.

Technology Creates Resources

Behind the impulse to wage war and expand empires there has always lurked, beyond mere ideology or religion, a fear that there simply aren't enough resources to go around. The advanced countries of Europe fought repeatedly over their own border demarcations and attempted to stake out sources of raw materials and cheap labor in distant lands to the east, west, and south. Having expanded into the New World, Asia, and Africa, Europe finally ran out of new lands to colonize and literally tore itself apart in the 20th century. America pitched in. As Marx had predicted, industrial countries beat their excess productive capacity into ever-more-destructive weapons and turned on one another.

What might be termed the Great 2000-Year European Civil War is now over, having yielded to the longest period of European peace in history. Advanced countries no longer need to carve out new cheap-resource niches or maintain huge occupying armies in conquered territories. The winds of technological change are drying up the chief incentives for conquest—the need for land, natural resources, and cheap labor. The Persian Gulf has the last remaining resource concentration big enough to fight over.

The "energy crisis" of the 1970s reflected our concern about resource scarcity—the fear that we would all "freeze in the dark." (Texans proposed this fate be reserved for Yankees.) This fear colored the debate about how, and even whether, worldwide economic development ought to proceed. The concern was misplaced. Technology creates resources. On a worldwide basis, there is only so much oil, copper, or gold in the earth; but as technology improves, deposits get easier to find and exploitation of lower-grade, hard-to-get-at resources becomes possible. Some of America's currently more-productive gold-mining enterprises profit handsomely by processing the tailing piles of 19th-century gold mines—the stuff they used to throw away. The amount of oil hidden near closed U.S. wells exceeds this country's total known reserves. The same applies to all physical resources.

These increases in accessibility have been dwarfed by increased efficiencies in use of materials. Copper-intensive telephone lines transmitting 64,000 bits of information per second are replaced by fiber-optic cables carrying close to a trillion bits per second. Automobiles exhibit better fuel economy and use less steel. The entire U.S. economy has expanded by nearly 50 percent since 1978 with virtually no increase in energy use.

The modern economy derives an increasing proportion of its wealth from the production and consumption of information, which is not a scarce resource; it can be duplicated and transported with little use of physical resources. Information technology—cheaper, better, and less resource-intensive every day—enhances the efficiency with which material resources are used.

Indeed, the environmentalist position of the 1970s that "there's not enough" has been rewritten to read "there's too much; we're going to grow too fast, poison ourselves, and die—not of starvation, but of worldwide gluttony."

Call it Eco-Marxism, if you will. Central-government control of the economy, which Marx said was necessary to make things more productive, is now being called upon to *limit* production. Ozone depletion, the greenhouse effect, toxics, drowning in garbage—while these are all issues well worth talking about, they're the polar opposites of "we'll freeze in the dark."

The Empire Had No Clothes

A modern nation needs very few of Thomas Jefferson's independent "yeoman farmers," but it does require large enterprises that give substantial independence to employees, as well as many small, adaptable businesses to serve them.

If you try to run a modern large enterprise as an empire, making all your decisions from above, you will surely fail. By the time a question gets to the top, nobody will quite understand it; and by the time the answer comes down, it will usually be both too late and wrong.

The small personal computer is the Protestant reformation of technology; it allows the individual to approach the gods of technology directly, rather than kneeling to priestly intermediaries of the data processing fraternity. These high priests can no longer make you wait and charge you a hundred times more than you've paid for your IBM PC—or, more to the point, your Asian-made clone.

If the tools of the modern economy breed individual economic initiative, they also make revolt against authority much easier. You cannot run a modern economy with an ignorant work force. You cannot run it without fax machines, personal computers, and direct-access long-distance telephone systems. You can't run an information-intensive economy if you keep your copying machines under lock and key.

The Soviets tried to keep information technology under lock and key, and they fell behind. Their problems took a while to become apparent, but information is more liquid than solid; it "leaks." With the stimulus of international travel and global media coverage, it has become clear to even the most glassy-eyed deputy commissar that the Soviet Union is failing economically. Gorbachev's genius was to realize this before collapse became irreversible.

A prominent Soviet economist, Viktor Belkin, now says that Soviet national output is less than 30 percent of America's—far less than CIA estimates. According to dissident Ylena Bonner—who with her late husband, physicist and human-rights activist Andrei Sakharov, rocketed from pariah to hero status in their homeland before his death—over 80 percent of the country's hospitals in rural areas (where 40 percent of the people live) have no running water. Soviet life expectancy is declining. The average individual has just over six square yards of housing space.

The Soviet people, too, know there is a richer world outside, and even Mikhail Gorbachev is well aware that the Soviet economy must decentralize or it will collapse. But this is politically subversive. If people can use fax machines for business, they can use them for politics, and they will. They have been doing just that. Popular movements, both in Eastern Europe and the Soviet Union itself, have swept opposition politicians into power with a speed that would have been unthinkable in 1985.

The Warsaw Pact, formed in 1955 to counter the NATO "threat," is dead as a military force. Indeed, the Soviet Union's former satellites in Eastern Europe are rushing to hook up with their rich NATO cousins and, ultimately, to merge with them into a single European security system. Inside the Soviet Union itself, powerful centrifugal forces may catalyze a breakup into politically independent republics allied in a loose economic confederation.

Nor do the Soviets have any use for Eastern European satellites. Vast expanses of territory no longer confer the advantage they once did. Buffer states afford little protection against intercontinental ballistic missiles. Besides, the satellites were economic losers. Ideas are the key capital goods in a modern, information-based economy, and sullen slaves produce few breakthroughs in the research labs. Ideas are products of educated, motivated people.

Each conquered nation of semislaves becomes just another several million mouths to feed. The Soviets physically dominated Eastern Europe; what good did it do them? What good will it do China to move the tanks in and conquer Hong Kong? The effective wealth of Hong Kong, its citizens, will either go—and they are streaming to North America right now—or stay there and stop producing. China's own intellectuals are the government's chief opponents. What good would it do to conquer Silicon Valley militarily? The success stories of recent years are small countries with few physical resources, but with free, motivated, literate populations; these include Switzerland, South Korea, Sweden, Hong Kong, Taiwan, and Singapore.

The Marxist-Leninist version of communism has been one of the world's great killer religions, whose converts thought noble ends justified any means, no matter how ruthless. Wrapped in this religious banner, Stalin and his fanatical followers killed more civilians than even Hitler. Now, as a religion, Marxist-Leninism—once an ideology with vast numbers of committed followers throughout the world—is dead. An autopsy of the patient reveals severe contamination by an overdose of information—from the West and elsewhere.

Television has sped the flow of news from West to East. In a historic example of how older political leaders make technological blunders, the East Germans adopted the same television technology and standards the West Germans were using—a fatal error. The grass on the west side of the Wall—or was it dollar bills?—was too green to be denied.

The globe is shrinking before our very eyes. The spasms of Marxism's death agony have been witnessed by the eyes of the whole world: in Beijing's Tiananmen Square, where students hoisted their own Statue of Freedom before the television cameras; in Nicaragua, where election results were monitored worldwide; and finally in Berlin, where the wall dividing Marx's native land was finally torn down.

Salvos of World War IV

World War III, the Cold War, is over; but a new conflict, World War IV, has already started. The end of Marxism's religious fervor and the collapse of the Soviet empire bring more than just a return to old-fashioned national conflicts: The nature of the conflict among developed nations has fundamentally changed. War between highly developed countries is technically obsolete. The missiles aren't going to fly—at least not between Europe, the Soviet Union, Japan, and the United States—and the tanks aren't going to roll.

War itself will not disappear. Defenses against the regional fanatic-of-the-year (one year, Libya; another year, Iraq) will still be required. Regional conflicts supported by the superpowers will decline. The Soviets are withdrawing financial support from Cuba, Syria, Nicaragua, Ethiopia, and Angola, while the former Soviet satellites eliminate safe havens for international terrorists. However, new regional conflicts will intensify, and both the Soviets and the U.S. may experience more problems with terrorism. If anything, as the United States and the Soviet Union begin to see eye-to-eye in international affairs, the two countries may be forced to become *more* active in policing the globe.

Neither will nuclear weapons vanish. The Soviets will not give up their nuclear strength—which, given their deteriorating economy, is their only remaining claim to superpower status; and China will still be an uncomfortable neighbor. The proliferation of regional nuclear powers will become the world's great danger. Both the U.S. and the Soviets may see an increasing appeal and feasibility in Star Wars–type missile defenses against these new nuclear minipowers.

The chief conflict of the next decade, World War IV, is economic in nature—and we're losing. While we've been putting our dollars into fighting World War III, the Germans and the Japanese have been putting their efforts into winning World War IV, and they've done very well. They successfully fought World War III to almost the last American dollar and Russian ruble. For forty years, the U.S. poured 6–10 percent of its annual output down the defense rathole, while Germany put less than half that much into defense, and put the difference into building the world's most productive factories.

The contest of coming decades will be among competing variants of capitalistic systems. Both Europe—where, over the past few centuries, both the capitalist and Marxist economic models were generated—

and Japan offer alternative and apparently superior candidates for tomorrow.

A commonly held conceit in the United States during the 1970s and early 1980s was that the U.S., by virtue of inventing new technologies, would be the first to commercialize them and would always maintain its technological edge. This hope has been proven false. Communication is so swift that technology moves like wildfire, and we are often slower than others to put our own inventions to use. The videotape recorder was an American invention, but today the market is totally dominated by the Japanese. As the pace of technological development accelerates, no one will be a clear leader; everybody, if they are smart, will learn from their neighbor.

Large-scale, multinational enterprises spread technological advances across national borders. Countries willing to participate in the global economy—to let goods, capital, technology, people, and ideas flow across their borders—share in the worldwide advance in knowledge and prosperity. Ironically, while it is the best hope for improving a national economy, participation in the globalization undermines the very sovereignty of nations. Thus Italian, Japanese, and American giants battle for markets in Spain and Britain; but the aircraft, articles of clothing, and television sets they're selling are assembled with parts from all over the world.

The healthier industrial economies of Europe, Asia, and North America are clustering into regional affinity groups. The impending fusion of long-feuding societies into a cooperative confederation is a harbinger of peace and prosperity in the next century. Military conflict is being supplanted by economic cooperation. Empires are being replaced by trading blocs.

Shifting Gears

World War III was an expensive victory for the U.S. For most of the past fifty years, many of the greatest minds in the nation were preoccupied with how to stop communism without vaporizing the world. This was a grand and noble effort; but, like the Soviets, we were so preoccupied with this external conflict that we allowed internal problems to intensify. We ended World War II with the world's best economic infrastructure, the strongest financial system, the most flexible political system, the best educational system, the best health-care system, and the most unified society. We are no longer leaders in any of these categories.

How can it be that within a few years, Japan—a land-poor, natural-resource-deprived nation whose industrial capacity was obliterated in World War II—will surpass the United States in total output of electronic goods, once a virtual American monopoly? How can tiny Taiwan's foreign-exchange reserves dwarf our own?

While the Japanese, Koreans, Taiwanese, and Germans were investing in better factories, civilian technical research, efficient health-care systems, and outstanding educational systems, we Americans were designing better weapons and building lavish houses and empty offices on borrowed money. It should be no surprise that the Japanese and Europeans will soon be richer than we are.

Now even our outstanding asset, our technical leadership, is up for grabs. Silicon Valley *can* be conquered economically—and at a relatively modest cost. Our leading industrial companies, desperate for money, are forced to sell their breakthroughs to Japan and Europe because our brilliant financial community lost over a trillion dollars *of our money* speculating in real estate, Brazilian loans, and junk bonds. The Japanese have been especially shrewd at learning from everyone in the world how to improve their technology. That's not stealing—it's good management.

We can't even manage to track the entries in our federal checkbook, let alone balance it. Our bank and savings-and-loan fiasco is by far the largest financial scandal in *world* history. Instead of being used for anything productive, half a trillion dollars of capital were vaporized through a deft combination of old-fashioned incompetence, adroit modern robber barons, corrupt officials, and well-intended but flawed economic policies—about which experts had warned us for decades.

America can't keep making this kind of mistake. The S&L crisis has produced no bloodshed, no limping veterans. But in World War IV, a financial war, it's the equivalent of losing Midway and Pearl Harbor.

The next several decades will see a dramatic shifting of gears within the United States. We must serve a rapidly aging and shifting population, restructure our economy, revive our failing educational system, radically reform a disastrous health-care system, reunify an increasingly divided society, and form our own hemispheric economic alliance.

These are daunting challenges, but far less so than those we have already surmounted. The long twilight struggle against a seemingly invincible foe called Communism is over. The nightmare threat of nuclear holocaust is over. World War IV's battles will be bulletless; no one has to die. America still retains a vital capacity for infinite renewal.

CHAPTER

2

The Birth of a Global Economy

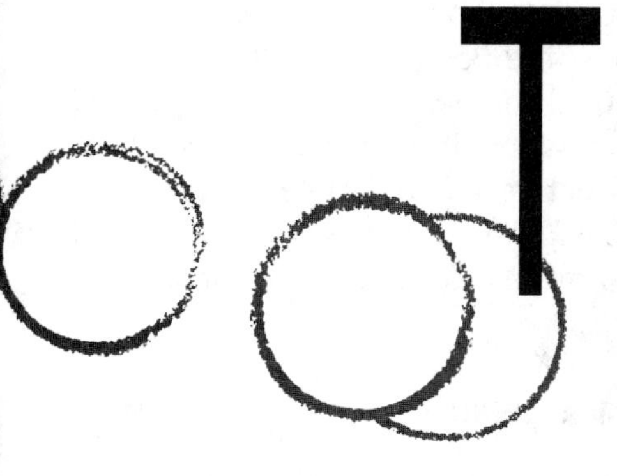

Treasury secretaries have to watch what they say on TV these days. On Sunday, October 18, 1987, James Baker appeared on "Meet the Press." The Secretary was angry about the West German central bank's tight-credit stance, which was having an undesired, albeit inevitable, effect on U.S. policy. Rising German interest rates were tempting investors to forsake their dollar-denominated interest-bearing accounts, bail out of dollars, and buy West German marks to put to work earning appetizingly high German interest.

Failure to mimic the German interest rate increases would thus put selling pressure on the dollar, which had already been falling against other major world currencies for more than two years. Yet U.S. rates were trending upward as it was; continuing to match the German rate increases might push the U.S. economy into a slump—just about in time for the 1988 elections.

So Baker repeated a threat made a couple of days earlier at a White House news briefing: If the West Germans didn't ease up, the United States would simply abandon its support of a worldwide attempt to maintain stable currency-exchange rates and reduce its interest rates unilaterally—even if that meant letting the dollar plunge.

In retrospect, he probably should have known better. While a cheap dollar might help U.S. manufacturers sell their wares overseas, it is anathema to U.S. financial industries, whose chief assets have dollar signs in front of them. Only two days earlier the stock market, already skittish, had tumbled in reaction to the White House hint of abandoning the dollar. But Baker's Sunday comments triggered an avalanche. On Monday, October 19, the financial markets of the world came unhinged. It started with a morning run on the dollar in Tokyo. By the end of the day, a vicious cycle of computerized sell orders had swamped the New York Stock Exchange, causing the steepest one-day drop ever—stocks lost over one-fifth of their value, or some $500 billion. That script was followed faithfully all over the world the next day.

Such are the skirmishes of World War IV, a war without bullets or borders—at least not the kind that protect a nation from the depredations of international commerce. The interweaving of the world's markets subjects weak national economies to the rule of the strongest, even as it blurs national boundaries.

Tiger by the Tail: The Technological Imperative

The next several decades will be a time of change and great danger.

- The pace of technical innovation and commercialization is accelerating throughout the world.
- The introduction of modern technology—especially disease-prevention techniques and telecommunication—destabilizes primitive societies by fostering both a demographic explosion and an unstoppable tide of rising expectations.
- Once this occurs, nations can restabilize only by adhering to a universal set of economic, political, and social rules. To ignore these is to court a process of economic, political, social, and environmental collapse from which there are few escapes.

Most of the contemporary and future history of the world through 2020 can be written in terms of the inexorable process of adaptation to the technological imperative. The 1984 initiative to decentralize the Chinese economy and the 1989 collapse of the Soviet empire were only two steps in this process. The nations of the world lie on a continuum. Which ones will integrate smoothly into the global system? Which will delay so long that they collapse? The scorecard reads as follows:

- *Taking the lead*—the United States, Canada, Western Europe, New Zealand, Australia, and Japan.

- *Rapidly modernizing*—Korea, Taiwan, Thailand, Singapore, Malaysia, Hong Kong, Portugal, Eastern Europe, Turkey, Israel, Chile, Mexico, and Costa Rica.
- *Slowly modernizing but still at risk*—the Soviet Union, most of Latin America, North Africa, South Africa, Indonesia, North Korea, Vietnam, and the Middle East.
- *At great risk*—Central Africa, China, the Philippines, Nepal, India, Pakistan, and Bangladesh.
- *In collapse*—Haiti, Uganda, and Ethiopia.
- *Still primitive*—New Guinea, Melanesia, Tibet, Mongolia, Afghanistan, and the Sudan.

The principal force of the technological imperative is demographic. Traditional societies, using primitive technologies, have high infant-death rates. Once infant-death rates decline, population grows so dramatically that primitive technologies cannot support the higher population. These societies must modernize or die.

Modern technology, with its vastly greater efficiency, eventually makes it possible to support a much larger population at much higher standards of living. Economic well-being does not depend on physical resources (if it did, Saudi Arabia, Brazil, and the Soviet Union would be the wealthiest nations in the world), but on how efficiently those resources are used. Taiwan, for example, has the second-highest population density of any major nation, but it also has the second-highest standard of living in Asia. Norway, nearly devoid of level land, has the highest per capita real gross national product in Europe.

Europe was lucky. The economic and political structures that culminate in long-run stability actually preceded modern technology there, evolving alongside technology over the centuries. The curse of colonialism is that primitive nations acquired the most destabilizing products of modern technology—guns, television, antibiotics, and vaccines—far in advance of economic modernization, the rule of law, stable families, or national identity.

The Rules of the Game

Using modern technology effectively requires following some very specific economic, social, and political rules.

- The first rule: political stability. That means orderly changes of leadership. It also means no civil war. The state, not mobs or private armies, must have a monopoly of physical force.
- The second rule: a predictable and simple legal system that protects both individual freedom and property. Laws must be known and enforced by an efficient bureaucracy, but also must not become a bureaucratic nightmare.
- Third: a decentralized, open, at least significantly capitalist economy. All attempts at independent isolationist development have failed. An economy must be open to international flows of trade, capital, people, and technology.
- Fourth: universal education, at least through grade school, with substantial numbers receiving high-school and college educations that emphasize technological training.
- The final rule: essential equality of women, including equal educational and economic rights, and laws and social customs protecting a stable family structure. That's how population explosions are stopped, and social stability created.

The Knitting Needles of Globalization

TRADE

Even in ancient times, trade yoked lands as distant from one another as Egypt and China. But in recent years finance, technology, and the media have amplified those linkages a millionfold. International trade has always been the lifeblood of small countries. Only a continental nation such as the U.S. or the Soviet Union could have treated trade as unimportant. Indeed, both countries are now paying the price for having done just that. The trader nations of Western Europe and Southeast Asia are far ahead of the pack. Most nations face a simple choice: trade or starve. Global specialization adds to efficiency. Nobody can do everything. Chileans and Zambians cannot eat copper; Denmark cannot live on cheese alone.

Many modern technologies—automobile production is a good example—require large scales of production. For European-sized nations, and even the United States, this has meant creating national monopolies or oligopolies, with all the problems that come with them. Although the most obvious problem of monopoly or oligopoly power is that of price (monopolies charge too much; wouldn't you?), even bigger problems are the reduced incentive to innovation and poor product quality.

The pressures of international competition, however, have been a superb antidote to the recalcitrance of such giants as General Motors and Ford, who have greatly improved their products lately. The more a country opens its national borders to global competition, the more it benefits domestic consumers and the more pressure it places on domestic producers. Hong Kong, a totally open economy, represents the extreme of benefiting consumers. Among larger nations, the United States sits near that extreme; Japan sits at the other end, as the most protectionist. Albania, North Korea, and Burma have totally cut themselves off from the world economy; their citizens will be hard-pressed to avoid starvation, much less prosper, until they engage in international trade.

The most valuable cargo of all is a human being. In this age, when information and expertise are prized commodities, world travel is mushrooming; and, with it, the acceleration of the mixing and merger of cultures. The $2-trillion-per-year travel and tourism industry now provides more jobs—100 million worldwide, according to American Express CEO James D. Robinson III—than any other.[1]

FINANCE

As early as the Middle Ages, national policy was frequently dictated by bankers. One reason for Henry VIII's break from the Catholic Church was to capture the Church's English property in order to pay off England's big debt to the Northern Italian banker-princes, the Medicis. Bankers catalyzed the key link in the British Empire of the 19th century: Around 1870, when the French company that built the Suez Canal was near bankruptcy, the English government was anxious to assume control of the canal. The British prime minister, desperate for cash, appealed to the Rothschilds during a card game, whereupon his card partners agreed to finance the canal.

The flow of international capital began during the Roman Empire, dwindled in the Dark Ages, started to revive around the 14th century, and has assumed flood proportions in this century. Today's international financial transactions dwarf the volume of goods and services;

in dollar value, more capital crosses national borders in two weeks' time than internationally traded goods do in an entire year.

Finance is one of the world's great equalizers. Within thirty years, this equilibration process will be largely complete among those nations choosing to play by international rules. A well-run financial system preferentially invests money in poor countries, which have the largest potential for the expansion of output and, therefore, the largest potential for profits. Foreign investment brings both money and technology to underdeveloped countries. This is exactly what happened in the great period of global expansion during the 19th century; capital moved out of the earliest-industrializing countries (especially England, but also Germany) and financed expansion worldwide, with permanent success in the United States and Japan—but, unfortunately, only temporary success in Latin America, which is today relatively worse off. Japan and newcomers such as Taiwan and South Korea are now net capital exporters, as is Europe.

The alternative to foreign investment is to desperately attempt to get along without international capital and the technology that accompanies it. This path was chosen by the Soviet Union under Stalin. In the short run, millions starved; in the long run, the Soviet Union ended up with inferior technologies. That country, having reached a crisis point, is now subordinating its historic expansionist drive to the quest for massive amounts of capital from Europe and perhaps the United States.

Japan will fade as a capital exporter in the next century, when a rapidly aging population and a growing consumer ethic will cause its savings rate to plummet. Over the next thirty years the United States, whose share of world capital has dropped from almost two-thirds of the total in 1976 to just under one-third today, will once again become a major source of capital as the celebrated baby boomers mature and metamorphose from net spenders into net savers.

London's Eurodollar bond market and the Japanese stock market are now challenging the primacy of the New York Stock Exchange, until recently the world's greatest pool of capital. Financial markets will coalesce into an international capital pool primarily based in Europe—probably in London. The British have the most robust financial markets in Europe. They also have another advantage: Their first language is English, the international language of business. Wherever it is based, the international equity and debt markets won't be housed in a single building, but will be basically electronic—an international equivalent of the national over-the-counter systems called NASDAQ in the U.S. and SEAQ in Britain. In the long run, some kind of international regulatory agency will be necessary to manage this capital market; it can't be done nationally.

One of the worst problems in international trade today is the absence of a stable currency. The Bretton Woods agreement, which in 1944 fixed exchange rates among all the world's major currencies in terms of the U.S. dollar, broke down in the early 1970s. Since then, currencies have bobbed like corks—and sometimes sunk like stones or soared like sword-fish—in the ocean of international exchange. The resulting chaos lends pointless melodrama to what would otherwise be mundane business decisions: What seemed like a great idea at 135 yen to the dollar makes for a bankrupt company two months later at 150 yen to the dollar.

All previous periods of strong worldwide economic growth have occurred during periods when a single, stable currency dominated the world. Roman coinage was the effective world currency for hundreds of years. The Spanish dollar played that role from the 16th through 18th centuries; in the 19th and early 20th centuries, the English pound prevailed. Earlier in this century, the success of the American economy made the U.S. dollar the global currency, but the United States has since lost its leading position and will probably be unable to recapture it.

The Japanese could make the yen a de facto world currency, but their ethnocentrism makes them unwilling to do so. Global leadership implies a loss of national sovereignty over markets, and also a loss of cultural definition. You can't be protectionist and be a world financial leader at the same time.

The Europeans are both willing and able. It takes a very large economic base to comfortably support a world currency. By 2020 the integrated European economy will be far larger than that of the United States. In a major nation, the disadvantages of its own currency functioning as a global standard are minimized and the advantages are maximized. The center of world finance is, in its own right, a very profitable place to be; and control of financial markets is the modern equivalent of control of resources and territory that nation-states fought over for so many centuries.

Within thirty years a single currency will exist for all of Western Europe, most of Eastern Europe, and possibly the Soviet Union. That de facto world currency—the currency of the expanding Common Market of Europe—will ultimately become the de jure world currency.

TECHNOLOGY

Technology spurs globalization through more than disrupting demographic equilibrium. Improvements in transportation technology have played a key role; information and communications technology will dominate in the future.

Land transportation has improved enormously over the last century, but sea and air transportation has improved much more. The modern container ship and jumbo jet are so efficient that it's often cheaper to move something between countries than within them. For example, western Canada can get things much more cheaply from overseas than it can from eastern Canada.

Progress in transportation continues on all fronts: In Europe, the Channel tunnel is linking once-impregnable Britain to the Continent. The French national railroad has agreed to provide advice to Poland on how to develop an ultra-high-speed rail network. Air transportation improvements such as the hypersonic "Tokyo Express" will continue to boost globalization.

The airplane is looming ever larger as a carrier of cargo as well as of people. Boats and camels were once fast enough for hauling bulk commodities such as wood, ore, and grain. If transit time was a month or longer, no harm done. But today, items of international commerce are frequently lightweight, delicate, research-intensive products of great value per pound—semiconductor chips, vials of pharmaceuticals—that are in danger of becoming commercially obsolete. The best way to ship them is not by ship at all, but by air.

The ultimate products of an information age can be sent around the world at speeds approaching that of light. Transportation seems a quaint concept when we consider the transmission of voice, video, and data. We are just starting to exploit the full power of modern communication technology as satellites go up and fiber-optic cable costs drop. A modern economy requires a modern telephone network. With good phones, international operations are simple; except for a modest cost difference, calling London from Los Angeles is about as easy as calling New York used to be.

Europe is emerging with the world's best telecommunications facilities. Starting with telephones that were the butt of jokes, France put an enormous investment into its Minitel system, which everyone now agrees is outstanding. Norway has a nationwide mobile cellular network, with direct-dial access to and from ships. Europe, both East and West, will have the world's highest rate of telecommunications investment over the next decade. An important topic among East Germans is how to get West German financing to modernize their badly out-of-date telephone system. West Germany's Dresdner Bank didn't wait; when it started opening branch banks in East Germany in the wake of reunification, Dresdner just rented a satellite channel and gave each branch its own receiving dish and new telephones.

Even as American telecommunications companies are joint-venturing with Czech and Hungarian counterparts hungry to leapfrog into national cellular networks, the United States has fallen behind in its domestic telecommunications. Here, regulations have encouraged improvements in existing technologies but discouraged investment in radical new technologies. Rewiring local phone networks will be a huge job, but the future is bright. AT&T and its U.S. competitors are pushing towards adopting an integrated network; all long-distance systems now use fiber-optic cables and are adopting fully digital switching.

Fortunately, fiber-optic cable technology is now getting so cheap that in twenty years fiber-optic cable will be everywhere; computer and video hookups will be fast and commonplace. Bell Labs is at work on a fiber-optic system that within a decade will carry 700,000 simultaneous telephone conversations thousands of miles without losing their clarity. (In contrast, today's intercontinental hookups require the costly installation and maintenance of underwater amplifiers every thirty to fifty miles in order to carry a mere 40,000 conversations.) Motorola, the world's biggest supplier of cellular phone systems, has announced plans to lift scores of small satellites into low orbits beginning as early as 1992, creating a pan–North American cellular network.

Starting in the mid-1990s another advance—automatic translation via telephone—will greatly accelerate global integration. At the outset, this feature will be used for text transmission. But electronic voice translation, already at the laboratory level, will soon be employed in limited-vocabulary conversations between specific persons after being "broken in" to the sounds of their speech; it will improve dramatically over the coming decades. The technology will be prodded ahead by new U.S. legislation mandating that telephone companies translate from sound to text and back for the deaf. By 2020, translating telephones will be available for all major languages.

If technological advance spurs global integration, the converse is equally true. At today's communication speeds, scientific and technical advances can be thoroughly monitored from great distances. Increasingly mobile technical personnel diffuse technologies across borders. The result has been a shrinking of the lead the discoverer of a new technology holds over remote competitors. The inventor's advantage is effectively neutralized by the cost of being first and the importance of moving quickly from invention to commercial production.

The Japanese deserve credit for realizing earlier than anyone else that you can always see farther if you stand on someone else's shoulders. Inventing and developing internationally competitive technologies is expensive. Yet American management has put next to nothing into trying to keep up with foreign technical developments. There are many times more Japanese scientists and engineers working in the United States—and familiarizing themselves with our technologies—than there are American scientists and engineers working in Japan. How many Americans can speak, let alone read, Japanese? America's ambassador to Japan, Michael Armacost, has estimated that Japan sends 25,000 students to the United States each year, while the U.S. sends 1,000 to Japan.

Japan's exports are to a great extent based on innovations by American companies, which virtually gave away the licenses to such products as the transistor and the integrated circuit. Similar giveaways are still occurring, because many key technologies are still developed by small, cash-short U.S. companies. Japanese corporations have easier access to cheap money provided preferentially by cash-rich Japanese banks, so they can bid away these new technologies.

MEDIA

Over the next thirty years, television may become the most important force for globalization. The recent free elections in Nicaragua and the peaceful revolutions that have shaken Eastern Europe are indications of how important the international media can be. Visual images have enormous power, and they don't require translation. The whole world watched the Germans tear down the Berlin Wall and witnessed China's bloody sacrifice to Stalinism in Tiananmen Square.

Global television transmission, made possible through satellite technology, is coming of age. Televised sport is going global. The

World Cup soccer competition is already the world's most watched event. By early in the next century, this globalization of sport will extend to professional basketball, hockey, and possibly volleyball.

You can now pick up television broadcasts from existing U.S. satellites with a ten-foot dish costing $2,000; picking them up from the satellites going up in Europe and the U.S. today will require only a two-foot, $200 dish. By early in the next century, so-called direct-broadcast satellites will allow you to get signals from around the world with an even smaller dish—you just have to aim it—and, in one stroke, break the government television monopolies that still exist almost everywhere except in the United States.

This latter development will integrate Europe culturally, linguistically—and in product standards. Despite supposedly free trade, the European economies have been so isolated from one another that their consumer preferences differ substantially. With the exception of automobiles, there is no pan-European product. By 1992, thanks to negotiated agreements, you will at last be able to use a German washing machine in France; right now, even the plugs are shaped differently.

Mass advertising will create a true global mass market for consumer goods, along with demands for open markets and world-quality goods. All the world's children will come to know Count Chocula, Big Bird, and Teenage Mutant Ninja Turtles. Sony will no longer need to ask government permission to advertise its products. More importantly, direct broadcast, by breaking government television monopolies, will provide open access to information, open up politics, raise expectations, and unify cultures. Televising the activities, successes, and mistakes of neighboring nations will encourage progress and reduce tensions.

As standards become increasingly universal, maintaining a diversity of cultural traditions will grow difficult. How long, after all, do cultural practices of different ethnic groups last within the United States? First-generation immigrants are closely tied to their cultural roots—the language, the dances, the music. Now the great-grandchildren of America's European immigrants are all listening to the same rock music, eating an international cuisine, and, most frightening of all for their grandparents, marrying across all ethnic and religious lines. In the long run, what we may now view as vital cultural differences will become artifacts, exhumed at will for entertainment value.

To what degree will the world accept a consumer-oriented economic ethic—the basic freedom to consume whatever you want as long as you can afford it and you don't directly damage someone else or the environment? There's a backlash against that in the United States, the leader in consumerism, and more so in Europe and Japan, whose older generations, especially, are much more traditional than Americans.

However, values are beginning to change even in the anti-consumer stronghold of Japan. The average Japanese worker today spends more than 2,100 hours a year on the job—10 percent more than workers in any other industrialized country—leaving little time for leisure pursuits. But in April 1991—probably owing both to external pressure over the country's huge trade surplus and internal pressure from young workers—Japan's government will reduce the legal workweek to 44 hours from the present 46, a step toward a 1,800-hour workyear targeted for 1992. If there's hope for the balance of trade between the United States and Japan, it's in the Japanese teenagers of today—the Japanese workers and consumers of tomorrow. Consumerism is winning converts in developed country after developed country. There will be increasing debate over whether this is a good or a bad thing.

The Dark Side of Globalization

Modern societies are fragile: They allow great freedom but lack the emotional ties of broadly shared religion or ideology. It's hard to call for sacrifice merely to achieve a materially comfortable life. The pressures of modernization are severely disruptive to all societies. Modern nations share difficulties in maintaining family stability and in fighting drugs and crime. Throughout the developed world, arrangements for medical care, welfare, childcare, and education are in need of revision.

In a more subtle way, globalization causes the worldwide division of have and have-not countries to be mirrored within the borders of even the richest countries. In the past, empires were able to retain the loyalty of domestic workers by paying them high salaries relative to those of exploited laborers in Third World colonies. But in a world of free trade and instantaneous, global capital transfers, this may no longer be possible.

As protectionist walls come down in developed countries, according to Harvard economist Robert Reich, it becomes increasingly difficult to protect domestic workers.[2] Laborers whose jobs consist of routine operations in manufacturing and, increasingly, in data processing—in any field, that is, where the product can be profitably produced far from its ultimate destination—will find themselves competing in a global labor market that favors low-wage sites in developing countries. In America, where corporations long ago began to ship such operations overseas, real earnings for such laborers have been dropping; and companies in Japan, where wages are now higher than those in the U.S., are rapidly moving production offshore. The worldwide advance of the consumerist ethic, because it favors consumers at the expense of workers, breathes life into protectionism, the last vestige of nationalist sentiment. Wages of a second category of workers—hairdressers, cabdrivers, hospital orderlies, retail salespersons, janitors, and security guards, whose output is a service that can be consumed only locally—will be conditioned by the affluence of their host country and the availability of cheap immigrant labor.

In contrast, those laborers Reich calls "symbol analysts"—engineers, artists, advertising copywriters, efficiency experts, executives, authors, educators, actors, investment bankers, and the like—find their services in increasing demand all over the globe and are commanding ever-higher prices. America's excellent university system and mature economy make it the natural launching pad for an inordinate number of these workers, who already account for more than 40 percent of America's gross national product (GNP) and about 20 percent of its jobs. But thanks to the very technologies that have created a global marketplace for their skills, symbol analysts' national identities, regardless of the origin of the passport, are becoming increasingly blurred.

Waiting in the wings to exploit any weakness are three anti-modern religions: Islamic fundamentalism, Maoism, and fanatic environmentalism. Islam was once the world's cultural and technical leader, but the new version is overwhelmingly anti-modern and anti-Western. Islam has great appeal to the underdeveloped world, and it may reconquer the entire Middle East from Morocco to Pakistan. Maoism has far fewer adherents, but Maoists are incredible killers and may succeed in taking over a faltering Latin American nation or two—although once in power, they will surely fail in running them. Fanatic environmentalism has the greatest appeal to Western intellectuals; their ersatz religion of Marxism having lost all intellectual legitimacy, former Marxists are moving to the environmental cause. The demonstrators will be the same; they will just march under a different banner.

CHAPTER

3

The Emerging World Order

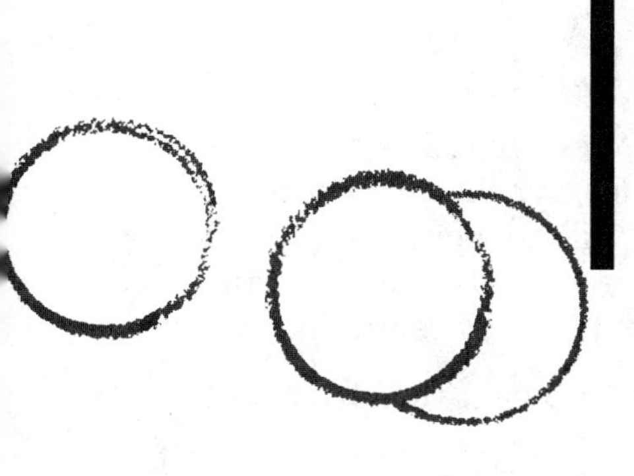

In 1993 the English Channel will be spanned by a 31-mile underwater tunnel, through which trains will bring passengers from London to Paris in three hours or less. Thus the once-isolated British Isles will be joined—physically as well as economically and, eventually, politically—to the continental colossus that is tomorrow's Europe. The 21st century will be the European century, not the Pacific century. Over time, the rest of the world will follow Europe's lead, as several forces combine to generate vastly higher levels of global cooperation and hasten a worldwide convergence already in the making.

This global convergence of economic, social, and political structures is a victory for capitalist democracy in a war whose battleground was not ideology but materialism. Both communists and capitalists agree that material progress is the ultimate goal of human society. Communism as an ideology has collapsed because it failed to provide what it promised: economic superiority. Capitalism is compatible with the decentralization required by modern technologies, as are such Western values as individualism and freedom.

Western capitalism's economic victory has brought the Cold War, the last of Europe's centuries-long series of civil wars, to an end. But with the Soviet Union rapidly senescing into an oxymoron of history, the United

States finds itself in the position of a Pyrrhic victor. U.S. technological research and development in the last three decades has largely taken place in a military context; as a result, Japan and Germany have seized the industrial initiative—and have become America's bankers in the process. But Japan, unwilling to renounce its cultural and commercial insularity, thereby abdicates its claim to world leadership.

The Megastate

The developed world will converge in several key ways:

- Nation-states will coalesce into *megastates*—massive confederations with many common economic rules, synchronized foreign policies, and joint military forces. These will not be as centralized as the U.S., but will fall somewhere between Canada and the current European Economic Community in degree of central power.
- Individual nations will cede much of their power over currencies, trade, commercial laws, movement of people, foreign policy, and strategic military forces.
- Within large nations, power will decentralize, with such former nations as Scotland or the Basque provinces gaining at least as much power as U.S. states.
- Developed nations will share common problems of population decline, immigration pressure, social turmoil, environmental issues, growth conflicts, and welfare-state difficulties (especially a need to restructure health-care systems).

Megastate organizations will dominate the economic sphere. Issues such as currency, control of financial markets and capital, and control of people can be resolved only at the international level. What we now think of as individual nations will end up being more like states of a confederation. The closest thing to a prototype is the European Economic Community (EEC), which has targeted 1992 for the creation of a single market in which trade, capital, and workers will flow freely across the borders of the EEC's twelve member states. This step is to be followed by the creation of a solitary European central bank, a common currency, and, in due time, political union.

Globalization will also mean global people—international citizens, at high levels of the business and academic worlds, spending not just two-week business visits, but major portions of their lives, outside their native countries. Management of flows of people—at least among the developed countries—will be relaxed, because multinational organizations can effectively transfer technology only by moving people. The concept of national citizenship—at least for a growing, elite proportion of the population—will be difficult to maintain. International personnel will require international taxation policies, education rights, and medical benefits, not to mention internationally transferable pension rights.

All this, of course, will not easily mix with the traditions of nations that have been sovereign for centuries. The army, as the last symbol of the declining nation-state's sovereignty, will be the last institution to be shed; but it will be shed—preserved, perhaps, as a vestigial, ceremonial force. In the end, it will be the megastate whose independent, international armed forces have the teeth.

The European Megastate and Its Followers

The new world order will be dominated by the most unified Europe in world history. Over the next thirty years, Europe will evolve into the world's largest megastate. The first stages are clear. By 1995, the existing twelve-nation European Community (including a unified Germany) will have a unified currency, free movement of people and goods, common external economic policies, a unified military command structure (a successor to NATO), and substantial coordination of foreign policy.

Europe is already the world's most mature region. As shown in Table 1, Europe has the world's lowest population growth. For capitalist Europe, real per capita income ranges from near U.S. levels in northern Europe to the relative poverty of Greece and Portugal. Communist Europe starts at one-half U.S. levels in East Germany (probably overstated) and drops to the grinding poverty of Albania and Romania. Because of its low population growth rate, Europe's per capita economic growth exceeds that of every region except East Asia.

As it grows, Europe will evolve several different levels of membership. The levels will follow the original pattern of evolution of the EEC:

- Customs union (free trade)
- Commercial and currency union
- Political confederation

Neighboring nations, including Norway, Sweden, Finland, Turkey, Yugoslavia (possibly only part), Malta, Cyprus, Hungary, Poland, Czechoslovakia, Switzerland, Austria, and Iceland either have applied or will soon will be applying for membership in at least the economic parts of the union. By the year 2000, all these nations will probably be

TABLE 1 NATIONAL SUMMARY: EUROPE

	1987 Population (thousands)	1987 Life expectancy (years)	1985 Literacy rate (%)	1987 Per capita GDP* ($)	1990-2000 Annual Population growth (%)	1980-87 Annual GNP growth (%)
ALBANIA	3,268	72	85	2,000	1.5	
ROMANIA	23,269	71	96	3,000	0.4	2.6
POLAND	38,363	72	98	4,000	0.4	0.5
HUNGARY	10,546	71	98	4,500	-0.1	1.0
BULGARIA	8,978	72	93	4,750	0.1	1.4
YUGOSLAVIA	23,864	72	92	5,000	0.5	0.6
GREECE	10,066	76	93	5,500	0.2	0.5
PORTUGAL	10,528	74	85	5,597	0.5	3.0
USSR	290,939	70	99	6,000	0.7	2.2
CZECHOSLOVAKIA	15,695	72	98	7,750	0.3	1.2
EAST GERMANY	16,578	74	99	8,000	0.0	1.6
IRELAND	3,523	74	99	8,566	0.0	0.9
SPAIN	39,623	77	95	8,989	0.5	2.1
ITALY	57,657	76	97	10,682	0.1	1.3
BRITAIN	57,121	76	99	12,270	0.1	2.4
AUSTRIA	7,595	74	99	12,386	0.1	1.6
HOLLAND	14,864	77	99	12,661	0.4	1.1
FINLAND	4,977	75	99	12,795	0.1	3.2
BELGIUM	9,895	75	99	13,140	0.0	1.1
SWEDEN	8,382	77	99	13,780	0.0	1.7
FRANCE	56,184	76	99	13,961	0.3	1.2
WEST GERMANY	60,977	75	99	14,730	0.0	1.5
DENMARK	5,134	76	99	15,119	0.1	2.0
SWITZERLAND	6,628	77	99	15,403	0.1	1.7
NORWAY	4,214	77	99	15,940	0.2	2.7
REGIONAL AVERAGE		73	98	8,591	0.4	1.8
REGIONAL POP.	788,868					
U.S. COMPARISON	250,372	76	96	17,615	0.7	1.8

*Output adjusted to reflect actual purchasing power within each country

Sources: *Statistical Abstract of the United States*, 1989 and 1990; *Economist*, May 26, 1990.

affiliated with the unified European customs and commercial structure. They will be moving towards political integration—a United States of Europe with 25 states and some 400 million people. Even the Roman Empire never extended to the boundaries of the emerging European megastate.

Other nations may also participate in a customs union by 2000, but they will be far from commercial or political union. Israel already has a favored trade relationship with Europe, but a closer relationship will be a protracted and divisive political issue. Romania will probably stay mostly communist and tied to the Soviet Union (or what's left of it) for many years. Yugoslavia is close to being torn apart by economic and political pressures; its western provinces of Croatia and Slovenia may simply split off to join Europe, forcing the Serbs to cooperate more with Romania and the Soviets. Albania, Europe's poorest and most isolated nation, will take many years to integrate itself with the European community. Latvia, Lithuania, and Estonia may want to join, but Russian pressure will limit their relationship.

By the year 2020, the European political confederation should include such laggards as Albania, Romania, Bulgaria, and Turkey. The Baltic Republics are likely to become bridges between Europe and Russia. They are culturally European, but their economies are closely intertwined with the Russian economy. If they give up on such useless symbols of 19th-century sovereignty as their own armies and fight only for economic independence, they could become the Hong Kongs of Europe, economic miracles with close links to both the European customs union and Russia.

The path to modernization for the Soviet Union will be far from easy. It is unlikely that the Russians can maintain their empire. The southern Muslim republics, with 50 million people, are hostile, primitive, resource-poor, demographic nightmares—in short, perfect breeding grounds for Islamic fundamentalism. Most likely, the Soviets will pull back to a course of modernizing the Slavic core of Russia, Byelorussia, and the Ukraine, and will grant substantial autonomy, if not ultimately full independence, to the Muslim republics. The Muslims will then be courted by either or both of their two radically different neighbors: westernizing Turkey, which claims a natural affinity for the secularized, largely Turkic peoples of the Muslim republics; and anti-Western, fundamentalist Iran. Armenian Christians, nearly surrounded by much larger Muslim populations, will pray for the return of the Soviet Union.

The Soviets are in exactly the same state of arrested development as Eastern Europe; neither can advance further without Western European capital and technology. Natural economic forces will ultimately overwhelm ideology. Karl Marx was right: Political structures must evolve to fit the technology of production. Western Europe is desperate to invest in the Soviet Union, a vast treasure house of such resources as oil, natural gas, and arable land; but that won't happen without political agreements to recommence the natural integration of the European economy, derailed by World War II and its aftermath. Among the first steps is Germany's reunification.

Germany, the First Technocratic State

The reunification of Germany is both the key ingredient and the best symbol of the end of Europe's long civil war. The latest round of that war started with Germany's invasion of France in 1870, lasted over a hundred years, and resulted in the political and economic division of Europe along the Iron Curtain. But with the triumph of economics over military power, that civil war is over. The chief belligerent, Germany, is now becoming the leader of the new Europe.

Otto von Bismarck created the modern technocratic state in mid-19th-century Germany when he pioneered the development of modern education and the modern welfare system. His goal was to produce better soldiers and more productive workers, as well as to choke off political support for the socialists. Germany outpaced the other European powers because the Germans—especially their elite—were much more willing to involve themselves in technology and industry. German universities were far more than finishing schools for the aristocracy; they were the technological spawning grounds of the late 19th and early 20th centuries.

Technology, the new source of economic power, had received little attention from pre-Bismarckian governments; new weaponry was the only exception. Early scientific development was not even related to universities; it was the creation of amateurs. The English Industrial Revolution was almost entirely a creature of the private sector.

Germany was the first government to think of civilian technology as a military asset. In the late 19th century the Germans became technological leaders, especially in chemicals. If there was a single technical advance that triggered World War I, it was the German invention of a process for making nitrates, essential ingredients in gunpowder. Before that development, the only large-scale source of nitrates was guano deposits—bird droppings—found primarily off the coast of Chile and Peru. Thus, English control of the high seas could mean the cutoff of Germany's gunpowder supply at any time. The new technology swept aside that obstacle.

Tragically, Kaiser Wilhelm used the economic power built by Bismarck's technocratic state to start World War I. The role of Germany had been the central military issue in Europe since the Germanic tribes first invaded the Roman Empire; these and subsequent wars had always been fundamentally economic—more territory meant more wealth. Even as technology was severing that connection, the Kaiser insisted on fighting over past sources of riches: the extensive colonial empires of Britain and France.

Germany could have won the power it desired without warfare, simply by letting its surging industrial growth continue. But its political and military leaders were still in the habit of thinking in physical-resource terms rather than technological terms. Germany's technical and economic strength got caught up with Prussian militarism, and an unnecessary war followed.

After its defeat Germany collapsed socially, economically, and politically; but its continued technological strength ensured that the tragedy of the first world war would be replayed in World War II, this time in living Nazi technicolor. Germany was again defeated, its economy destroyed, some of its territory ceded to Poland, and the rest split into two pieces—perhaps, for all anyone knew, permanently.

Out of the weakness of total defeat in World War II came the strength of near-total emphasis on economic power in the post-war era. The 1960s and early 1970s saw Germany's transformation into a world-class technological and economic power—and Japan's as well. In both countries, the combination of an efficient welfare state, a strong education system, and close ties between government, industry, and universities—the German model—has worked wonders.

The United States represents the competing organizational model for the developed world, being much more decentralized than Germany, other European nations, or Japan. This decentralization and openness has made the U.S. far more innovative technically and economically; Silicon Valley could happen only in the United States. The U.S. system is also far better suited than the ethnocentric Germanic and Japanese social/economic systems to absorb a broad range of racial and ethnic groups. On the other hand, the U.S. is showing signs of serious weakness:

While its universities remain the strongest in the world, it lags far behind Western Europe and Japan in health, welfare, and primary and secondary education. Ill-conceived financial policies have fueled a decade-long borrowing binge, billion-dollar paper chases, and the favoring of real estate speculation over productive industrial investment.

1984 Revisited

Physical warfare among developed countries, once critical to a nation's economic prowess, is obsolete; technology and organization, the key assets of a modern economy, cannot be conquered. Hong Kong's and Silicon Valley's great wealth would vanish with the loss of their freedom. First the Japanese and Germans, and now the Americans and the Russians, have realized that economic and technical power, over the long haul, transcend military power.

As technology, trade, finance, and the media accelerate the decline of the individual nation-state, two alternative outcomes can be envisioned:

- A Europe-centered economy gradually pulling in, nation by nation, pieces of what we now call the Third World as well as North America and Asia, until the entire planet is linked in a global system.
- A world of regional blocs: most likely a U.S. bloc, a European bloc, and a Japanese/Chinese bloc—exactly the regions predicted in George Orwell's *1984*.

Even in the event of a breakdown into those three regions, warfare among them is unlikely. The larger, stabler, and more advanced a state becomes, the more difficult it is for either a maniac or a killer ideology to take over. The modern megastate and its member technocratic nations need bureaucrats, not charismatics. Japan is run by bureaucrats. George Bush is a bureaucrat. Helmut Kohl, Germany's chancellor, is a bureaucrat. Gorbachev may be the last world-scale charismatic political figure.

Only still-unifying and -modernizing nations need charismatic leaders. The danger to the world order lies in such emerging powers as Iraq or Brazil: countries big enough to manufacture nuclear weapons on their own, but with divisive economic, political, and social problems. A Middle Eastern or Latin American Hitler in control of a nuclear nation is the nightmare of the next decade and the next century.

Tomorrow's world will be far from peaceful. Military force in developed countries will be refocused on local police actions and guarding against the emergence of dangerous regional powers. The Iraqs, Libyas, and Lebanons of the world won't disappear, but instead will become far more dangerous, armed with chemical and nuclear weapons. As yesterday's superpowers pull back, while Europe still fears asserting itself, many ancient hostilities are beginning to re-emerge. These include regional conflicts in Africa, Asia, and the Middle East, as well as smaller-scale civil wars throughout the world. Not just for decades, but for hundreds of years, the Turks have been fighting the Kurds; the Kurds have been fighting the Persians; the Persians have been fighting the Baluchis. Just across the Soviet border, the Azerbaijanis have been fighting the Armenians for over 2,000 years.

Much of the danger of the developing world's military is a bitter residue of the Cold War. The United States, Europe, and the Soviet Union put 21st-century weapons in the hands of 18th-century nations. In time, these arsenals will deteriorate through misuse, poor maintenance, and lack of spare parts, but for now they are deadly. Moreover, as Cold War tensions recede, the world may soon see the largest fire sale of second-hand military equipment in history, and advanced nations will continue to be tempted to sell modern, new weapons in order to maintain production capabilities and high employment. Embargoes against the worst actors—Iraq, Libya, North Korea—may succeed, but elsewhere the international arms bazaar will be open for business.

Megastate military forces will need to project their power into vital but dangerous locations such as the Persian Gulf. But the United States will of necessity grow unwilling to continue spending itself near-bankrupt defending European and Japanese interests, and our chief Cold War antagonist, the Soviet Union, will be exhausted. The United Nations, with the possibility of consensus among Security Council members finally demonstrated in the Iraq-Kuwait crisis, may once again become relevant. Europe will eventually be forced to create more-aggressive military forces, because Iraq is the last large-scale foreign intervention the United States can afford. Next time, it's Europe's turn.

The warfare most commonly affecting developed nations in the future will be terrorism, both internal and international. Terrorist groups such as the Irish Republican Army or the Maoist Shining Path guerrillas in Peru are, in practice, anti-modernist nationalists who reject the international, capitalist, consumerist amalgam that economic and technical forces are creating. Terrorism is the bane of political democracy within a decentralized market economy and pluralistic social structure. Such a society is so fluid that a small number of committed combatants, armed with all-too-easily obtained weapons, can inflict great damage and then fade quietly back into the woodwork—or across the border, as so many West German Red Army Faction members did successfully until the new leadership in East Germany flushed them out of anonymity.

North Korea and Cuba will be with us at least for a while, although with much less support from places like the Soviet Union and its former satellites. The Colombian drug cartels and Arab-state- and Iran-sponsored terrorists will still be there. Developed countries will be forced to coordinate police activities on an international basis, permitting harsh interdiction and extradition procedures in some cases to prevent large-scale attacks by terrorists—or worse, their acquisition of chemical or even nuclear weapons.

Whereas the prospective division of the world into three distinct regional entities doesn't in itself imply megastate military confrontations, it does pose a problem from an American perspective, because in any such arrangement Europe, with or without the Soviet Union, will be the economically dominant power. While Southeast Asia has great potential, Eastern Europe is the real prize of the future. Meanwhile, our own Latin American backyard is in bad economic shape.

Powerhouses and Trouble Spots

EASTERN EUROPE

Eastern Europe has far to go before it becomes as attractive to investors as Indonesia, Taiwan, South Korea, and Thailand. But the will to create the preconditions for that investment—property rights, clear commercial laws, and a convertible currency—is strong. Eastern Europe is crying out for investment, and the feeling is reciprocated.

East Germany, Hungary, Czechoslovakia, and Poland will soon be fantastic places to invest. They are already part of the European culture. They are stabilizing politically, and their highly literate populations represent the world's greatest bloc of underused human resources.

Several East European countries, where communism has turned out to be a road to capitalism and national unity, may yet seek intermediate socialist stopping-off points; but that need not impede their integration into Europe. Many Western European enterprises are themselves somewhat socialized. While direct government operation of competitive enterprises doesn't appear to work, natural monopolies such as utilities and railroads can be successfully operated by governments.

In the courting of capital-starved Eastern Europe, financial power is everything. The United States has a cultural leg up on Japan; almost any major American city houses citizens who speak fluent Hungarian, Polish, Czech, or German. But Japan has already anted up a $1 billion aid program to Eastern Europe. The United States is having a hard time coming up with $100 million.

Geography confers a natural trading advantage on Western Europe, and especially on a reunited Germany, which shares borders with nine other European countries, including Poland and Czechoslovakia. It will be much cheaper to ship heavy goods from Germany than from the U.S. Trade flows between Germany and Czechoslovakia will compare to trade flows between New England and New York.

THE MIDDLE EAST

Iraq's invasion of Kuwait in August 1990 called attention to the troubles at Europe's periphery. An aggressive, unified, nuclear-armed Arab state would pose a mortal danger to Europe. It is this potential—not the price of oil—that has motivated the world's united response to the invasion.

The Arab world is a fundamentally unstable region. Most of its constituent nations are feudal hand-me-downs or arbitrary colonial creations, and most of them have been armed to the teeth by one Cold War adversary or another, or both. Unfortunately, as much as two-thirds of the world's known reserves of petroleum sit in the vicinity of the Persian Gulf, making it the only physical resource left that is worth fighting for. The threat lurking behind the Iraq-Kuwait crisis is not restriction of supply leading to higher oil prices, but rather that Iraq will use its Kuwaiti windfall to fuel its military machine and ultimately conquer the entire region. Had we not opposed the invasion, oil prices would be lower than they are now and would have stayed lower for many years.

Iraq will probably be forced, militarily or diplomatically, to leave Kuwait. But two dire outcomes are still possible:

TABLE 2 NATIONAL SUMMARY: MIDDLE EAST AND NORTH AFRICA

	1987 Population (thousands)	1987 Life expectancy (years)	1985 Literacy rate (%)	1987 Per capita GDP* ($)	1990-2000 Annual Population growth (%)	1980-87 Annual GNP growth (%)
YEMEN PDR	2,585	52	42	1,000	3.3	
YEMEN ARAB REP.	7,162	52	25	1,250	3.4	
EGYPT	56,219	62	45	1,357	2.4	5.9
MOROCCO	26,249	62	34	1,761	2.4	2.8
LEBANON	3,392	68	78	2,250	1.9	
IRAQ	18,868	65	89	2,400	3.4	-8.7
ALGERIA	25,714	63	50	2,633	2.7	3.8
TUNISIA	8,095	66	55	2,741	2.1	
JORDAN	3,065	67	75	3,161	3.6	
SYRIA	12,471	66	60	3,250	3.8	3.5
IRAN	55,249	66	51	3,300	2.9	0.0
TURKEY	56,549	65	74	3,781	1.9	5.4
LIBYA	4,206	62	66	7,250	2.8	
OMAN	1,345	57	30	7,750	3.0	0.0
SAUDI ARABIA	16,758	64	55	8,320	3.2	-7.7
ISRAEL	4,445	76	95	9,182	1.5	2.4
UNITED ARAB EMIRATES	2,250	71	60	12,191	4.7	
KUWAIT	2,083	73	70	13,843	2.7	-8.1
REGIONAL AVERAGE		64	56	3,263	2.6	3.0
REGIONAL POP.	306,705					
U.S. COMPARISON	250,372	76	96	17,615	0.7	1.8

*Output adjusted to reflect actual purchasing power within each country

Sources: *Statistical Abstract of the United States*, 1989 and 1990; *Economist*, May 26, 1990.

- Iraq withdraws with its forces intact, only to try again in a few years.
- Iraq attacks Jordan and/or Israel, and the Palestinian diaspora leads uprisings in Egypt and Jordan, resulting in a hellish, region-wide war.

Regardless of how the Iraqi war ends, in the long run the European union will reach into the Middle East. Turkey and Israel hope to join. Turkey—cohesive, modernizing, and looking westward—has applied for membership in the EEC, which will ultimately be granted. Turkey's successful entry into the European megastate may be the best antidote to the darkening anti-Western mood of the Islamic world.

As shown in Table 2, the Middle East and North Africa have an unpleasant combination of high population growth, general poverty, and widespread illiteracy. The apparently high real incomes of such nations as Kuwait represent more the volume of oil pumped than actual standards of living. While the economic growth rate is relatively high, population growth eats up much of the gain.

What we tend to think of as the true Middle East—Israel and every country that immediately surrounds it—is and will be, as far as the eye can see, the world's great powder keg: a region of not merely population explosions, but military explosions.

Lebanon is a free-fire zone, suspended in total chaos. The higher birthrate of Muslims in Lebanon has led to a Muslim majority in what was once a Christian-dominated country, but the rivalries go far beyond simple religion. Christians kill each other as often as they fight with Lebanese Muslims, and vice versa. Mired ever more deeply in internecine rivalries among and within its warring constituent groups, the country is mercilessly poked and prodded by outside forces. Lebanon makes simple war look good. Straight-out conquering and occupying Lebanon would cost fewer lives than its endless civil war. Since Israel does not want to occupy Lebanon but cannot allow Syria to do so, the civil war will continue for decades.

Israel, created as a refuge for oppressed Jews around the world by Europe and the United States out of well-earned guilt, is the Middle East's most advanced nation. Europe, for most of its history, has treated Jews more harshly than even the Arabs do today. The United States refused to admit Jewish refugees before World War II. After the Holocaust, who among them would trust anything except their own homeland?

In its battle for survival against the increasingly modern military forces of Arab countries with fifty times its population, Israel can win many times, but it can lose only once. Would the U.S. send its troops to save the Jewish state? How would the United States handle a flood of Jewish refugees from a defeated Israel?

Despite the distraction of repeated border wars and the need to maintain an extraordinary level of military readiness, Israel has made economic progress. But Israel's Arab minority has a high birthrate and within twenty years will become an Arab majority—at least within the boundaries of post–1967 war Israel—unless the current huge influx of Soviet Jews continues, and they all stay. More than one million Soviet Jews, expecting an increase in rabid anti-Semitism in a decaying social environment but barred from entering the United States, have already received visas to emigrate to Israel; more than 40 percent of the arriving adults are scientists, engineers, and academics.[1] The Russian exodus has bought Israel time. But there is not enough room or water for both Israel's Arab population and all those Russian emigrés. Where will they be housed? Will Israel's Palestinian Arabs simply be forced out of the West Bank? Iraq's recent invasion of Kuwait, and the overwhelmingly exuberant response of Palestinians to that invasion, has unfortunately rendered this last question much more likely to be answered in the affirmative than anyone thought possible only months ago.

The peace process is dead. Pan-Arabist thought leaves no room for a Jewish state on the Arabian Peninsula. But the creation of a Palestinian state in the West Bank would leave Israel only eleven miles wide at its midsection. Surrounded as it is by hostile Arab neighbors, viewing the lopsided support of neighboring Jordan's Palestinian majority for both Saddam Hussein's push into tiny Kuwait and his Pan-Arabist rhetoric, and observing the speed with which the most-feared Palestinian terrorist organizations have offered their free-lance services to the Iraqi dictator, Israel would be naive in the extreme to think it can buy peace through withdrawal to its pre-1967 borders.

PLO chief Yasser Arafat's embrace of Hussein has cost him the support of Western politicians, oil-state financers (Saudi Arabia alone has poured some $7 billion into PLO coffers since 1970; Kuwait was another big contributor), and even Israel's doves. Israeli opinion, split 50/50 on almost every issue of importance for the past decade, is now unanimous in rejecting any overtures toward Arafat, the PLO, or any nascent Palestinian state. Western PLO sympathizers can no longer look the other way when Palestinian leaders take far more aggressive stances toward Israel in the Arab press than the ones they adopt for Western consumption. It is possible that moderate Arab governments (i.e., those that support America's confrontation of Iraq) will use their new leverage with the U.S. to pressure Israel toward a settlement with the Palestinians. More likely, the Palestinians can expect to see the former largesse of their Arab neighbors dwindle to practically zero during what promises to be a long period out in the diplomatic cold. Depending on how the Iraqi crisis plays out, West Bank Palestinians may indeed wake up one day to find themselves in a Palestinian state—on the east bank of the Jordan river in the rubble of King Hussein's Jordan.

The overthrow of Soviet-style communist systems in the countries of Eastern Europe has led to a cutoff of modern weapons for the Arab states and training and munitions for Palestinian terrorists. However, perennial pan-Arabist passions in the region make it quite possible that, twenty or thirty years from now, Israel's external situation will be identical to that of today: an embattled, militarized state surrounded by antagonistic, but chaotic Arab states. Actually joining the EEC political confederation—a near political impossibility from today's perspective—may be Israel's best long-run hope.

Nowhere else in the region is there anything approaching stability or sustained modernization. All along the western shore of the Persian Gulf are states of enormous petroleum-related wealth—Saudi Arabia, the United Arab Emirates, the cipher holding the place for Kuwait—all created out of tribal fiefdoms in the stroke of a pen by European mapmaker/diplomats, and all depending on hired experts, hired guards, and hired armies.

A political fault line runs through the entire Arabian Peninsula. Jordan, an artificial creation unlikely to survive much beyond 2000, has possibly had its life span shortened considerably by King Hussein's equivocation regarding the Iraq-Kuwait situation, which has alienated him from Western support. Syria and its bitter rival Iraq—both, like Jordan, Lebanon, Kuwait, et al., created by Britain and France in 1922 after the crushing of the Ottoman Empire—are in the grip of iron dictatorships, each pan-Arabist in rhetoric and each itching to destroy the other. Both dictators are unlikely to survive through the 1990s. In the ensuing vacuum, both nations will probably collapse into civil war.

Iraq is, for now, the world's most dangerous nation. Its economy destroyed in a futile eight-year war with Iran, Iraq chose to use its Soviet and French weapons to capture the oil and bankroll of tiny Kuwait, the richest country in the Middle East. Of the several possible outcomes, most involve the death of Saddam Hussein. Hussein has created national unity (by using poison gas to kill opponents like the Kurds en masse) and a well-equipped army bigger than those of Britain or France. Iraq—bent on acquiring world-class weapons, spending more than any other country on earth to import them—has already made and used advanced chemical weapons, and probably will have a nuclear capability within the decade if the U.S. Air Force doesn't quickly repeat Israel's 1981 performance (severely panned by the critics of the day): the surgical destruction of an Iraqi nuclear-weapons research facility.

North Africa has the potentially tragic combination of great economic potential and anti-modern ideological fervor. As is the case with most former colonies, once the colonialists were thrown out, we heard little about the ruthless and largely incompetent dictators that took over. Yet Morocco, Algeria, and Tunisia, having weathered long periods of incompetent state socialism without collapsing, are now socially and politically unified; and they're tied to the European community by historic patterns of trade and interchange of people. They are labor-short Europe's Mexico. Libya, too, has great potential: a tiny population, vast resources—and a mad dictator.

The North African nations are being swept up in a wave of Islamic fundamentalism, a dualistic force that at once promises to unite a billion Muslims and threatens to turn back the clock, politically and economically speaking, to the 7th century. All of North Africa could yet veer off into decades of religious fanaticism, terror, and starvation. Islamic fundamentalism, which made dramatic inroads in recent Algerian elections, has great appeal to the region's still-impoverished masses—particularly men threatened by modernism's clear mandate to improve women's rights.

Egypt—the most populous country in the Middle East, with over 55 million people on less farmland than Minnesota has—is being torn apart by religious fanaticism, decades of misguided economic policies, environmental destruction, and a population out of control. Egypt is on the edge of collapse.

Adjacent to Egypt is its potential salvation, the Sudan: a huge country with a tiny population, half–Middle Eastern, half-African. Because of geographic isolation and a terrible civil war, the Sudan has the greatest untapped resource base in Africa. Nobody even knows what's there, except oil and vast acreages of arable land. Developing the country will take enormous investments, but nobody will invest as long as people keep shooting each other, and they've been shooting each other for twenty years.

Iran is the world's best-known casualty of the social and political stresses of modernization. In the 1970s, Iran's economy and technology got too far ahead of its social and political structure. The result was Khomeini's ascendancy; the 7th century triumphed over modernity, at least temporarily. Iran's political shift will delay modernization for many years, but not forever. Ultimately, religious fervor will die out and economic issues will come back into focus. Whether Iran will spend all its oil wealth on guns and mosques first is an open question.

ASIA

Asia has had by far the highest economic growth rates of the world over the last decade, as shown by Table 3. Asian population growth has slowed sharply, and the region is headed for demographic stability. Most of this growth has been concentrated in East Asia. India and South Asia are making only limited economic progress.

The conventional wisdom of the 1980s was that Asia would become the world's leading economic and political bloc, thanks to Japan's industrial and financial dominance, China's opening to the West, and the rapid economic strides of their Southeast Asian neighbors. Only part of that prediction will be borne out. Asia is an economic wonder, but a political weakling. Japan is the world's second-largest economy and first truly modern non-Western nation. South Korea, Taiwan, Malaysia, and Thailand are the world's fastest-growing economies. These once-impoverished nations have overtaken Latin America in wealth and are gaining on Europe. This economic growth will continue for decades to come.

The region's political weakness is threefold:

- China, the region's largest nation, has regressed into Stalinism and will probably near economic collapse in the 1990s.

- The single most important factor in the overall economic success of all of Asia—first Japan, then South Korea, then Taiwan, and now Thailand and other countries—is continued openness of U.S. markets. The region's current prosperity thus survives at the whim of the U.S. Congress.

- There is no movement toward regional unity. Even when Japan finally opens up enough to permit Asia's independence from the U.S., there will be huge cultural animosities to overcome. For example, after their bitter experience with Japanese colonialism, the Koreans could not conceive of political confederation with Japan.

The future of China, still the quintessential Asian issue, is a purely political question. The Communists reestablished basic national unity

TABLE 3 NATIONAL SUMMARY: ASIA

	1987 Population (thousands)	1987 Life expectancy (years)	1985 Literacy rate (%)	1987 Per capita GDP* ($)	1990-2000 Annual Population growth (%)	1980-87 Annual GNP growth (%)
BHUTAN	1,566	49	25	700	2.0	
NEPAL	19,158	52	26	722	2.4	
BURMA	41,279	61	79	752	1.9	5.0
BANGLADESH	115,753	52	33	883	2.2	3.9
AFGHANISTAN	32,291	42	24	1,000	1.1	-4.2
KAMPUCHEA	6,993	49	75	1,000	2.0	
LAOS	4,024	49	84	1,000	2.1	
VIETNAM	68,488	62	80	1,000	2.3	
INDIA	850,067	59	43	1,053	1.8	4.7
PAKISTAN	113,163	58	30	1,585	2.5	7.1
INDONESIA	191,266	57	74	1,660	1.7	4.3
PAPUA NEW GUINEA	3,824	55	45	1,843	2.2	
PHILIPPINES	66,647	64	86	1,878	2.5	0.3
MONGOLIA	2,185	64	90	2,000	2.6	
NORTH KOREA	23,059	70	90	2,000	2.1	2.8
SRI LANKA	17,096	71	87	2,053	1.3	3.8
CHINA	1,114,512	70	69	2,124	1.1	9.7
THAILAND	56,449	66	91	2,576	1.5	5.0
MAURITIUS	1,141	69	83	2,617	1.5	
MALAYSIA	17,053	70	74	3,849	1.7	4.0
SOUTH KOREA	43,919	70	95	4,832	1.2	8.9
TAIWAN	20,454	73	95	5,126	0.9	8.0
NEW ZEALAND	3,402	75	99	10,541	0.7	2.3
AUSTRALIA	16,643	76	99	11,782	1.0	3.0
SINGAPORE	2,703	73	86	12,790	0.8	
JAPAN	123,749	78	99	13,135	0.4	3.7
HONGKONG	5,770	76	88	13,906	0.9	
REGIONAL AVERAGE		65	63	2,343	1.5	6.7
REGIONAL POP.	2,779,128					
U.S. COMPARISON	250,372	76	96	17,615	0.7	1.8

*output adjusted to reflect actual purchasing power within each country

Sources: *Statistical Abstract of the United States*, 1989 and 1990; *Economist*, May 26, 1990.

and were moving China, whose rural population alone exceeds 800 million people, toward a modern economic structure. However, when modernization inevitably led to demands for political openness, the old leadership clamped down politically. Enforcing that choice meant restoring severe economic controls. Now the economy is collapsing. Starvation will soon reappear. The only support the politicians have is the army, and starving countries don't provide much support to armies, whose leaders at some point realize that politicians can't provide the army what the politicians don't have—food. The drive to modernization and political reform will probably reappear by 2000.

Taiwan and Hong Kong are prospering, although the latter awaits its fate at the hands of China as of 1997, when control passes from the British. Singapore, Thailand, and Malaysia are making significant economic progress. Resource-rich, population-dense Indonesia is quietly chugging along, following the successful Asian pattern of export-led economic growth; but its rain forest—the third-greatest in the world, after Brazil and Zaire—is being plundered for export to Japan.

Asia is not everywhere a success. The Philippines are collapsing into chaos; Afghanistan, Sri Lanka (Ceylon), Cambodia, and Burma are embroiled in civil wars; Bangladesh and Nepal are environmental disasters; and India and Pakistan are near war. India's abundant, well-trained professionals and entrepreneurs are all but paralyzed by its near-Soviet-style bureaucracy. India is the world's largest English-speaking nation, an instant advantage—if English continues to be taught in that country. If India ever frees itself from state controls, there may be hope for its economy.

By 2000 Japan will finally start seriously opening its economy to outside goods and placating its long-suffering workers by ending controls on urban growth and curtailing subsidies of antiquated agriculture and retail-distribution systems. This change will be driven both by the rising expectations of young Japanese and by the flight of Japanese corporations that, because of the insularity of Japan's policies, are moving offshore. As Japan's trade restrictions incite other countries to discriminate against Japanese imports, it is increasingly in a Japanese company's interest to become truly international, as American firms have been doing for a decade.

Asia's real success story is likely to be Korea. Before 2000, North Korean dictator Kim Il Sung will die, and civil war will probably break out within the northern republic. The reunification of Korea would create a single nation of 80 million people with the world's highest economic growth rate. By 2010 Korea should have per capita wealth comparable to that in the U.S., Europe, and Japan today. By 2020 Korea could be vying with the Russian-led remnants of the Soviet Union for the position of fourth-largest economy in the world. Far more open than Japan, Korea could become the real leader of an emerging Asian megastate.

WEST MEETS SOUTH: LATIN AMERICA ON THE EDGE

One has to be concerned about nations that are growing economically but still immature politically and under demographic pressure. The countries of Latin America hold the potential for stability and economic improvement, but also the potential for collapse. Over the last fifty years, this region has been transformed from one of substantial per capita growth to one of economic sickness. Some Latin American countries are near economic or political collapse. There's no clear prognosis for their status thirty years from now.

Table 4 demonstrates the stagnation of South America. Central American nations are listed in Table 5 along with the rest of North America. Per capita economic growth in the region has been small to nil. Population growth has slowed sharply, but still the region's

TABLE 4 NATIONAL SUMMARY: SOUTH AMERICA

	1987 Population (thousands)	1987 Life expectancy (years)	1985 Literacy rate (%)	1987 Per capita GDP* ($)	1990-2000 Annual Population growth (%)	1980-87 Annual GNP growth (%)
BOLIVIA	6,730	54	75	1,380	2.0	
PARAGUAY	4,660	67	88	2,603	2.6	
ECUADOR	10,790	66	83	2,687	2.3	
PERU	22,353	63	85	3,129	2.3	2.5
BRAZIL	157,940	65	88	3,524	2.1	2.8
COLOMBIA	32,598	65	87	4,306	1.7	2.3
VENEZUELA	19,753	70	96	4,647	2.2	-0.4
CHILE	13,016	72	98	4,862	1.3	0.0
ARGENTINA	32,291	71	95	5,063	1.1	-1.1
URUGUAY	3,002	71	95	5,063	0.5	
REGIONAL AVERAGE		66	89	3,797	1.9	2.5
REGIONAL POP.	303,133					
U.S. COMPARISON	250,372	76	96	17,615	0.7	1.8

*output adjusted to reflect actual purchasing power within each country

Sources: *Statistical Abstract of the United States*, 1989 and 1990; *Economist*, May 26, 1990.

TABLE 5 NATIONAL SUMMARY: NORTH AMERICA

	1987 Population (thousands)	1987 Life expectancy (years)	1985 Literacy rate (%)	1987 Per capita GDP* ($)	1990-2000 Annual Population growth (%)	1980-87 Annual GNP growth (%)
HAITI	6,509	55	38	775	1.6	
HONDURAS	5,286	65	59	1,119	2.6	
EL SALVADOR	5,659	64	72	1,733	2.4	
DOMINICAN REP	7,501	67	78	1,750	2.3	
GUATEMALA	9,249	63	55	1,957	2.1	
NICARAGUA	3,606	64	88	2,209	2.7	
CUBA	10,548	74	96	2,500	0.8	
JAMAICA	2,513	74	82	2,506	1.5	
TRINIDAD/TOBAGO	1,270	71	96	3,664	1.9	
COSTA RICA	3,039	75	93	3,760	2.1	
PANAMA	2,423	72	89	4,009	1.9	
MEXICO	86,888	69	90	4,624	1.8	1.2
CANADA	26,527	77	99	16,375	0.6	2.8
USA	250,372	76	96	17,615	0.7	1.8
REGIONAL AVERAGE		73	92	12,731	1.1	1.7
REGIONAL POP.	421,390					

*output adjusted to reflect actual purchasing power within each country

Sources: *Statistical Abstract of the United States*, 1989 and 1990; *Economist*, May 26, 1990.

economies are growing slowly, if at all. For a hundred years all of the ingredients for modernization have been there. The continent has vast resources. Many of its countries have well-educated populations, with literacy levels equivalent to that in the U.S. The economies of Argentina and Uruguay were roughly comparable to the U.S. at the turn of the century. Yet things have gotten worse, not better. Average citizens are worse off today than twenty years ago in most Latin American countries, the failure of whose feudal regimes is moving them towards civil war. Their populations are overwhelming their economies.

Latin America finds itself swinging back and forth between incompetent military dictators and populist chaos. The nations in this region have been unable to create a stable legal and political order. They are not modern states. Many of them operate on fascist economic principles: The general runs the electric utility. His technical background is near zero (he's the dictator's brother), but he knows how to find his

Swiss bank accounts, and so do his friends. There is no functioning economy with clear rules. There are Byzantine restrictions on both local business and international capital, at times interspersed with wholesale expropriation and nationalization of foreign-owned property. Needless to say, investors become very skeptical.

American, European, and Japanese capital were flowing into Latin America during the 1970s and early 1980s. Since that time there has been a negative outflow of capital. As a whole the region received a net flow of capital of roughly $300 billion in the form of loans to governments and to commercial enterprise. The great majority of it was wasted. Perhaps $100 billion ended up in Switzerland.

Peru can look forward to years of trouble. Peru's rural-based, radical Maoist Sendero Luminoso is the Khmer Rouge of the Western Hemisphere. It's not impossible for such a group to take over—briefly, but brutally—in a nation suffering from economic collapse under wrenching population pressure.

Brazil, a country of 150 million people, lurches from fascism to populism and back. Brazil's economy has such potential that it grows in spite of its political chaos and huge inflation rate; but this growth may not continue. The country has managed to gain access to advanced rocket technology from European consortia, and is believed to be approaching nuclear-weapons capability. Look for trouble from Brazil.

Colombia was doing fantastically economically—developed export industries, diversified economy, political stability, and not caught up in international debt—until the drug mess tore the country apart. Colombia must choose between legalization and all-out war with the drug lords. The smart money is on the drug lords.

Columbia is on the edge of becoming a western Lebanon. Haiti has tumbled over that edge into an economic, political, environmental, and human abyss. Argentina's inflation in the summer of 1989 was 100 percent per month, which, compounded, equals more than 400,000 percent annually. Judging from its levels of education, infrastructure, and resources, Argentina should be as wealthy as Canada. Yet Argentina is South America's greatest disappointment. Our own country's increasing ethnic diversity and lack of political cohesion make Argentina a chilling case study. In such a place, trying to buy everybody off, rather than efficiently running the economy, is a great political temptation.

The only hope for Latin America lies in dramatic political change. This region has the world's most pernicious combination of Marxist slogans supporting robber-baron oligarchies. Foreign aid and loans have primarily enriched the Swiss banks; the region would have been better off without them. Once-penurious Asian nations such as Korea have surpassed every nation in Latin America in wealth.

The list of countries in this region with stable growth prospects is short: Chile, and perhaps Venezuela and Mexico. Recovery will begin only when each constituent nation crosses the greatest psychological threshold of all: acceptance of its own responsibility for success or failure.

VIEW FROM BEYOND THE EDGE: AFRICA

Black Africa is the world's basket case. As shown in Table 6, the region has by far the highest population growth rate, the greatest poverty, the greatest illiteracy, the worst health, and the least economic growth in the world. Africa is slipping backwards: At current rates, in twenty years the average African will subsist at one-half today's impoverished level. Black African nations, like those of the explosive Middle East, are largely artificial constructs with few stable political, legal, or social traditions.

Behind the silence of the Western media about Africa, ever since whites stopped killing blacks en masse, hides the world's house of horrors. For thirty years the routine has been simple: Throw out the colonialists, replace them with a dictator, run down the economy through theft and incompetent socialism, and spend the next five to fifty years killing each other. The entire region is nearing collapse. Thirty years after the end of colonialism there is not a single functioning multiparty democracy in all of post-colonial Africa.

If there's economic and political hope in black Africa, it might be in South Africa, where blacks have waged a decades-long fight for freedom. Even that common struggle has failed to generate cohesion between two principal tribes, the Xhosa and the Zulu, whose members are now killing each other by the hundreds as anti-apartheid Westerners' voices remain mute. But the South African economy is by far the strongest in Africa; the infrastructure is the most modern. As badly as they have been treated by white South Africa, black South Africans are, on average, far better educated than citizens of other black African nations. The outcome of the South African drama may depend purely on accidents of history: If Nelson Mandela lives for a long time and can make peace with Zulu chief Mangosuthu Buthelezi,

TABLE 6 NATIONAL SUMMARY: AFRICA

	1987 Population (thousands)	1987 Life expectancy (years)	1985 Literacy rate (%)	1987 Per capita GDP* ($)	1990-2000 Annual Population growth (%)	1980-87 Annual GNP growth (%)
ZAIRE	35,330	53	62	220	3.1	0.3
CHAD	5,053	46	26	400	2.2	
TANZANIA	25,994	54	75	405	3.4	0.5
BURUNDI	5,474	50	35	450	2.9	
NIGER	7,691	45	14	452	3.2	
ETHIOPIA	51,375	42	66	454	3.3	1.5
MALAWI	8,198	48	42	476	3.3	
SIERRA LEONE	4,168	42	30	480	2.6	
GHANA	15,234	55	54	481	3.0	0.9
BURKINA FASO	8,941	48	14	500	2.8	
MOZAMBIQUE	15,830	47	39	500	2.9	-5.6
GUINEA	7,269	43	29	500	2.4	
UGANDA	17,593	52	58	511	3.4	
MALI	9,182	45	17	543	2.9	
RWANDA	7,603	49	47	571	3.7	
CENTRAL AFR. REP.	2,879	46	41	591	2.5	
MADAGASCAR	11,802	54	68	634	3.2	-2.2
BENIN	4,840	47	27	665	3.8	
NIGERIA	118,865	51	43	668	3.0	-1.6
TOGO	3,566	54	41	670	3.3	
LIBERIA	2,628	55	35	696	3.2	
ZAMBIA	8,112	54	76	717	3.6	
SUDAN	25,037	51	23	750	2.9	-0.5
CONGO	2,305	49	63	756	3.3	
KENYA	25,393	59	60	794	4.1	3.2
MAURITANIA	2,038	47	17	840	3.1	
SOMALIA	8,415	46	12	1,000	2.1	
ANGOLA	8,802	45	41	1,000	2.7	
SENEGAL	7,740	47	28	1,068	3.1	
IVORY COAST	12,070	53	42	1,123	3.6	
ZIMBABWE	10,482	59	74	1,184	3.7	
CAMEROON	11,109	52	61	1,381	2.6	
NAMIBIA	1,400	56	30	1,500	3.7	
LESOTHO	1,757	57	73	1,585	2.5	
GABON	1,069	52	62	2,068	1.4	
BOTSWANA	1,276	59	71	2,496	3.4	
SOUTH AFRICA	36,696	61	70	4,981	2.1	0.5
REGIONAL AVERAGE		51	50	940	3.1	-0.5
REGIONAL POP.	533,216					
U.S. COMPARISON	250,372	76	96	17,615	0.7	1.8

Sources: *Statistical Abstract of the United States*, 1989 and 1990; *Economist*, May 26, 1990.

he has the potential for bringing about both peaceful change and successful economic and political structures. Even that's a long shot. The more likely outcome is 6 million refugees knocking on North America's and Europe's doors.

The rest of the continent will slide into chaos: endless civil war, marauding bands of killers in the uniforms of soldiers, accelerating erosion and loss of farmland, mass famine, and social breakdown. Africa exemplifies not just political chaos, but social collapse—the perfect climate for transmitting AIDS. Over the last decade the AIDS epidemic, which probably started in Central Africa many decades ago, has spread rapidly through heterosexual promiscuity. Uganda, with as much as 70 percent of its urban adult population infected, appears to be the worst off. The rate seems likely to reach that level soon in Zaire, Zambia, and Rwanda-Burundi. As many as 30 percent of the adult population in Kigali, Rwanda's capital city, carry HIV, the virus that causes AIDS. The disease is spreading south into Zimbabwe and north as well. The Ivory Coast, for example, has the third highest real per capita income in independent black Africa; but in 1988, more than a third of all adult deaths in its capital city, Abidjan, were from AIDS.

In the northeast, Ethiopia is already in collapse mode: over twenty years of civil war, net negative economic growth for several years, no per capita progress for decades. That country's famines were overwhelmingly creations of government policy, rather than natural occurrences. The civil war, overgrazing, and overpopulation are causing environmental losses that may make the famine permanent.

Kenya's high economic growth is eclipsed by the highest population growth rate in the world—over 4 percent annually.[2] At this rate a population doubles every eighteen years. There is a single political party: kleptocracy. In the spring of 1990, President Daniel arap Moi of Kenya had his foreign minister and political rival, Robert Ouko, killed, dismembered, and burned.

Can the developed world afford to ignore the problems of poor countries? The September 1, 1990, *Economist* left black Africa completely out of its "New Map of the World." Table 7 shows the great disparity in living standards and growth rates across the regions of the world. The overwhelming difference in living standards between the developed world and the Third World will propel emigrants across the borders into the promised lands of the burgeoning megastates. Meanwhile, an outgrowth of the modern economy and modern technology is that as women make more money, they make fewer babies. Throughout nearly the entire developed world, birthrates are below replacement levels. The declining incidence of maternal labor pains will give birth to an adult-labor shortage in all the developed countries. The United States, Europe, and Japan will need new blood.

TABLE 7 WORLD SUMMARY

	1987 Population (thousands)	1987 Life expectancy (years)	1985 Literacy rate (%)	1987 Per capita GDP* ($)	1990-2000 Annual Population growth (%)	1980-87 Annual GNP growth (%)
NORTH AMERICA	421,390	73	92	12,731	1.1	1.7
EUROPE	788,868	73	98	8,591	0.4	1.8
SOUTH AMERICA	303,133	66	89	3,797	1.9	2.5
NORTH AFRICA & MIDDLE EAST	306,705	64	56	3,263	2.6	3.0
ASIA	2,779,128	65	63	2,343	1.5	6.7
AFRICA	533,216	51	50	940	3.1	-0.5
TOTAL	5,132,440	65	70	4,151	1.5	4.3

*output adjusted to reflect actual purchasing power within countries

Sources: *Statistical Abstract of the United States*, 1989 and 1990; *Economist*, May 26, 1990.

CHAPTER

4

The Changing American

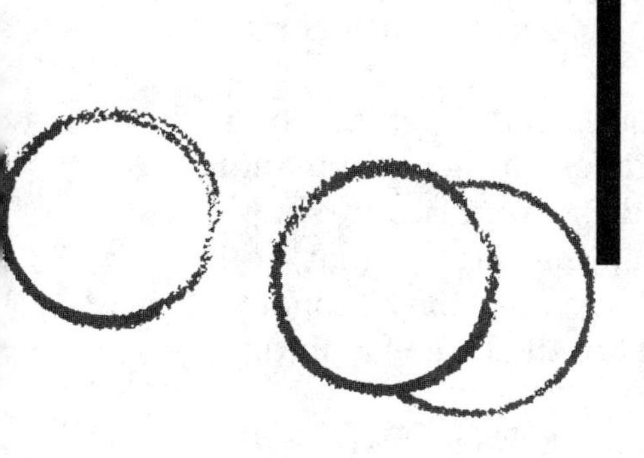

In the developed nations, now converging into a triad of megastates, population growth has virtually stopped—except for that due to immigration. But in much of the rest of the world, population growth rates outstrip economic, political, social, and technological capabilities—and create immense pressure to emigrate.

As societies modernize, they undergo a demographic transition that proceeds through three classical stages.

- *Stage One:* Initially populations are stable, with high death rates balancing high birthrates. Birthrates are high in primitive societies because children, who frequently die before reaching adulthood, are the only form of old age security.
- *Stage Two:* Modern technology—vaccines, sanitation, and increased food supplies—quickly drops the mortality rate, but birthrates remain high, ushering in a period of explosive population growth.
- *Stage Three:* Ultimately birthrates drop, too—in part due to the recognition that, thanks to modern technology, more babies are surviving to adulthood—and a new stability is achieved.

Advanced societies are now experiencing a surprising fourth stage of the demographic transition: decline. Birthrates are below replacement levels throughout Europe,

Japan, and in European America. The decline is brought about not by starvation and disease but by a uniquely modern scourge: affluence. Modern societies have changed the cost-benefit ratio of having children. Children no longer provide useful labor or old age security, nor do they fulfill a required role for women. Women have vast economic opportunities beyond the family, and children require growing quantities of expensive education and housing. No society has provided sufficient childcare or other social services to reduce the severe economic and time penalties of childbearing. Modern birth control makes the economically obvious choice easy.

Reducing population growth doesn't automatically spell economic prosperity. China and India have put the brakes on their population growth—but too late; current populations in these countries are simply too large for the national resource bases. Argentina and Uruguay, both of whose populations are growing slowly, have only their economic and social systems to blame for their poverty in the face of abundant resources.

Because so many nations are still stuck in Stage Two of the demographic transition, the world's population, now estimated at 5.3 billion, will increase by one billion people (90–100 million people per year) in the 1990s, faster than ever, with 90 percent of the increase occurring in developing countries. This growth is leading to mass urbanization. By the year 2000, 19 of the world's 21 biggest metropolitan areas will be in poorer nations.[1] If we are lucky, the world's population will stabilize at around 9 billion in the next century.

Some regions show no signs of slowing population growth. African and Middle Eastern cultures are proving particularly resistant to improving rights for women and reducing birthrates. In fifteen countries—thirteen of them in Africa—birthrates rose between the early 1960s and the 1980s. At present rates of increase, Kenya's population is due to almost quadruple by 2010. Social conditions are deteriorating in Central Africa, where demographic projections may be invalidated by epidemics reminiscent of medieval Europe.

The prescription for overpopulated countries is clear: stable government, institutionalized support for the elderly, and empowerment of women (including birth-control education). But what is the prescription for Stage Four societies—the advanced countries of Europe, Asia, Australasia, and North America—where below-replacement birthrates and longer life expectancies translate into aging populations, worker shortages, and diminished worker-to-retiree ratios?

The Soviet Union and the United States—the third- and fourth-most-populous countries in the world, respectively—are just two of the countries facing declining birthrates and the real possibility of declining populations, or at least declining European populations. In both countries the European majority's birthrates are below replacement levels, while non-European minority groups (mainly Central Asian in the Soviet Union; chiefly of African and Hispanic descent in the U.S.) are growing rapidly.

As two demographers have suggested in *Science* magazine,[2] there may be no better time than the present for the Soviet Union—projected to be one of the fastest-aging countries in the world during the 1990s—to undergo a rocky transition to a market system. The painful unemployment produced inevitably by the shutdown of inefficient enterprises will be ameliorated by the shrinking labor force. The number of working-age men in both superpowers and Europe is declining so rapidly that maintaining huge standing armies in Western and Eastern Europe is becoming untenable. It is not surprising that European troop reductions are now being hammered out between the former adversaries.

Other NATO and Warsaw Pact countries—Britain, Scandinavia, both Germanys, Hungary—and also Japan are growing even more slowly, and will continue to do so through 2010. Once-prolific Italy's fertility rate—the average number of children an Italian female can expect to have in her lifetime—is now the lowest the world, at 1.3. (Compare this to Rwanda's 8.3 rate.) As of 1989, the fertility rate of U.S. women was a more robust 2.0—still well below the replacement rate of 2.1 (some will die before reproducing). The population in West Germany is actually declining; it soon will start declining in most of Scandinavia.

Japan has the highest life expectancy in the world and a fertility rate that in 1989 fell to an all-time low, for that country, of 1.57 children per woman, according to a recent Japanese study. Thus, the Japanese population is aging more rapidly than that of any other country; the percentage of Japanese who are 65 or older will soon exceed that of the United States and should approach Sweden's by 2020. Japan, whose culturally and ethnically homogeneous society shuns outsiders, races to solve its looming worker shortage by improving productivity through worker training, through increasingly automated production techniques, and by moving production facilities offshore and turning to imports.

In June 1990 the *New York Times* reported that Finance Minister Ryutara Hashimoto, addressing the Japanese cabinet, blamed his country's trend toward smaller family size on the growing tendency of Japanese women to delay having babies so they can complete their education. He suggested that women be discouraged from seeking higher education. The leaking of his remarks caused such ferment that he quickly denied having made them.

With developed countries' growth slowing and the Third World already overloaded and continuing to grow, there's strong pressure in the world for rebalancing populations through migration. The nations with the most open immigration policies will get as many as they want.

The countries of Europe are scarcely known for being melting pots; the European concept of nationhood has long been associated with commonality of language and ethnic stock within a nation's borders. But with the dramatic decline in the birthrates of native populations, Europe—along with the U.S. and Japan—has grown old. West Germany's economy was saved by a massive influx of Turkish workers, now being supplanted by East Germans. In France it was Moroccans and Algerians; in England, Pakistanis and West Indians.

Immigrants from South Asia, the Middle East, and North Africa now constitute almost 4 percent of Britain's population, more than 5 percent of West Germany's, and at least 8 percent (and growing by 100,000 a year) of France's 56 million.[3] Indeed, Great Britain, France, West Germany, and Switzerland—and, even more so, Australia and Canada—all have greater shares of foreign-born persons than the United States. In Switzerland foreigners constitute 16 percent of the population, compared to 6 percent in the U.S.

Absorbing immigrants into an essentially homogeneous society is difficult once the immigrant population reaches a certain threshold of visibility. Like Japan, France is struggling with a labor shortage. Unlike Japan, France's solution has been a policy of importing immigrant laborers, particularly from Algeria, a former French colony. Some 4 million Muslims, most of them of Algerian descent, supplement a native work force whose size has not kept pace with economic demand (and at any rate is loathe to engage in menial tasks). Muslims now constitute the second-largest religious group in the country, after Roman Catholics.

Recent election victories in Algeria by Islamic fundamentalists have generated apprehension among native white Frenchmen that fundamentalist Islam could spread to France, compounding the language barrier with cultural hostility. The concern is heightened by outright fear of an unwanted flood of culturally distinct Algerian immigrants into France should chaos envelope Algeria. A backlash is developing; France's xenophobic National Front Party has the support of about 17 percent of the electorate. West Germany's right-wing Republican Party has also made election hay out of that country's Turkish immigrant workers.

The potential for immigrant-catalyzed racial and cultural clashes in West Europe has probably been derailed by the sudden overthrow of existing Communist governments in Eastern Europe. The collapse of the Iron Curtain has created, almost overnight, an immense supply of inexpensive, highly educated, European laborers—to Western Europe's lasting benefit, and to the detriment of displaced "guest workers" from poorer countries on other continents.

As this century draws to a close, there will be two worlds, demographically speaking: the poorer countries, where women will average nearly four children apiece and life expectancy will average 61 years; and the richer countries, where children will be born at slightly below replacement rates but can expect to live 74 years. By the end of the next century, however, all the world will have gone through the demographic transition. Population will have stabilized, standard-of-living differences will be declining sharply, and the period of dramatic worldwide immigration will end. The international language of commerce, English, will have overwhelming economic power, but it will contain far more Spanish words. The reasons for that are to be found in the Western Hemisphere.

Generation Wars

McDonald's has a big problem: There aren't enough teenagers. The United States went through a dramatic decline in births, from a peak of 4.7 million in 1957 to a trough of 3 million in the 1970s. The fertility rate in 1957 was 3.77 children per woman; it had sunk to 1.7 by 1976, but has since crept back up almost to replacement levels. The steep decline in births in the 1960s and 1970s followed a steep increase in the 1940s and 1950s.

The low birthrates of the 1970s means there will be far fewer native-born new employees in the 1990s than our economy naturally provides jobs for. The Census Bureau projects the number of young adults aged

25–35 will drop 15 percent in the next decade for the country as a whole, and more in the Northeast and Midwest.

We are going through an "echo" baby boom. Four million babies were born in the U.S. in 1989, a number sure to be surpassed in 1990. After peaking in the mid-1990s, the rate will back off to about 3.5 million births per year in the next century. Still, U.S. population growth during the 1990s is projected at only 7 percent, surpassing the previous record low of 7.2 percent during the 1930s, when birthrates were unusually low and immigration was restricted.

Sharp labor shortages are showing up in the U.S., first in occupations that rely on younger, low-wage workers. The formerly labor-intensive, low-wage restaurant and retail-trade sectors are being forced to automate, pay higher wages, or both. Wages for young, entry-level workers will rise in the coming decade; and the unemployment rate, now a little over 5 percent, will head to below 4 percent—virtually automatically. If it *doesn't*, whoever is president in the year 2000 should be voted out of office.

The shortage will be buffered, to an extent, by a continued increase in the proportion of Americans—especially women—who take jobs. By 2000, 69 percent of all Americans aged 16 or older will be in the labor force, up from 66 percent in 1988.[4] But there is an upper limit to the labor-force participation rate, and we are approaching it.

In a single year between 1989 and 1990, the number of 18-year-old Americans dropped 8 percent.[5] There are 14 percent fewer Americans aged 16–24 today than there were a decade ago. This remarkable demographic trend is accentuated by an incredible explosion in the number of elderly Americans.

Twenty years from now, there will be 40 percent more people over 75, and 8 percent fewer children under age 5. The 65–75 age group will grow slightly if at all in the 1990s, because birthrates during the Great Depression were the lowest in our history, but their numbers will burgeon after the year 2000 and explode after 2010. The aging of America will strain the Social Security system, place tremendous pressure on our health-care system, and affect housing markets as large numbers of older Americans begin to retire and move.

A severe generational conflict is developing between the older white population on one side and the younger white population and minorities on the other. The United States happens to have the wealthiest group of "young old," aged 55–70, in world history; and they're better off relative to the rest of us than ever. Three mechanisms of wealth transfer from younger to older Americans are responsible.

First, in relative terms, government expenditures have shifted sharply: more for the elderly (chiefly as Social Security and Medicare), less for the young (bigger payroll-tax bites). The European-American elderly are the wealthiest in the world. Yet young American families have a lower real income than their counterparts in most other developed countries. The poverty rate among the elderly in the U.S. is about half that of American children under 6, of whom nearly one in four—and about half of all young African-American children—live in families whose incomes fall below the federal poverty line.

Second, young people's finances and lifestyles have also been devastated by the high cost of housing, which has been severely restricted in many parts of the country. Local and regional zoning laws and environmental policies—a trend that began during the 1970s—have driven prices and rents up, especially on both coasts, effectively locking potential first-time homebuyers out of the market. Housing-growth restrictions in urban and suburban areas force young workers, of whom a growing number are nonwhite, into nightmare commutes. Restricted infrastructure growth heightens the commuting nightmare. It is as if older, affluent homeowners were saying: "We won't build highways, because they pollute; but *you* have to spend an extra two hours a day generating more pollution while your car sits stalled in traffic jams."

Meanwhile, the smartest investment decision an individual ever made was to be born before 1950. People who today are 45 and over own a huge concentration of wealth, because they already owned real estate when inflation took off in the 1970s. They didn't save any more than the current younger population does. They simply managed to plunk down $2,000 for a down payment on a house then selling for $20,000; now it's often worth $200,000. Because of a generational stroke of fortune, they've got a sizable chunk of home equity, and they're expecting to retire early on it. This pattern, which the country can't afford to maintain, will be reversed as the year 2000 approaches: With all these real-estate holders trying to cash in at the same time, who are they going to sell to? What will be left to retire on after the next few rounds of tax hikes?

The third and final shift in financial power from the young to the old derives from our country's financial debt—government, corporate, and personal, owed both internally and internationally—and a hidden debt we've built up by allowing our infrastructure to depreciate instead of maintaining it. All of that will be paid for by the young.

The wealthiest older generation in world history is also the healthiest. But we're learning that the human body hits a wall between age 80 and 90. You can stay alive after that, but few can stay healthy. Advanced medical technologies allow you to remain alive and *un*healthy for as long as you're willing to tolerate the misery and somebody is willing to pay.

The costs of extended dying for the elderly will soon become unacceptable to society. According to the Census Bureau, the number of people aged 85 or older—which increased by 44 percent during the 1980s, while the general population grew by only 10 percent—will grow 42 percent during the 1990s, six times the projected overall rate. The premier ethical quarrel of the coming decades—How much medical care is enough for this "old old" population?—will make the abortion issue seem like a playground argument; the numbers are vastly larger, and the citizens in question will have been certifiably, unequivocally alive for eighty or more years.

As the burden of supporting older, nonworking citizens becomes intolerable for young workers, the age of retirement will eventually go much higher. The great majority of people will work into their seventies—which will probably add to their longevity. An increase in the mandatory retirement age—and probably in the required working age for Social Security eligibility—could mean European-American males will hold their own as a proportion, now a solid majority, of the working population in the late 1990s and beyond. But for now, the proportion of workers who are women will rise; and the proportion who are members of ethnic minorities will climb dramatically.

Working Women

Short of extending the retirement age, the saturation point for male workers has been reached in the United States. By 2000, according to *American Demographics* magazine, 76 percent of men aged 16 or older will have jobs or be looking for them[6]—the same as today. (The proportion of men working past age 55 has been declining for over thirty years.) The participation rate for adult women will climb to 63 percent, up from today's 57 percent. The only Western countries with comparable numbers of adult women working outside the home are in Scandinavia.

The proliferation of office jobs over "muscle" jobs, the high cost of housing, and the advent of effective birth-control technologies that allow family planning—all of these have spurred the entry of women into the work force. In 1950, only about 30 percent of all paid workers in the United States were women; by 1970, 38 percent were; today 46 percent are. The Bureau of Labor Statistics projects the number to rise to 47.5 percent by the year 2000.

Women have fanned out into the professions. Almost one-third of new doctors and about two-fifths of all new lawyers today are women.[7] But most women work because they have to. A University of Michigan researcher, Sheldon Danzinger, has found that half of the country's two-income families would drop below the poverty line, as defined by the federal government, if the wife didn't work. (Ironically, the influx of women into a glutted labor market during the 1960s and 1970s may have contributed to a downward spiral in real wages. Inflation-adjusted median family income has barely budged since 1973.)

The trade-off between making more money and having more time to raise children has thus not always been a purely aesthetic decision. From 1975 to 1988, the proportion of mothers who were in the work force rose from about 47 percent to 65 percent. By 1987, over half of all women in the U.S. with children less than a year old were working or looking for jobs.

The mass entry of women into the work force in advanced economies once appeared to be creating a vicious circle: If birthrates drop because women who are working full-time or in school preparing for professional careers don't have as many babies, the labor shortage they are helping to fill will eventually deepen. This worrisome development seems not to be occurring. In the last few years, despite extremely high female labor-force participation rates in the United States and Sweden, fertility rates have actually climbed in both countries. Career women are deciding to have children; they just have them later than ever before.

In the next decade or so, labor shortages will force employers to accede to what women en masse want to do. The phenomenon of working women choosing to take time out of careers to have babies will accelerate. More women with children will look for part-time opportunities and take longer career breaks.

A significant portion of men will also insist on and receive more flexible careers. Sabbaticals, job-sharing arrangements, and flextime will become commonplace. An information-intensive economy creates opportunities for telecommuting; telephones, computers, fax machines, and modems allow a parent to engage in office-type work from the home.

If there really is a spontaneous trend toward reconnecting with children and the home, we're lucky. A degree of incompatibility may exist between the unbridled modern economy and the closely knit family/community structure that's necessary for the psychological health and well-being of children and adults.

Market economies, while wildly innovative and dynamic, value only those things that are paid for in cash. In converting childrearing—traditionally the province of mothers in the home—into a market activity to be subcontracted to entrepreneurs and their paid employees, the entire developed world is in the midst of an enormous experiment whose outcome is far from certain. We won't know what works until we've done it for a generation or two. The economic elites of the advanced countries have evolved a combination of part-time work and very expensive childcare that seems to work reasonably well; but no one has developed an effective mass-childcare system for the population as a whole. Japanese women with small children rarely work full-time, nor do many West German mothers. So far the countries putting the biggest efforts into maintaining traditional family and community structures—clearly Japan, and also West Germany—are turning out to be the economic and social winners.

More Immigrants, Please

The United States is in the midst of a wave of immigration. It will accelerate. This is one of the most important demographic factors in the U.S. for the next fifty years. We will get 700,000 to 800,000 immigrants per year at the peak of our coming labor shortage from the late 1990s through 2010. Pressures for immigration are building on both sides of the American-Mexican border. The number of Americans aged 20–29 will decline 12 percent in the 1990s, while the number of Latin Americans aged 20–29 will rise from about 42 million to 48 million, or 14 percent. In fiscal year 1988, Immigration and Naturalization Service agents apprehended almost one million illegals at the border.[8] This number has nowhere to go but up.

As Europe went through its demographic transition in the late 19th and early 20th centuries, its surplus population was exported to the underpopulated U.S., whose culture became essentially an extension of Europe's. Now no more than 10 percent of America's immigrants come from Europe. Today's immigrants, most of them young, are nearly all non-European. The success or failure of their absorption into the mainstream will pose a major test in America's future.

Primary and secondary educational institutions will have their hands full. While modern technology will ultimately handle language much more efficiently than it does today, there are few examples of successful multilingual societies. Perennial language conflicts in Canada, Belgium, Sri Lanka, and India forecast an unpleasant future if our educational institutions cannot meet the test. We will need more ways of maintaining national unity during the next century, a period of heavy immigration.

In the last decade, almost 6 million legal immigrants (the vast majority from the Pacific Rim and Caribbean nations, especially Mexico, the Philippines, Korea, and Haiti) and an additional 2 to 3 million illegals (about half of them Mexican) entered the United States—the highest numbers since 1901–10, when 8.6 million entered the country. The immigrants who arrived between 1901–10 constituted 9.6 percent of the U.S. population;[9] the 1980s arrivals, less than 3 percent.

Immigration was high during the 1980s, when the largest age-group of native-born Americans in history was entering the work force. The resulting labor surplus produced high unemployment rates. Now, just as we're moving toward a severe labor shortage in the late 1990s and early in the next century, there are voices calling for tighter restrictions on immigration. (These same voices may sometimes be heard lobbying in support of relaxing the rules for their own pet ethnic groups.)

The simple fact is that the United States needs immigrants. With respect to job growth in the 1990s, most of the big percentage gainers (e.g., paralegals, medical assistants; home health aides; radiologic technologists and technicians) demand skills that few immigrants are likely to bring with them, but the biggest gainers in absolute numbers include such low-skill categories as retail salespersons; janitors, cleaners, and maids; and waiters and waitresses.[10] Employers will be desperate to fill jobs that many native-born don't want to do themselves. We have evolved an economy that requires people who are willing to work for very low wages in service industries—the hotel/motel sector, fruit and vegetable harvesting, and construction.

America is lucky. People *want* to come to this country, which has such a successful tradition of absorbing immigrants and assimilating their children. Japan, whose homogeneous culture never fully accepts immigrants into its arms, toys with such notions as restricting educational opportunities for women, or shipping its old people overseas to live out their days.

Ethnic Minorities: Growing

Whatever we do, short of putting up a Berlin Wall around the U.S. and shooting people, the population—currently 250 million—will grow significantly until sometime between 2025 and 2050, when it will stabilize at 300–350 million. Nearly 40 percent of that increase will be from immigration, and most immigrants will be Asian or Latin American.

The growth of European America has nearly ended. America's white, non-Hispanic population, now estimated at 190 million, will stabilize at about 195 million by 2010. At current birthrates, it will then start declining. America's European working population will decline after 2000. For the next ten years, the non-European proportion of the labor market will jump. Whites will be a minority in California by about 2000. Indeed, by the year 2000, California will have become the world's first 100-percent-minority modern economy—a role model for the pluralistic society—as European-Americans' proportion of that state's population drops below 50 percent.

First-generation Americans from most immigrant groups do unusually well. The family strength is still there; they haven't been totally Americanized; there's a drive to succeed. There's almost always a sharp improvement from their parents' condition, frequently to income levels and social and occupational status well above the national average. The success of recent Asian immigrants proves that race doesn't matter, but culture matters a great deal.

Asian-Americans constitute the fastest-growing racial minority in percentage terms, the result of heavy immigration by Filipinos, Koreans, Vietnamese, and Chinese. Continuing chaos in the Philippines and the expected takeover of Hong Kong by the Chinese government in 1997 will accelerate Asian migration to the Pacific coast of North America. While the number of Asian-Americans is small nationally—about 5 million, or 2 percent of the total—they are heavily concentrated in California, where the proportion is already 9 percent and will reach 15–20 percent by 2020. The averages within this group hide a large range of demographic characteristics. On the one hand, the first wave of Vietnamese immigrants and their children, who tend to speak

English, are very well educated and have high incomes; Koreans, too. These Asian-Americans take advantage of America's propensity to redistribute wealth in the form of education—the kind of capital that really counts in an information-intensive world. Other Asians though, are having significant problems.

Despite having to overcome a history of discrimination in this country, Asian-Americans will become a very important group economically and in every other way. They prove both the American dream and the American tragedy. American society has more opportunity and more flexibility than any developed nation. But if your family cracks under the strain, the safety net is a long way down and the holes are very large.

Hispanics are now America's second-largest ethnic minority; by 2025 they will be its largest. Legal immigration from Latin America is running at 250,000 annually. Illegals bring the figure to more than 400,000, perhaps even 500,000. There are about 20 million Hispanics in the U.S.—about 8 percent of the population. By 2010, there will be 31 million, about 10 percent of the total—and closer to 12 percent if present immigration trends persist.

The Hispanic immigration experience is really twofold: first, to the United States in general; and second, from rural to urban areas within the U.S. Hispanic-Americans are mainly concentrated in the Southwest, where they already are the largest minority group. One out of three reside in California, where they constitute about 25 percent of the population, probably to grow to 35–40 percent by 2020. Texas, New York, Florida, Illinois, Arizona, New Jersey, New Mexico, and Colorado all have large Hispanic populations.

The overwhelming majority of American-born Hispanics are bilingual. Even in the barrios, virtually all kids learn English. Across generations, according to a major study carried out by Rand Corporation in the mid-1980s, their birthrates, incomes, and educational levels converge to the U.S. average. Hispanic birthrates are high, but there's a clear generation-by-generation progression of integration into the American mainstream. Asked how many offspring they want to have, young American-born Hispanic women give roughly the same answer as European-Americans do—they want 2.4 children. Median incomes of Hispanic-Americans varied in 1988 from a low of $15,400 for Puerto Ricans to a high of $23,872 for Central and South Americans, with Mexicans, the most numerous subgroup, at $19,839. In general, those urbanized the longest have the highest incomes.

There remain consistent pockets of rural poverty in the Southwest, where many Hispanics are employed in low-wage, seasonal, labor-intensive agriculture. Because the European-American owners who dominate the economies of these regions need seasonal workers, they do their best to keep other industries out. Everybody works for three months, nobody works for the other nine. Housing is terrible. Schools range from bad to horrible; if the farmworkers' kids get through eighth grade, they're lucky.

Nationwide, Hispanic school dropout rates are high: While 86 percent of European-Americans aged 22–24 have finished high school, 42 percent of Hispanics in the same age bracket haven't. Urban Hispanics who have been raised in America have a high-school dropout rate closer to the U.S. average, but it is still high. The African-American dropout rate is only 17 percent.

There is evidence that the Hispanic-American family is breaking down under U.S. economic and social pressures. While the Hispanic-American family structure, like the Asian-American, is still largely intact—more Hispanic households (82 percent) than non-Hispanic households (70 percent) consist of families—divorce rates are jumping. Of even more concern is the fact that nearly one-third of Hispanic births are to unwed mothers—a once-rare occurrence. When generation after generation is left behind, as appears to be happening to America's rural Hispanic population and has happened to large numbers of both rural and urban African-Americans, it's a problem for the entire country. If Hispanic community and family structures crack in the same way as African-American ones have, the United States will have an underclass in its central cities and rural areas that is larger than ever before.

One way to look at the African-American population of the U.S. is as discriminated-against, rural-to-urban immigrants. In their social and economic evolution, real progress didn't start until the rural-to-urban immigration of the 1950s and the end of officially sanctioned discrimination in the 1960s. African-Americans, at 30 million the largest U.S. minority group today, will reach an estimated 39 million in 2010. But with birthrates now at replacement levels and no further immigration, African-American population growth is slowing sharply. This group will be about equalled in numbers by Hispanics sometime around 2025. Although many states have virtually no African-Americans, they are broadly spread across the nation. By 2000, they'll constitute 20 percent of total population in the South, 6 percent in the West,

11 percent in the Midwest, and 12 percent in the Northeast—still fairly rural in the South, heavily urbanized elsewhere, more or less unchanged from the current distribution.

African-Americans have scored their greatest successes in politics. Many of our largest cities, including Detroit, Chicago, New York City, and Los Angeles, have black mayors. California's small black population—8 percent—has political influence far beyond its numbers: The mayor of the state's largest city, a black speaker of the house, and many influential black legislators. They are, at least in political power, overrepresented. This pattern will extend beyond California's borders.

African-Americans will be the "Irish" politicians of the next century. The rise of the influence of African-Americans in politics and the Democratic Party is just starting. There will be a black presidential nominee by 2020. Hispanics are also gaining political influence. The tradition of a white Republican Party and immigrant-minority Democratic Party won't last; either that, or the Republican Party won't last.

Most African-Americans are making a steady transition into the economic and social mainstream. Black married couples had a median income of $27,000 in 1987—an incredible achievement given their relatively young age, history of discrimination, and lack of formal education. West Indian communities stand out in economic achievement.

But a significant proportion—one-quarter to one-third—of African America is collapsing under economic and social pressures. Underlying this failure is the phenomenon of fundamental family breakdown. As recently as the 1950s, black America had exceptionally strong families. The weakening of the African-American family in particular—and the breakdown of the African-American community in general—is a phenomenon of the second half of the 20th century. Were the integration policies and aid programs of the 1960s and 1970s fundamental failures?

In 1987, 63 percent of all African-American births were to unmarried women, and the number is growing. Over one-half of African-American children are growing up with only one parent present. In America, that's a problem. Substituting for a stable family is expensive. Denmark and Iceland, where over 40 percent of births are to unwed mothers, have all-encompassing governmental support systems; we don't.

The problems of America's black underclass are going to get worse. The schools can't replace families—especially not the inner-city public schools, which are cauldrons of chaos. The drug epidemic is not going to disappear anytime soon. There are advance indicators that an AIDS epidemic is starting in black ghetto America. Black America will be unwilling to face that reality, just as gay America denied the first stage of the AIDS epidemic.

African-American men aged 15–24 are seven times more likely to be homicide victims than like-aged European-American men, and 170 times more likely than a young man in nonviolent Japan. There are places—so far, still small and isolated—where the police don't dare go today. But that could get much worse tomorrow. We face the dismal prospect of mini-Lebanons incubating within the U.S.

The division of the planet as a whole into two worlds, the developed and the underdeveloped, is mirrored within the United States. Inside many American cities, a set of have-nots is becoming increasingly isolated from the outside world. The Detroit area looks like a doughnut; the center is emptying out. The city, now overwhelmingly black, has lost nearly half of its population since 1970. If New York continues to deteriorate—some parts, such as South Bronx, have already become mini-Lebanons—then today's exodus of executive headquarters is just the beginning of that city's demise.

The racial pattern of the U.S. will become frozen as the interregional mass movements of past decades end. The West has finally been settled, the South repopulated. Detroit and Chicago don't need any more workers, and they are not about to provide either the public housing or high welfare payments that might bring more minorities. High-income populations will move north, away from perceived minority problems; snow and safety will appear more attractive than sun and bullets. The main geo-demographic change will be sprawl *away from central cities* as advances in telecommunication and manufacturing technologies make central cities less necessary.

Accelerating the shift away from central cities and minority concentrations will be America's worsening crime problem. The past decline in younger people, aged 5–24, didn't help much—the individuals within this group made up the difference by becoming more crime-prone—and that demographic decline is coming to a halt, anyway. The route to security will lead away from central cities, the warehouses for the underclass.

For significant portions of all racial and ethnic groups, the economic and political system is working. We're going to see an abundance of intermarriage across racial lines. By 2010–2020, as many as 10–20 million people, mostly young and from throughout the entire income spectrum, won't fit into the old categories.

But those who have gotten ahead are building higher and higher walls to protect themselves. Locked, private communities for middle-class people are growing in number. The potential exists for a polarization of retired, still mostly European-American homeowners vs. a young, heavily taxed labor force of increasingly minority composition. The development of entire age-differentiated communities will accelerate in the 1990s.

The United States is the first country that has tried to blend Europe, Africa, and Asia into a single egalitarian nation. For the forseeable future—the next 100 years—immigration pressures will be overwhelming. More than ever, the solutions to this country's problems reside not in divisiveness, but in reaffirmation of a pluralistic ideal within a vibrant economy. How are we going to treat our growing elderly population? How are we going to take care of our kids? How are we going to work with our minorities to accelerate them into the mainstream? These are tough questions to answer, and all the answers will be costly—but answer them we must, or lose our leadership role in the 21st century.

CHAPTER

5

Solo Descent from a Mountain of Debt

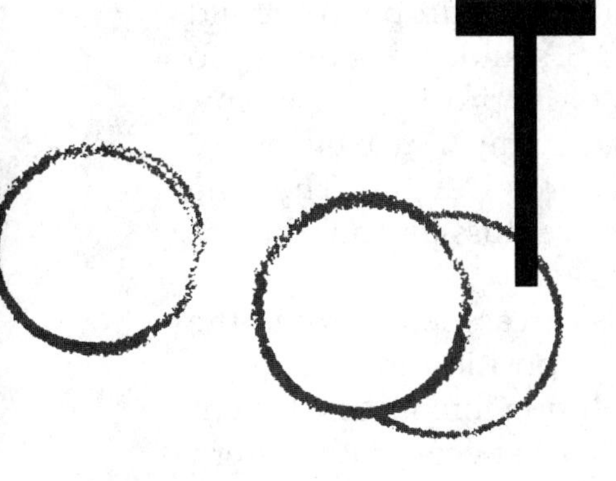

The United States emerged from World War II victorious over both its enemies and allies, blessed with the developed world's only intact, integrated, continental economy and other outstanding economic, social, and political features:

- World dominance in finance and in most technologies (only Britain came close), products that set world standards for quality, and an efficient legal/insurance system.
- The healthiest citizens in the world, at a modest cost.
- A relatively pristine environment, and the world's first national parks and wildlife refuges.
- The world's best housing, transportation, and communication infrastructure.
- The world's only near-universal K–12 education system, and by far the best university system.
- Close-knit communities and families; social problems such as divorce and drug addiction being relatively rare.
- A political system that allowed both maximum freedom and effective action.

The U.S. has lost the across-the-board superiority it had in 1945. Many nations now have standards of living comparable to ours. Our share of global output has declined from almost one-third after World War II to just over one-fifth in the 1980s. This was inevitable and, to an extent, even desirable. After the war, America's Marshall Plan steadied European political and economic systems; the United States-led Bretton Woods monetary agreement stabilized currencies, laying the groundwork for viable, long-term trade relationships among all the non-communist industrialized countries. Capital and technology flowed eastward across the Atlantic and allowed Europe to rebuild itself and return to rough equivalence with U.S. standards of living. To help occupied Japan sift through the ashes of its prostrate economy, the American government dispatched to that country such efficiency and quality-management experts as W. Edwards Deming. Then the U.S. turned to the task of standing off aggressive Russian and Chinese Communism in what became World War III.

Now that war is over, with communism's carcass left to rot in the dust. The U.S., for its part, is reassessing its position in a changed world. The Soviet Union is fending off dissolution into its constituent republics by espousing the principles of a market economy. Eastern Europe no longer wants to be politically distinct from an immensely affluent Western Europe. Japan, having mastered the American science of baseball, went on to pioneer the transistor radio; the rest, as they say, is history. Several tiny, resource-poor Asian countries have shown the world what an educated, motivated, disciplined work force can do when its potential is set free by a stable market economy.

The cost of leadership was steep. Over the last 45 years, American military expenditures have averaged about 6 percent of GNP—an aggregate total of three years' worth of output. World War III's victors are the vanquished of World War II, Germany and Japan. Our new allies, along with many of our old ones, wisely fought the Cold War to the last American dollar while efficiently investing their own savings in their civilian economies.

Concentrating on the political conflict of the moment and on bringing our new allies into the modern fold, we ignored the imperative to modernize our own economy. In the 1980s, only 1.8 percent of America's GNP was devoted to civilian research and development; the comparable figures for Germany and Japan were 2.6 percent and 2.8 percent, respectively.[1] During the 1980s, gross investment in the United States as a fraction of GNP was 17 percent; in Japan, 30 percent.[2]

The United States still holds an edge in information processing and biotechnology, two cutting-edge technologies; still attracts capital from flush economies around the globe; and still causes many of the best and brightest workers to emigrate from their homelands to what, in 1990, is still the world's wealthiest nation. U.S. manufacturing output has actually been roughly constant as a proportion of total world output, at 22–24 percent—and, according to CIA estimates, has even increased when adjusted for the actual purchasing power of the currencies in which volume of industrial nations' output is measured.[3]

But the competition has heated up. We have lost much of our leadership in industrial technology, finance, and product quality, and we have fallen behind in our overall economic infrastructure; thus we are at risk of ceding tomorrow to our more-vital trading adversaries. Our problems are economic as well as sociopolitical:

Economic

- Once a Gulliver among Lilliputians, our economy is too small for tomorrow's global marketplace. We must create at least a North American Common Market to remain competitive.
- Federal finance is out of control. Deficits are unsustainable; priorities are misdirected. We have the weakest, most unstable banking system in the developed world. Vast sums are wasted.
- Our inefficient legal and insurance system has become a drag on the national economy.
- Too much of American management has grown lazy, insular, and focused on financial manipulation instead of product improvement.
- We spend too much on the military and have little to show for it. The military has become a vast pork barrel rather than an efficient fighting machine.
- Our transportation infrastructure, once the world's best, is deteriorating. Our communication infrastructure is failing to keep pace with technological change.

Sociopolitical

- Our health-care system stands out for its high cost and poor results.

- Environmental issues have become so politicized that we gain minimal improvements at maximum expense. New threats to the climate and the atmosphere could bring massive disruption if not solved efficiently.
- As a nation, we spend too much on housing, yet there are severe regional housing shortages. Solutions to housing and infrastructure problems are increasingly constrained by local politics.
- Our education system is ineffective and costly. We spend more than almost any developed nation, yet have lower rates of both basic and technical literacy.
- Family and community structures are deteriorating, without effective replacement by government social services. All the key indicators of social problems—crime, drug abuse, child abuse, teen pregnancy—are the worst in the developed world.
- Money-oriented, single-issue politics has become a high art. The courts and Congress use their ever-growing powers without responsibility. Presidential decision making is increasingly constrained and ineffective.

All these issues add up to a single, ironic conclusion: Having tutored the world in the democratic arts and served as a role model for economic development, *the United States is not itself an efficient, modern technocratic state*. Globalized technology and finance force all nations, even the mightiest, to adopt the most-efficient social and economic structures, as measured not by ideology but by what works. The U.S., having squandered two or three decades and a good deal of its wealth avoiding politically difficult decisions, will eventually be forced to confront them anyway. But the greatest benefits always go to those who modernize first.

Economic Overview

Economic prosperity requires efficient economic structures. Under the pressure of international competition, our private sector has made significant, if belated, efficiency gains, particularly in manufacturing, and more will come. However, sectors of the economy heavily directed by the government—particularly the military, finance, and health-care sectors—are in trouble. The problem here is one of inefficiency, not one of "socialism"; Germany's national health-insurance system produces a healthier nation, for far less cost, than our mostly private health-care system.

The much-discussed peace dividend pales in comparison to the "efficiency dividend." Wringing inefficiencies out of our economy's flabbiest sectors will be like finding money—lots of it. These inefficiencies are not traditional "waste in government"; teachers work very hard and are probably underpaid, but the education system as a whole is still inefficient. Nor do efficiency gains necessarily mean cutbacks in output. Money saved through a more efficient health-care system can be to some extent plowed back into higher-quality care.

Bankers on a Binge

Over the last decade the fractionated, confused American financial system, the worst among the major industrial powers, has lost about a trillion dollars: about $200 billion in foreign loans, $600 billion in real estate, at least $100 billion in junk bonds, and billions more in student loans, farming, and energy. Our banking system's principal structural problems are threefold:

- U.S. banks are too small. A megamarket world needs megabanks. The world's ten largest banks are all Japanese.
- The U.S. deposit-insurance system is unworkable.
- The system is encouraged by incentives to overinvest in real estate and underinvest in industry.

The U.S. has favored small, inefficient banks for centuries. Size is important in capital markets because it allows banks to spread their risks. Yet until very recently, states severely restricted large intrastate banks and made interstate banking almost impossible. New York prohibited New York City banks from expanding upstate; until the 1970s, it was illegal for banks in Illinois to have more than one branch. Without strong branch networks to pull in deposits, it was no mere accident that the first large bank failure in the current wave was Continental Illinois.

Our banks are restricted not only in size, but in what they may invest in. They can make loans, but unlike foreign commercial banks they cannot take equity positions. As a result they dare not invest in small start-up companies. If you get only 15 percent interest on investments, as in a typical loan deal, you cannot afford many failures. But half of all venture-capital-style investments fail; a bank would need at least 30 percent annual returns on each of its good investments to compensate for losing 100 percent on the bad ones. Only equity investments can provide this potential high rate of return.

That restriction has spurred the evolution in the U.S. of a separate and heavily mythologized venture-capital sector. While we Americans may think of venture capital as our strength, it's really a symbol of our financial weakness. All in all, what these tiny, specialized groups of American investors have pulled off is nothing short of amazing. But in many cases they've lacked sufficient staying power to carry potentially successful companies through temporary dry periods. They've had to bail out. And to whom? The Japanese and the Germans, whose megabanks and trade surpluses give them the financial strength to carry those small companies over the threshold of profitability.

The Mortgage Morgue

America's shortage of industrial capital is also related to a national fetish for real estate and to our disastrous national experiment with deposit insurance.

Our idiosyncratic financial system and the glaring subsidies of our tax system have encouraged a binge on spending for real estate as pure consumption—typically as residences, but also in the commercial sector, in the form of outsized workspaces. We created a heavily subsidized set of dedicated home-building machines called savings and loan institutions, which eventually were expanded so they could invest in commercial real estate. Federal deposit insurance, by increasing savings-and-loan deposits beyond what they would otherwise be, subsidized S&Ls and, therefore, the real-estate sector. Tax subsidies added to real estate's appeal. Federal deposit insurance made its entrance in the early 1930s, when over one-third of the nation's 25,000 banks went under, victims of the Great Depression. In 1934 Congress passed legislation insuring the first $2,500 of an individual's account against bank failure. This ceiling was gradually hiked up over the years.

Meanwhile, strict regulations had limited the rate of interest a savings institution could offer its depositors, while also directing S&Ls to make the vast bulk of their loans as mortgages. The happy result, for homebuyers, was low-interest mortgages—a de facto subsidy to the housing market. But the inflationary wave of the 1970s caused interest rates on all new loans to skyrocket (growing government deficits have kept rates high long after that wave subsided). A bevy of money-market funds cashed in by luring bank and S&L depositors' funds, for which they could offer higher returns. This forced the end of interest-rate ceilings on deposits in the 1970s. Meanwhile, insured-deposit ceilings were boosted to $100,000 in 1980. Caught between their holdings of old, low-interest loans and their new, high-interest deposits, the S&Ls sustained heavy losses.

To recoup these losses, the S&Ls asked for, and received, deregulation. In 1982 Congress passed the Garn-St Germain bill permitting S&Ls to invest in "high-return loans," which in polite bankers' circles is a euphemism for risky business. While probably a necessary step in avoiding periodic, disastrous deposit flights from S&Ls, deregulation mixed poorly with deposit insurance. In the Reagan-era climate of laissez-faire, savings institutions were handed a vastly enlarged selection of potential avenues for investment without much fear of government scrutiny. As Herbert Stein, chairman of the Council of Economic Advisers under President Richard Nixon, has written: "Some will say that the insurance was too big. Others will say that the regulation was too weak. I do not want to enter that argument now. But surely the insurance was too big for the regulation or the regulation was too weak for the insurance."[4]

Real estate is probably the most politically active industry in the United States. Developers are the financial heart of the Democratic party, and Republicans are working hard to catch up. Both parties competed for the contributions of such famous financial geniuses as Lincoln Savings and Loan president Charles Keating, who single-handedly threw or gave away $2 billion of taxpayer money, including a $1 million salary to his son.

A coalition of real-estate interests—savings and loans, banks, developers, and construction unions—lobbied successfully to make more capital available for their speculation. Like any compulsive gambler, the S&Ls kept raising the stakes, turning small initial losses in the late 1960s into the vast losses of today. Instead of owning up to their initial losses on their early gambles, financial institutions were allowed to invest in speculative enterprises to try to recoup their losses. The more insolvent the S&L, the more desperate the attempt to make up for its bad debts with fresh depositor money lured by ever-higher rates. Risk-free insured deposits chased the highest rates, ending up at the riskiest institutions.

Speculation can become so integrated into the national financial picture that the government develops a fiscal interest in keeping the speculation going. In the case of the S&L crisis, the government has tried to keep the real-estate spending boom of the 1980s going because the government (by dint of federal deposit insurance) and the politicians (by virtue of their vice: an addiction to developer contributions) have so much invested in it.

But as speculation devoured ever more capital, a mushroom cloud of bad debt exploded. Hundreds of billions of dollars of real money was lost forever, thrown away on now-abandoned shopping malls, vacant office buildings, and high-flying S&L executives' perks. Overinvestment in commercial real estate drove rents down to levels that could never cover the loans. Empty buildings are a loss to the nation as well as to individuals.

Estimates of the total cost to taxpayers of the S&L mess vary, depending on accounting assumptions, but, even ignoring interest on what will be a long, painful payback, the amount of bad S&L debt so far accumulated exceeds the combined 1989 profits of all the Fortune 500 largest industrial companies. Other fiascos are in store. Junk mortgages held by failed S&Ls have been repackaged and passed like hot potatoes to commercial banks by the Resolution Finance Corporation, the mortgage morgue set up to dispose of government-repossessed S&L assets.

High on the Mountain of Debt

In the past decade, private debt of nonfinancial institutions has risen from $2.9 trillion to about $7 trillion.[5] Foreign investors own hundreds of billions of dollars' worth of U.S. corporate securities. Each of these securities represents a claim against future earnings of the company owned. Any recession will be a disaster for the government, whose budget deficit would soar to astronomical heights; but it will be worse for debt-soaked firms, who are unable to print their own money.

Peering into the future of the U.S. economy means craning your neck at a mountain of debt. We will have to find a way to climb that mountain or tunnel through it; there is no getting around it.

To pay off your debts, you must first save money. In this, we have been upstaged by the Japanese and Europeans. In 1989, for example, Japanese households saved 17 percent of their household income; U.S. households, 6 percent. Our federal deficits, which have ranged from 2 percent to 6 percent of GNP during the 1980s, cut deep into total savings; net national saving in this decade fell to an all-time low of 2 percent.

The Japanese are able to maintain high rates of household saving even in a climate of artificially low interest rates on deposits, capped by stringent regulations. This is possible because Japanese tax laws subsidize savings—just the opposite of American tax laws that, while taxing all interest income fully, until recently have subsidized *consumption* by permitting deductions for personal interest expenses.

The superiority of the Europeans and the Japanese in competing with us globally is no longer in the cost of labor—by 1988, hourly wages of production workers in the U.S. ($13.62) had been surpassed by those of their counterparts in Japan ($13.80), West Germany ($20.19), Italy ($14.77), and France ($14.03)[6]—but in the availability of capital. Higher saving rates translate into more available capital.

Financial Futures

The importance of global markets and the increasing efficiency and power of global financial flows dictate major financial reform in the United States, both legally and institutionally. The 1986 Tax Reform Act, by sharply reducing the tax advantages of real-estate investment, was the first, modest step in that direction. Many other reforms will be accomplished over the next decade.

- Myriad small- to medium-sized institutions will coalesce into an interstate banking system composed of some fifty to 100 dominant national banks. State-chartered banks that are independent from the Federal Reserve will cease to exist as separate banking institutions, and so will S&Ls.

- Deposit guarantees will be limited to one per person. Under current law, it is a simple matter to set up a dozen or more separate $100,000 accounts, each backed by federal deposit insurance. This is ludicrous. Lending institutions' use of guaranteed funds will be restricted.

- Growth of "non-bank banks" such as GE Credit or GMAC, which sell commercial paper (short-term corporate IOUs) to large investors rather than take deposits, will continue.
- The bank-regulatory function will be consolidated in a single agency—the Federal Reserve system—instead of today's complex alphabet soup of agencies, a lobbyist's dream. This agency will also oversee federal loan guarantees—a source of large past and future losses.
- Banks will be permitted to own stock and engage in underwriting. Only the possibility of securing high returns will lure banks into the risky venture-capital business and keep America's innovators from getting their capital infusions from foreign companies.
- Banks will be required to maintain decent equity capital and forced to mark investments to market values, instead of carrying them at outdated (and often overstated) book values. The former requirement increases the likelihood that a bank will remain solvent; the latter both makes it possible to detect solvency problems and increases liquidity by reducing incentives to hold onto loans with inflated values just because they beef up the balance sheet.
- Asset markets will be lubricated by more carefully defined standards for credit data. Easily tradeable bank loans reduce banks' risk of illiquidity.

Government Finance

The structure of public finance is as bad, or worse, than that of private finance. Actual federal government debt has grown from $663 billion at the end of 1979 to more than $3 trillion today—over $10,000 for every living American. The official debt is the tip of a jagged iceberg of exposure. We already know of at least another $200 billion of bad debt, courtesy of the S&Ls. The federal government, including all the off-budget agencies it underwrites, holds close to $6 trillion in potential liabilities: $2.7 trillion for insured checking and savings accounts and credit unions; $1.3 trillion in insurance for crops, pensions, and so forth; and $1.4 trillion in loans and loan guarantees for farms, housing, education, and small business.[7] If as much as 5 percent of those potential liabilities become actual, taxpayers will be on the hook for another $300 billion.

America's gross public debt is equivalent to about six months of annual national output. In West Germany—where the word for "debt," *Schuld*, is the same as the word for "guilt"—the ratio is substantially lower. Japan, on the other hand, has a higher ratio of public debt to national output, but because their personal-savings rate is so high the Japanese have been able to easily support their deficits—and ours, as well.

The Japanese, through their purchases of U.S. Treasury bonds and notes, have been financing about 30 percent of the federal budget deficit. What if they stop bailing us out? There is every reason to believe they will. Throughout the 1980s Japanese capital gushed into world markets as the new giant raked in huge trade surpluses year after year. In the last half of the decade, Japanese stock prices tripled and land prices more than doubled, adding more monetary muscle to the acquisitive Japanese outreach. Now the gusher is drying up. Japan's population is aging more rapidly than that of any other industrial nation, begetting an acute labor shortage, with upward pressure on wages and interest rates. The speculative bubble buoying the Tokyo stock market has popped; land-price advances have stalled in Japan's new higher-interest climate. At the same time, domestic workers are demanding more imported goods than ever before. The vaunted trade surplus will shrink inexorably, and with it the amount of capital available for outside investment. Besides, the Japanese have joined the West Europeans in funneling money to Eastern Europe, the promised land of high returns.

At a time when the U.S. should be running a surplus, staggering federal deficits continue—in part hidden by spurious accounting techniques that define additions to the Social Security Trust Fund as operating revenue, when the fund should instead be segregated in a separate account. The deficit problem will get much worse over the next few decades:

- At the peak of our growth cycle the deficit was about $150 billion. As the economy slows in 1991–92, it will jump above $200 billion—even when the tens of billions generated annually by the Social Security Trust Fund are considered as revenues. Without that accounting gimmick, the deficit will exceed $300 billion.

- The long-delayed peace dividend, even if it is not poured into the sands of Saudi Arabia, will be more than absorbed by skyrocketing Medicare costs in the 1990s. Both Social Security and Medicare costs will explode in 2005, as the World War II baby boom reaches retirement age.

- Interest on the federal debt is compounding to the point where interest will soon vie with health care and Social Security to be the largest expenditure category.

- The real Reagan "economic miracle"—foreign willingness to finance the U.S. trade and budget deficits—cannot continue forever. Our relatively low productivity gains over the past decade and our debtor status make us a poor investment; our foreign bankers will not be willing to keep the tap open much longer.

- The federal financial structure is incapable of controlling the deficit. The Iron Triangle of lifetime legislators, lifetime bureaucrats, and well-financed lobbyists will always want to spend more than any American president, and they will always win. The federal government has no enforceable budget procedures.

Current restrictions on the Social Security Trust Fund require that it be invested only in U.S. Treasury securities. If the proceeds of every government bond sale went unfailingly toward worthwhile investments in America's future instead of consumption, vote-pandering, and inefficiency, that might be okay. In fact, however, the Social Security surplus goes not into productive investments but toward underwriting the federal deficit. Meeting promised Social Security payments beyond about 2010 will be fundamentally impossible unless a national Social Security savings account is started *now* and invested in something real—not more federal paper. Building such a savings account requires shifting to much lower federal deficits, moving into surplus over the next economic cycle and staying there. Otherwise, we will need more than a 30 percent Social Security payroll tax by 2020.

The solution to the federal deficit problem is obvious, because it is used successfully in most states: (1) allowing line-item vetoes on all financial commitments (so named because the chief draws a line through any particular item he or she wishes to omit from an omnibus spending bill), and (2) requiring a supermajority to pass the budget.

What has worked for decades in Illinois and California would also work in Washington.

It is the politics of budgetary reform, not the mechanics, that now make change impossible. Therefore, the most likely scenario is a series of financial shocks in the early 1990s: collapsing financial markets, soaring interest rates, slow economic growth, and exploding federal deficits. These shocks will only worsen, regardless of who is president, until the national financial house is back in order.

A big part of the government's solution to its financial difficulties will be taxes on energy. The political madness of the Middle East will continue to generate wildly fluctuating energy prices: years of oil priced at $15 to $20 per barrel, punctuated by $30 to $40 spikes lasting weeks or months. Such gyrations serve neither energy users nor energy investors. Europe long ago learned how efficient energy taxes can be. Oil-import fees could finance an even larger Strategic Petroleum Reserve than we have now; an import fee that varied inversely with price could smooth the market, too—as would the writing of clear rules for exactly when the Strategic Petroleum Reserve should be used. General energy taxes (for example, a gasoline tax) would bring money into the treasury while benefitting the environment.

Legal/Liability System

The much-criticized U.S. legal and insurance liability systems have both strengths and weaknesses. The legal system handles contractual disagreements between private parties as well as any other nation. (All legal systems are ponderous and frustrating.) The United States has perhaps the best securities laws in the world. The problem lies not in the insurance sector, which handles known risks with reasonable efficiency, but in the continual creation of new risk categories by the legal system and in the inefficiency with which the system handles small (below $1 million) disputes.

American lawyers have become too creative. They create uninsurable risks for business and cripple business planning by conceiving new categories of liability:

- *Product liability.* Judges and legislators have decided to hold manufacturers strictly liable for any damage from a product, even if no one knew it might be a problem and the product was produced decades ago. Asbestos and several drugs are in this category.

- *Employment liability.* Judges in several states have created implied contracts between employees and employers, so that ponderous legal procedures must be followed in dismissing employees.

- *Environmental liability.* The federal government has extended liability for environmental damages to lenders who had nothing to do with such an event as a toxic spill. If you lent money to someone who spilled toxic substances, you are liable, regardless of your knowledge or actions.

While the issues addressed by these legal changes were real, neither the companies nor their insurers can handle multi-billion-dollar surprises.

The second problem category, disputes for which the cost of traditional litigation exceeds the payment to the victim, applies to small civil litigation and in particular to auto liability, which totals about $100 billion per year in claims.

Extensive legislation at both the state and federal levels will ultimately resolve both these categories of legal/insurance problems. The proposed reforms will be controversial and will be slowed by the enormous political power of the plaintiff bar, but the existing system is simply becoming unaffordable. Obvious benefits will accrue to citizens of those states that institute the following:

- *Enforceable waivers.* Waivers of the right to sue are largely unenforceable today. Waivers are justified for both high-risk sports (e.g., skiing) and risky medical procedures. Enforceability will have to be guaranteed by state defense funds and penalties for those who try to abrogate the waivers.

- *Federalization of risk.* Some crucial products, such as vaccines, carry inevitable risks. For such products, federal payment of economic damages (not including pain and suffering) combined with elimination of private liability is justified. Without such limits, no private organization will dare produce new vaccines like the hoped-for AIDS vaccine—possibly the most dangerous vaccine in history.

- *Binding arbitration.* Arbitration can handle small cases efficiently. States might consider requiring arbitration for categories of liability such as nonfatal automobile accidents.

- *No-fault insurance*. This means the victim is paid by his or her own insurance company. No-fault is a solution for some categories of modest, random risk, but becomes problematic when risk is non-random, e.g., for damage caused by known drunk drivers. Such high-damage individuals would have to pay higher rates.

- *Codification of employment and product-liability laws*. Legislative action would probably be more efficient than current judge-created precedents. New laws might limit such problems as the time delay, or "tail," of liability—claims arising years after the period of insurance—or precisely define liabilities.

- *Limits on new liability categories*. Judges have neither the capacity nor the obligation to determine the long-range societal implications of their precedent-creating rulings. A special tribunal may be required to review the societal cost/benefit trade-off from awards in any new category of damage.

- *Limits on juries*. Juries might be ruled out for small cases or special categories of highly technical liability.

- *Enforceable mandatory insurance*. The uninsured will be a growing problem for all types of risk. With prices spiraling upward, "going naked" without insurance is an increasingly attractive option. Where mandatory insurance (as for automobiles) is required, a noncancelable payment as part of car registration will be necessary.

State by state, year by year, reforms will proceed. By 2010 at the latest, the nation will be actively investigating an even broader issue: Is European-style codified law, which severely restricts judicial discretion, more efficient than American-style common law, which allows judges and attorneys to create new categories of liability? Should judges and juries have any discretion, as they now do, to award damages for liabilities not strictly identified by the legislature?

The Trouble with Management

American management makes more, relative to the average worker, than the management of any developed economy. According to *Business Week*, the average big-company chief made more than $2 million in 1988, 93 times the average pay of a factory worker and 72 times that of a schoolteacher. (In 1960 the ratio was a mere 41 for factory workers, 38 for teachers.) In 1988 Walt Disney chairman Michael Eisner "earned" $40 million in salary, bonuses, and long-term (deferred) compensation; RJR Nabisco chairman Ross Johnson was paid $53.8 million, *just to go away.*[8]

There is too much criticism of American investors for being shortsighted. U.S. law *forces* institutional investors to be shortsighted. German and Japanese corporations are run by powerful boards of directors that actively represent institutional owners—banks and pension funds. U.S. corporations are run by weak boards without active representation of major financial institutions. U.S. fiduciary laws require sale of stock to a corporate raider even if the stock price is undervalued; pension funds are supposed to sell the stock of unsuccessful companies, not find new managers. U.S. banks are not allowed to directly own stock at all. Lazy, overpaid, shortsighted managers are the product of weak investors. Current state moves to protect managers against the power of stock owners will make managers even lazier. Corporate raiders and leveraged buyouts are not the problem, but the symptoms of a larger problem.

When (probably by the late 1990s) the largest group of stock owners, major pension funds, take management leadership in the firms they own and banks are allowed to make direct corporate investments (though not with federally insured funds), the lazy-manager syndrome and inability to think long-term will correct itself.

Sectoral Change

The American economy will continue to experience both rolling recessions and industry-by-industry restructurings. The next wave will be concentrated on defense, utilities, retail, agriculture, manufacturing, and high tech.

DEFENSE

The defense sector will be both cut back and reformed. Cutbacks—much larger than now forecast—will occur as budget desperation forces the defense sector to be more efficient, the potential for superpower conflict evaporates, and, in the longer run, our interests in foreign conflicts become less vital. Threats will be regional, not global.

Rivalry between quasi-independent branches of the armed forces has led to redundant weapons systems and inefficient deployments.

But the worst thing that ever happened to military efficiency was the development of computers capable of printing out data on which military subcontract goes to which congressional district. The power of the defense pork barrel is a great hindrance to reducing, refocusing, and reforming the military. Obsolete, unneeded weapons systems and bases continue to be supported just because they provide jobs in the right districts.

By 2005 or thereabouts, the following shifts will have occurred:

- A 50 percent reduction in strategic force levels and real expenditures, with the sharpest cuts taken in parallel with the Soviets. We will still need nuclear weapons and enough missiles to deter the largest possible adversary—an underdeveloped power like China, or Iraq.
- More base closings and consolidations.
- Reduction in reserves, useless (except for noncombatant technical personnel) in brush fire wars, in favor of integrated, fast-reaction forces that are rapid and deployable—in other words, bring in the Marines.
- Revival of a slimmed-down Star Wars, hopeless against an onslaught of myriad Soviet ballistic missiles but useful and vital against new "small potatoes" nuclear powers who lack such huge missile arsenals.
- Consolidation of the defense industry, with several firms disappearing, and an end to congressional micro-management of the defense sector. The next three decades will be terrible years for the many officers who have invested their careers in building toward early retirement and working for a defense contractor.
- Early pullout of all except token forces from Europe, which can easily afford to defend itself. Slower withdrawal from East Asia, as that region develops its own defense capacity.
- Ultimate withdrawal from the Middle East, as Europe takes over the defense of its own vital interests in the Persian Gulf, which exceed U.S. interests. Our intervention to save Kuwait is an expensive favor to the Europeans. The United States met a global responsibility in stopping Iraq, because Europe wasn't ready.

UTILITIES: ENTER THE COMPETITION

The communications and energy utilities are evolving from stable, highly regulated, protected monopolies to highly competitive, increasingly deregulated enterprises. This shift has largely occurred in telecommunications, but it has just started in electric utilities, where regulators are shifting from detailed rate-of-return review to broader, incentive-based price regulation. New, smaller-scale technologies are bringing competition to large, central-station electric generation. The Federal Energy Regulatory Commission is trying to increase competition by forcing open access to the transmission system.

The United States will follow the lead of the United Kingdom, which is now leapfrogging to a system of electricity generation, transmission, and distribution by multiple, independent firms. The electric utilities of the future will largely be service and distribution organizations. New power generation will come through open bidding from competing, separate firms. If GE thinks nuclear power is more efficient, it can build and operate the power plant, and supply power to the open market. New commercial buildings and industry will supply most of their own power and sell their surpluses to the system. Transmission grids will operate as common carriers—open to all at a uniform price.

RETAIL: DEATH OF THE MIDDLE MARKET?

The traditional American retailer is caught in a squeeze between discount stores, specialty stores, and high-service luxury stores. Retailing was highly profitable over the last twenty years for two temporary reasons:

- So many women flooded into retail jobs that inflation-adjusted wages in retailing went down.

- Women spent so much of their earnings on new clothes that sales skyrocketed.

The end of this temporary prosperity and the rise of competitive stores spell the end of traditional mid-market retailers. The retail sector as a whole will be under extreme cost pressure, and the mid-market retailers are the most likely victims.

AGRICULTURE: END OF AN ERA

American agriculture is impressively efficient at producing the wrong things. Federal crop-support programs and other subsidies encourage too many farmers to produce too much corn, wheat, rice, cotton, and tobacco using too much land, too much energy, too much fertilizer, too much water, and too many pesticides.

During the 1980s, farm programs cost the Treasury about $20 billion a year, while consumers paid an additional $10 billion or so per year in jacked-up food prices. But don't let anybody tell you that our government is giving out any handouts to undeserving, rich farmers: A 1988 congressional act imposed a ceiling on drought relief to any farmer whose gross annual revenues exceeded $2 million.

Reforms in this sector will come only slowly, due to a potent lobby and a lingering Hollywood nostalgia for yeoman farmers, who have all but ceased to exist. However, federal budget problems, environmental problems, and international pressure will force an end to the existing pattern by 2010.

This will not be an easy time for rural America. The large corporate farm will dominate the future, but without further help from the taxpayer. Farm-support payments will be made directly as means-tested rural welfare, disconnected from crop production. Farm imports will increase, and production of subsidized crops, including corn, wheat, rice, cotton, sugar cane, sugar beets, and tobacco, will decline in many regions. Many Western farmers will find their newly salable water rights to be worth more than their farms.

GENERAL MANUFACTURING

Modern manufacturing involves the flexible production and continual improvement of semicustomized, high-value products. Japanese manufacturers emphasize production engineering, continual small improvements in design, and close relationships between design and production. American manufacturers search for design breakthroughs and assume that any idiot can handle the production—which too often describes the result.

Still, American manufacturing has already greatly improved its productivity and quality in the last five years. In the years to come, the emphasis will be on reducing overhead costs. For most products, the big expense is the 35 percent of total cost that goes for overhead—the largest portion of which is for the avalanche of paper that builds during the design process and ends up as a pile of manufacturing instructions. To halt that paper avalanche, design and manufacturing must communicate through electronic media with systems that combine graphics with words. We have, if we will only use it, the world's best manufacturing software. Work-stations manufacturers such as DEC, HP/Apollo, and Sun and software makers like ASK, Consilium, and Docugraphix lead the world in computerizing the design and production process.

Direct labor now accounts for only about 15 percent of most final products' manufacturing cost. For the few products where direct labor costs are still significant, shifting production to Mexico will prove far more productive than moving to Asia. Manufacturing contracts with Asia mean giving away the design along with the production contract, and seeing a partner quickly become a competitor. Mexican firms will not provide such aggressive competition for many years to come.

HIGH TECH MEETS HIGH FINANCE

The financial weakness of America's venture-capital firms is leading to a wave of consolidation in the high-technology sector, with foreign investors and large domestic firms picking up bargains. New start-ups will become increasingly scarce, as cash-thin venture capitalists desperately try to keep their successes and near-successes alive through the current economic slowdown and until the next hot new-issues market.

There hasn't been a hot new-issues market in stocks since 1983, and none is in prospect for many more years. But by 2000, the high-technology end of manufacturing will be a big beneficiary of financial reforms allowing large financial institutions such as banks to take equity positions in companies. This will open up a new era of small-company financing and renewed growth of small high-technology firms.

New ventures will increasingly emphasize high-tech-related services. Efficiency in the *use* of new technology will command a premium. Hardware alone is not enough. We are not yet fully exploiting the capabilities even of existing technologies.

The window of vulnerability for the United States is in the next several years, before reforms kick in. Near the beginning of the 20th century, Britain's investments in the "high-tech" industries of the day—chemicals, electricity, precision engineering—lagged behind the Germans', and Germany soon overtook Britain in industrial might. Unlike the Britain of 1900, however, the U.S. is second to none in the quality of its universities and its basic research. It would be ironic if America's debtor status prevented it from enjoying the fruits of that research; for the next thirty years are going to yield technological advances that will make those of the last three decades pale in comparison, and the United States will be at the hub of discovery.

CHAPTER

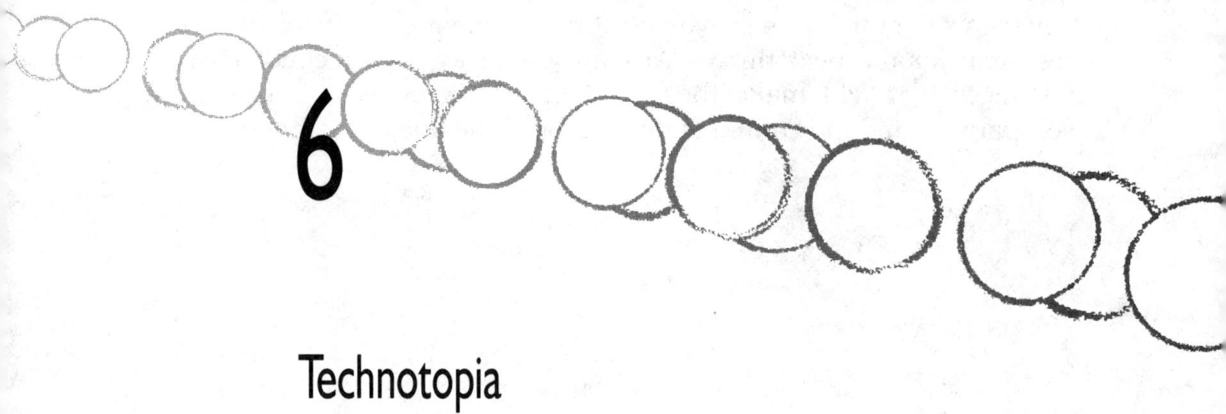

6

Technotopia

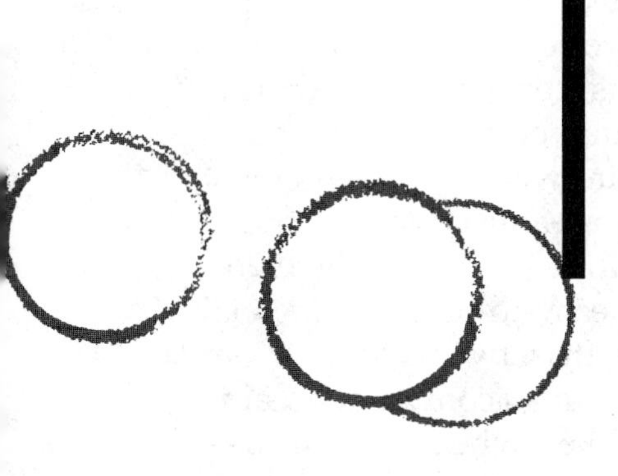

In January 1987, University of Houston researcher Paul Chu discovered a new class of ceramic materials that conduct electricity perfectly at much closer to room temperature than other previously known "superconductors." Word of Chu's discovery—a theoretical breakthrough as well as a potentially important commercial technology—spread among the scientific community not through refereed scholarly journals, as was customary, but by fax machine. (Anticipating the speed of the rumor mill, Chu intentionally inserted an inaccuracy into the draft of the article he was circulating among selected colleagues—he claimed the newly discovered substance was green. A comedy of greed ensued as laboratories all over the world, attempting to beat Chu to publication, quickly emptied their shelves of green substances. The real McCoy was, it turned out, black.)

The pace of scientific discovery is getting too fast for stately scientific journals. Exciting technologies have been invented throughout human history, but never at a rate like today's. There are more scientists alive now than the total who have lived and died since science first branched off from witchcraft and the magical arts. Modern information systems accelerate scientific discovery and commercial development. New scientific instruments accomplish in days, or minutes, what took a lifetime not long ago. With the world crystallizing around free-enterprise and instantaneous communications systems in which capitalist competitors drive technology as fast as it will go, products now move much more quickly from initial development to large-scale commercial use and finally to international use.

Consider the contrast between the key technology of the 19th century—the steam engine—and the key technology of the late 20th century—the small computer. It took about fifty years to make the steam engine, invented in the mid-1700s, workable and efficient. It took even more time—until early in this century—before this technology saw worldwide use. The integrated circuit, developed in the early 1960s, was in worldwide use within twenty years. Its most important expression was the microprocessor—a group of electronic circuits integrated into a single chip—developed in the early 1970s. The microprocessor was residing in small, easy-to-use, commercial personal computers by the early 1980s—less than twenty years from the invention of the first integrated circuit. The small computer became an internationally available "commodity"—like soybeans or sulfur—in less than ten years.

The next thirty years may or may not bring us interstellar propellers and laser razors, but the 1990s and the early part of the 21st century will see the fastest technical change in history. To be sure, the pace will be uneven. Put Martha Washington (or, to be historically accurate, one of her slaves) into the kitchen of 2020 and show her nothing more than how to turn on the water and the stove, and she could cook up a storm. Similarly, we are unlikely to see radical substitutions for the automobile, jet airplane, or electric motor.

Even in the hard sciences, some fields are reaching saturation: Nuclear physics, which receives billions of dollars in support annually, has discovered little of economic significance for decades. We may never fully understand the basic nature of matter at the subatomic level, or human interactions at the societal level. We will probably come nowhere close to understanding cosmology—how the universe really works; the fundamental cosmological questions of how the universe began may not be answerable.

Yet other technologies are exploding, interacting, and precipitating social change. The merger of information technology and telecommunications will accelerate a national trend toward geographical decentralization—a.k.a. sprawl. New materials will mean lighter, stronger products and ever-greater energy efficiencies.

Biotechnology will give us undreamed-of power over our environment, our bodies, and even our heredity—and will create fierce political and ethical controversies of the sort that call to mind the poet T.S. Eliot's words: "After such knowledge, what forgiveness?"

Rule One: Don't Panic

The reason so many past economic and environmental projections have been wrong is that they assumed constant efficiency—that technology does not improve. One 19th-century projection of the London environment employed the following, straightforward calculation: Then-occurring increases in population and prosperity translated into more use of transportation, which at the time meant more horses. Therefore, London was going to be completely buried in horse manure. Detailed further projections involved the question of how many feet deep it would be.

We are always about to run out of or be buried in something. But if we maintain our economic and political flexibility to exploit the potential of technology, increased efficiency will continue to make the panic projections of the day wrong. Whether we can maintain this flexibility is a much more open question.

A modern American equivalent of London's imminent burial was the 1976 National Energy Plan, an enormous federal effort projecting that by today we would be using approximately 30 percent more energy than we in fact are. The plan called for building hundreds more nuclear power plants and a much larger energy infrastructure; other forecasters at the time projected energy prices in the range of $100 a barrel for oil and $3 to $4 a gallon for gasoline.

The projections were wrong, for two reasons. First, after years of tying ourselves up with complex bureaucratic rules and waiting in gas lines, we dropped the rules and let prices rise; from a conservation standpoint, one price increase is worth a thousand regulations. And second, the elevated price expectations encouraged the development of new technology and increased exploitation of existing ones. Once we used the full flexibility of the economy to set technology free, the energy crisis quickly disappeared.

Iraq's invasion of Kuwait ended a four-year glut of cheap oil; barring all-out war, there will be plenty available tomorrow. There is no nation powerful enough to keep oil prices above $25 indefinitely; other, cheaper alternatives exist. Within the territorial United States are enough reserves of coal to last several hundred years. However, mining coal is dangerous, and burning it is dirty. Natural gas, also abundant at the right price, produces fewer pollutants than either oil or coal. Oil, coal, and natural gas—hydrocarbons one and all—release their energy through combustion, whose inescapable product is carbon dioxide, a prime suspect in the still-theoretical but widely publicized process of global warming (the "greenhouse effect") expected to occur within the next century.

In the next century, environmental, political, and economic considerations will spur new looks at both nuclear energy and photovoltaic power systems within the United States. In fact, in the next twenty years or so, a major reversal will occur in revealed environmentalist wisdom. Groups such as the Sierra Club, which once favored nuclear power as an alternative to western dams, will do so again.

The cost of photovoltaic power generation has shrunk by a factor of 40 in the last decade,[1] bringing that long-awaited technology nearly within striking distance of commercial viability. Residences, many of whose rooftops could serve as convenient mounting sites for photovoltaic panels, account for over one-third of all electricity used in the United States.

Atomic fission produces no greenhouse gases whatsoever. Several countries, including Sweden, France, and Japan, derive significant amounts of their electricity from nuclear power (more than 70 percent in the case of France), yet not a single new order has been placed for a nuclear unit in the United States since 1976. Most of America's existing commercial nuclear plants—now supplying close to 20 percent of U.S. electricity needs, second only to coal—will be retired within twenty years. These plants can tolerate numerous simultaneous malfunctions, but they are vulnerable to catastrophic meltdowns in the event of compounded human error—and, in one or two cases, have come close enough to undermine public support. Immense licensing and construction delays now make these plants financial dinosaurs before they ever go into operation; any electric utility executive caught considering building one today would be labeled a lunatic.

Public perception of nuclear power will change. Already brownouts are occurring more frequently along the eastern seaboard, while the federal government, under international political pressure to reduce greenhouse-gas emissions, is considering a so-called carbon tax to discourage fossil-fuel use. The government is also under internal political pressure to reduce America's dependence on foreign oil, a large and increasing percentage of which comes from unstable and sometimes hostile countries.

Meanwhile, several new nuclear reactor models are either on the drawing boards or being tested.[2] These models rely for safety not on "active" measures such as the automatic closing of a valve or an operator's turning a wheel in the event of an emergency, but on "passive" features such as gravity and convection. Even in worst-case scenarios, instead of melting down, the reactors simply run down like a car out of gas. One model not only runs on uranium 238—an isotope 100 hundred times more plentiful than the uranium 235 today's reactors use—but actually eats radioactive waste; specifically, it consumes those long-lived by-products that we're now looking for ways to store underground for 10,000 years or more, and its own wastes decompose within a more workable time frame of hundreds of years.

The new reactors are small and standardized; thus they can be factory-built and subjected to rigorous quality control, then shipped to their destinations in trucks for on-site assembly. Reduced public concern about safety will speed up the licensing process, which will make the new models competitive with conventional fossil-fuel plants. There is one slight economic problem with this technology: Unless U.S. investor and environmentalist reticence melts sooner rather than later, the new reactors will be built by the Japanese.

Demand for electricity varies diurnally and seasonally. All electrical-power technologies could be made more efficient if a decent form of electrical energy storage were developed. Today, the only half-decent method is "pumped hydro"—essentially, using excess electricity to push a giant puddle up a hill, and then allowing the water to flow back down over an electricity-generating turbine when demand peaks—which isn't anything to write home about to begin with, and doesn't work at all in Kansas, or any other flat state. The Department of Defense is working on a gigantic superconducting coil whose resistance-free loops would store electricity with almost 100 percent efficiency in the form of a circulating current, to be redirected into the power grid when demand merits it.

Both the land-intensive nature of photovoltaic technology and the small size and ease of construction of new-generation nuclear power plants are consistent with rural placement and, therefore, with decentralization—which is fortunate. Advances in telecommunications and information technology—and the rising cost of urban land—are making sprawl the demographic law of the land.

The Toys of Tomorrow

Industrial technology brought workers into the cities, there to concentrate them in factories and offices. Information technology is scattering them ever farther from urban centers. By 2015 or so, our planet will be enshrouded in a delicate spiderweb of fiber-optic cable and circled by a galaxy of artificial communications satellites. Either network will be capable of transmitting symphony-quality sounds and video images of astounding clarity to wall-sized panels no thicker than picture frames, mounted in homes and exurban mini-office clusters.

Doctors will be able to send X-rays stored electronically in a hospital computer almost instantaneously to a specialist's video display terminal on the other side of the world. Drivers and airline pilots will be trained on interactive "virtual-reality" machines whose displays depict visual fields that respond to the user's every move. Machines with 20,000-word vocabularies—more than most humans—will take dictation, return phone calls, and program other machines in remote sites at the urging of the authorized human voice.

The computer on your office desk is more powerful than the largest research computers in the world thirty years ago—the ones you had to plead to get moments of time on. Computers thirty years from now will make today's look like Model T's. Despite an explosion in the use of computers, skeptics claim, the advent of computers has had no measurably positive effect on productivity. But, as Stanford economic historian Paul David has pointed out, although electricity was in wide use by the dawn of the 20th century, it was not until the 1920s that industrial productivity statistics began to reflect the impact of electric power. After that, U.S. manufacturing productivity surged. Organizations are still learning how best to put computing power to work. But an auspicious marriage is taking place: the wedding of increasingly sophisticated data-processing systems to speedy, global telecommunications networks.

Information technology is just entering wide-scale commercial use; we are not close to fully exploiting it. While computers have been around in one form or another for about fifty years, for most of that period they have been used mainly as glorified bookkeepers. Now computers are serving as drafting tables, laboratories, and managers. Computer-aided design, engineering, and manufacturing draw on enhanced capabilities for imaging, data manipulation, and transmission of the results to remote sights. (When a national magazine employed computer "massage" to move the Great Pyramid a bit closer to the Sphinx for a recent cover, the photo fakery sent a shiver up the spine of the artistic and forensic communities.) Biochemists use computers to tell them what complex molecules look like; synthetic chemists go a step further and ask computers to help them design new molecules with specific, desired traits.

Supercomputers can perform as many calculations in one second as a good desktop computer can perform in a month. By the end of the century, these juggernauts of information processing will be ten times as fast as they are now. Speed translates into high resolution and accurate prediction. Supercomputers create complex electronic simulations of reality to analyze financial markets, the flow of air past a jet's wing, seismic characteristics relevant to oil exploration or earthquakes—and, yes, the weather: In early 1990 a state-of-the-art supercomputer was able to forecast, retroactively, a hurricane that swept over the British Isles on October 16, 1987; a feat that the most powerful machine at the time, using *exactly the same data,* had failed to perform.[3]

Production technology is being transformed by automation. Typically, products sit around in warehouses after production, waiting for somebody to order them. In automated factories, computers coordinate robots' activities with engineering, accounting, and sales departments, boosting changeover flexibility and shrinking production time. Customer satisfaction is high and expensive inventories are low. Nothing is produced until it is needed.

Robots, whose salaries are measured in drops of oil and squirts of electrical current, will rival cheap foreign labor. The dexterity of robots will improve; their cost will go down. It will become far more efficient to customize products on order than to produce large lots and store them at considerable expense in the hope that somebody will buy them all eventually. Hand assembly will be obsolete for the great majority of products by 2020.

In a high-cost country like the U.S., this will mean laying off traditional assembly workers. Thousands of reasonably well-paying blue-collar assembly jobs will be lost. What will those people do? Displaced older workers will be difficult to retrain (at least that has been the experience so far); the younger generation will need a far better education than it is getting today.

Centrifugal Forces and Synthetic Sensations

As information processing and transmission gets ever cheaper and more miniaturized, significant social changes are in store. Ultra-lightweight, durable, laptop computers using memory cards instead of disk drives will be able to run for 100 hours on two AA batteries; today's 5- to 10-pound laptops' batteries must be recharged after 3 hours of use. Built-in cellular modems will transmit data from virtually anywhere to virtually anywhere else.

In mid-1990 Motorola announced that it would soon begin to launch several dozen satellites into low orbit—the first phase in the creation of a nationwide cellular-telephone network. We will eventually have instantaneous, worldwide communication—if we want it. Imagine a battery-run device that fits in the palm of your hand, has built-in voice, video, and computing power, and goes wherever you go, worldwide, with your own personalized phone number. Your kids will have them, too; wherever they are, they will be able call home for help when they get into a tight spot.

Spending forty hours a week in a cubicle in a downtown skyscraper will become the exception, not the rule. Telecommuting information workers, who will comprise an ever-greater proportion of the population, will work more and more out of their homes or in small suburban and exurban office clusters nearby and communicate with their colleagues through regular videoconferences.

One of World War IV's big battles of the 1990s will be fought over high-resolution television, or HDTV, which generates images of razor-sharp clarity. America, Europe, Japan, and even Korea each seek to prevail in what promises to be an enormous market, with progress in each case reflecting the amount invested: Japan, whose government and private industries have spent over $1 billion on HDTV research, may have a product available by 1991; Europe, which has invested over $300 million so far, will be next; the United States will bring up the rear sometime in the mid-1990s, literally the last of the big-time spenders at $100 million. In addition, Japanese government and industry have launched what is collectively a $1.4 billion effort to develop a 40-inch HDTV panel not much thicker than a picture frame by 1996. However, innovative U.S. digital HDTV technology could leapfrog even the Japanese. If, as is very possible, one or more blocs go the protectionist route of adopting their own sets of technical standards for HDTV, the world will remain effectively divided into three huge media audiences, each receiving only transmissions emanating from within its bloc.

The uses of crisp, large-format HDTV are limited only by the imagination. Buyers will be able to electronically prescreen homes for sale, walk down supermarket aisles, and watch models exhibiting the latest fashions, then place orders through electronic catalogs. No need to try on that suit or skirt: your personal measurements are all on file. A time-traveler from the present, arriving in the year 2020, might ask: "Where did all the shopping malls go?" Home-entertainment centers with multiscreen, multimedia capability will become commonplace. Wall-sized panels will feature picturesque, changeable, eye-resting, and entirely realistic (or, for that matter, surrealistic) three-dimensional backdrops for small, urban apartments instead of the reality—a stack of bricks three inches past the window—and offer escapist, high-resolution action scenarios for vicarious adventurers. Why have a picture window that looks out across the street when you can have the Alps, the Yucatan, or any other synthetic hologram of your choice?

Structures will be electronically "tuned in" to individuals, both to improve energy efficiency and to prevent crime. Tuneable lighting and heating systems will sense where people are and quickly turn up light or heat levels in that area only. Security technology will finally come into efficient mass use, because anti-intrusion devices, no longer subject to numerous false alarms as they are today, will be able to specifically identify the occupants, their pets and friends, and other authorized individuals. Intruders will be identified and detained. The debate over what constitutes an acceptable degree of physical restraint by home robots is certain to be a hot civil-rights issue in 2020. Japan and Europe will quickly adopt these new crime-control technologies while the U.S. wastes years and lives arguing over liability insurance and the rights of criminals.

Information will become cheaply, universally, and instantaneously accessible. Fiber-optic cable, so fast it transmits the entire text of the *Encyclopedia Britannica* around the world in less than two seconds, is now about as cheap to install as copper wire, and getting cheaper. For staying current on nonrecreational reading material, by far the fastest growing sector of the media, access to electronic libraries will be the only rational option. When the equivalent of 1,000 books can be stored on a 3.5-inch disk, which will be more difficult: censorship, or enforcing copyright laws?

As the use of credit cards becomes universal, street crime will decline, because no one will carry cash. Economic crime will become overwhelmingly electronic. Ubiquitous electronic checkout counters will keep instant records of everything you purchase; illegal, immoral, or just plain unpopular activity will become difficult to hide. Indeed, *all* your financial activities—and many of your nonfinancial ones—will be tough to hide. Cellular communications, for example, are easily monitored. A major 21st-century issue: Who will have legitimate access to your electronically transmitted and stored records? Simple privacy will suffer an onslaught by marketers who will know your spending proclivities, your demographic characteristics, your credit history, and probably your political and psychological leanings in excruciating detail. This will, of course, be valuable and tradable information. Those same marketers will have an unprecedented ability to inject their messages into your psyche through fax, phone, and videoport.

A whole industry may spring up to save you from immersion in a constant bath of information. Agencies will supply designated privacy zones where advertising is not permitted, protected conversations and data exchanges can take place free of electronic monitoring, and personal communications devices will not operate—your boss can't find you.

With the advent of the long-distance worker, sprawl is inevitable. Even now, some 70 percent of all commutes are not from suburb to downtown, but from suburb to suburb—a market that mass transit cannot dent. Despite improvements over the next several decades in high-speed ground transit between densely populated areas, the automobile is here to stay in one form or another. Even if the number of rides a long-distance worker takes doesn't increase, distances driven per ride will. Cars will continue their evolution into mobile living spaces replete with phones, entertainment displays, and other distractions; yet, despite those distractions, drivers will want to go faster. When they do drive into the city, they will find it less familiar and probably more forbidding than do today's workers, who are more tied to the central site.

A navigation system now available commercially in Japan uses satellite signals to pinpoint your car's position in an urban grid, displayed on a flat, four-inch color screen. Eventually, cars and roads will be equipped with electronic gear that let a driver relinquish control to an autopilot. Telemonitored traffic control in congested urban environments and collision-avoidance feedback on busy highways will increase safe-driving speeds and make trips quicker—a much more efficient solution to congestion than building more highways.

By 2005, permanently bar-coded vehicles will be commonly monitored by satellites or roadside scanners that measure emissions and assess each car's personal pollution tax, as well as its daily highway use fee. Car theft will be obsolete; blackboard-eraser-sized, tamper-proof tracking devices will be concealed in all cars. Monitoring stations will automatically direct police to stop stolen or nontransmitting vehicles.

New Materials

Microelectronics now account for 6 percent of a car's dollar value; by the year 2000, they will account for 20 percent.[4] Electronic sensors and feedback mechanisms have improved auto-engine performance as well as that of household appliances and entire factories. Still, transportation consumes 60 percent of the oil used in the United States and produces 40 percent of all hydrocarbon emissions.[5] If an electric car were feasible, oil use and emissions would drop drastically; the extra demand for electricity to recharge batteries could be met with nuclear and solar energy instead of hydrocarbons. Our balance of payments and national energy security would be immensely improved.

Will we finally get a workable electric automobile capable of driving the distances realistically required in the decentralized environment of the 21st century? A lightweight, high-capacity storage battery would be a big help. Traditional batteries give ranges of about 100 miles; the best new battery uses hot, molten sodium, which explodes if water touches it—not a pleasant thought in the event of a crash in the rain. Electric cars that pick up energy from coils in the road may in the end be more feasible. But compared to either alternative, the internal-combustion or gas-turbine engines will become so efficient that if you have to bet, bet on them.

The application of several new materials to an old conveyance like the car will produce phenomenal results. Until very recently, most materials research was more art than science; exactly why a certain alloy or catalyst had certain properties, nobody really knew. But over the next decade we will understand how to design materials—all materials—from the ground up, which is to say at the atomic level. Materials breakthroughs will occur in the following areas:

- *Catalysts* accelerate chemical reactions. Almost all the major catalysts were discovered by accident; we did not know why they worked. Now we design them. A catalyst that could efficiently make methanol from natural gas would revolutionize the energy sector.
- *Alloys* are combinations of metallic compounds. Alloys lighter than aluminum and stronger than steel are under development.
- *Plastics* are hydrocarbon materials; some of the best new plastics are derived from wood, not oil.
- *Composites* such as wood are the key to the superiority of biological materials. New artificial composites outclass all other materials in strength per pound.
- *Ceramics* were the first human-created materials (pottery), products of an art that changed very little for thousands of years. A moldable ceramic that could safely substitute for steel in automobile engines would double fuel efficiency. We are now designing ceramics that are perfect electrical conductors. Commercial microelectronic devices employing ceramic superconductors are just beginning to show up. A University of Houston team has devised a continuous process for fashioning rods of ceramic superconducting material—a step toward the production of practical superconducting electric-power cables and electromagnets.

Materials recently discovered and now being perfected—high-strength composites, new plastics, and ceramics—will turn the automobile into a dream machine that has at least twice the energy efficiency, weighs about half as much, accelerates as fast as we dare—and lasts virtually forever. Automobiles will have no radiators; engines, half the size of current ones, won't wear out. Shells will be both safer and lighter and will never rust. Forget running out of steel or copper; forget a gasoline shortage. Indeed, the problem will be one of disposal: Once you're bored with it, what do you do with it?

Housing, much more than transportation, is an area in which consumer tastes impose limits on materials. If there is anything human beings are conservative about, it is the houses they live in. People will pay a great deal for something that looks and feels like home. The construction materials of the future, especially in the United States, will be wood, brick, plaster, and concrete—no surprises here. Housing structures are inherently big, and there is nothing on the horizon that beats wood for price. But more and more portions of the house—say, bathroom or kitchen modules—will be factory-built from molded plastics, composites, and alloys.

Biotechnology: America's Ace?

When the iron machines of the Industrial Age were superseded by machines made largely of silicon, the result was the Information Age. What will we call the coming age, in which the most advanced machines will be fashioned from carbon, around whose atoms all life revolves?

The deciphering of the genetic code will lead to the greatest technical advances—and the greatest technological controversies—of the next few decades:

- *Genetic engineering* will lead to improved crop yields, ultra-efficient manufacturing processes, and thorough toxic-waste clean-up. It will unlock the secrets of whole ranges of diseases, including cancer, diabetes, arthritis, and multiple sclerosis. Research in this sector, which requires use of human embryos, vast numbers of animals, and challenging emotional concepts of the limits on human intervention, will encounter increasingly bitter opposition across the spectrum of political activism.
- *Environmental engineering* of whole ecological systems will be a real possibility. This technology, fraught with controversy on our own planet, may blossom on others.

Genetic Engineering

As an industry, biotechnology stands to rival electronics in dollar volume and perhaps surpass it in social impact by 2020. The United States, blessed with the finest universities in the world, is today the overwhelming world leader in biological research; virtually no field in science is as dominated by Americans. Universities and biotechnology firms here will maintain and expand their position as the chief repositories of medical-biological expertise, an area where the potential breakthroughs and controversies are mind-boggling—if regulations don't force the entire industry to head offshore.

Fewer than thirty years ago, scientists determined the structure of deoxyribonucleic acid, or DNA, the genetic material of virtually every living organism from amoeba to zebra. In those thirty years we have learned not only the detailed structure of DNA, but how it works: Within every living cell, DNA directs the production of the proteins that collectively spell out the language of life. As *The New Republic's* Robert Wright has written in an incisive essay about the implications of genetic research, "proteins are us."[6] Every complex biomolecule is made by a battery of proteinaceous, molecular machines, or catalysts, called enzymes. In turn, the recipe for each enzyme is coded on a stretch of DNA called a gene.

By manipulating genes and their products ("genetic engineering"), we can intervene in living systems for the sake of medicine, agriculture, industry, or the environment. A technique available since the 1970s allows a gene to be snipped from an animal or plant and stitched into the genetic material of a bacterium or yeast cell, whose rapid multiplication yields large numbers of copies of the gene or, if desired, large volumes of whatever that gene codes for. Formerly rare hormones, for example, are now available in quantity for the treatment of human deficiencies—and for experiments in reversing the aging process.

Biotechnology is controversial. Genetic engineering is opposed by the Green movement in Germany, where research facilities were firebombed by opponents of biotechnology in 1989. Some of West Germany's giant chemical companies have moved their biotechnology operations here. Japan, as usual, faces no such problem. Japan's genetic-engineering industry is expanding rapidly, abetted as usual by takeovers of fledgling U.S. companies.

Less constrained by ethical shackles, our knowledge of animals and plants will grow even faster than our knowledge of human beings. By transferring genetic traits from one species to another, we will be able to make milk cows more productive or to make crops disease-resistant, self-fertilizing (as legumes are), or salt-tolerant. Many plants grow well in salt water, but none produce food of any consequence. Genetically transferring a head of grain to Spartina, a salt-tolerant marsh grass—or alternatively, transplanting Spartina's salt tolerance to food crops—would solve our freshwater irrigation problems, because we could irrigate with ocean water. Tomato plants are now being grown in almost-half saltwater. The all-important grain crops belong to a class of plants that has been more difficult to manipulate, but experiments with genetically engineered corn are already underway.

Paradoxically, this new technology may aggravate the developed world's chief agricultural problem: overproduction. The technically advanced countries produce too much food: too much poultry, too much meat, too much butter, too much wheat. At the same time, people in the underdeveloped world are starving—not because the technology isn't available, but because they lack the political and economic organization to use it.

The industrial potential of biologically altered organisms is huge. Genetically engineered microorganisms already concentrate ore and clean up toxic-waste spills. Many chemical processes today involve high temperatures, high pressures, imperfect catalysts, and toxic by-products—and are, therefore, energy-inefficient and hazardous. For thousands of years, "yeasts of burden" have been put to work in the brewing and baking industries. Thirty years from now, noiseless assembly lines of yeast or bacterial cultures—each batch genetically altered to contain a particular ultra-efficient enzyme catalyzing one step of a chemical process—will produce bulk chemicals of exquisite purity; additional genetically engineered microorganisms will gobble up any toxic wastes produced. Scientists will design new enzymes by computer, then build them from scratch in the laboratory and insert them into microbes that will do their bidding. Eventually, we will be able to design microscopic biomachines capable of reproducing themselves as well as performing precision repair and monitoring tasks inside our bodies.

A relatively new technique allows tiny amounts of DNA to be multiplied simply into sizable batches for detailed examination in the lab. Paleontologists can conduct genetic analysis of long-extinct species; anthropologists can do the same with 2,400-year-old mummies; and forensic specialists can identify criminals from minuscule traces of skin or blood.

This same gene-amplification technique will also speed progress in a $3 billion, 15-year mission whose impact will surely be greater than that of the Apollo lunar landing program: The United States has embarked on a bold attempt to decipher the entire human genetic code by 2005. Headed by Nobel Prize–winning biologist James Watson, one of the co-discoverers of DNA's double-helical structure, the Human Genome Project has as its goal nothing less than the location, identification, and determination of function of each of the 50,000 to 100,000 genes that go into making a human being. Once a gene's chemical sequence has been identified in one lab, labs anywhere in the world can synthesize their own batches with mechanical "gene machines" for further analysis or use. The medical benefits are obvious. At the very least, the nature of many of the 4,000 known human genetic diseases will be unraveled. Genetic diseases can be traced to coding errors at specific sites on DNA, whose entire three-billion-letter text consists of permutations on an "alphabet" of four different chemicals hooked together like plastic beads on a child's necklace. It's likely that by 2020, the functions and origins of most active molecules in the human organism will be known.

The Frontiers of Medicine

During the next decade we will learn to turn the immune system on and off virtually at will. Applications will come early in the next century in the form of cures for infectious diseases, cancer, and autoimmune diseases. The research required to develop these cures touches every political hot button: It requires sacrificing thousands of animals; the systems involved are so complex that only live mammals can be used. Further, some embryological research requires the use of aborted human fetuses. Altering human genes may be the only sure way to cure genetic diseases.

The autoimmune diseases and cancers are flip sides of a coin: In the autoimmune diseases, the immune system is attacking something it should allow to remain or develop further. In cancer, the immune system fails to attack and arrest the growth of a cell that starts to grow without limit. Cancer happens naturally, and most of the time the immune system nips it in the bud. To cure cancer is to know what faulty switch mechanisms start cells proliferating as well as to know why the immune system makes the mistake of not attacking the proliferating cells. Embryology, the study of the development of a complete organism from the initial fertilized cell, is teaching us the switch mechanisms in the genetic code.

The issues of animal research, embryological research, and genetic engineering are life-and-death matters. Consider the potential: In the next ten to twenty years, we can have cures for cancer and the autoimmune diseases, which kill about 500,000 people a year in the United States alone. Demonstrations, litigation, and legislation by single-issue fanatics will not halt biological research altogether, but they will slow it down. The torture of innocent rabbits by the thousands to perfect a new line of lipstick may well be morally inexcusable. But delay of only five years in cancer research means the death of 2.5 million people who might otherwise have lived.

Yet genetic-engineering opponents have not only single-handedly slowed biological technology significantly but also (this could only happen in America) made their efforts self-financing; courts reward them with legal fees for finding obscure laws that force the slowing of technological research. In 1982, for example, plant pathologist Steven Lindow proposed to field-test a genetically altered bacterium that, sprayed on potato or strawberry plants, would protect them from freezing. Jeremy Rifkin, a high-profile, Washington, D.C.-based neo-Luddite who opposes all genetic engineering on the grounds that some altered life form could escape from its experimental restraints and destroy life as we know it, filed the first of several procedural lawsuits. Five years, many lab tests, and more than 1,300 pages' worth of applications and data later, Lindow received permission to spray a quarter-acre potato patch. The bacterium did exactly what Lindow hoped it would do, and no more. Most recently Rifkin, in a wildly premature preemptive strike against eugenics, has been trying to block a proposed experiment that would employ genetically modified cells from the immune system to treat cancer.

The surgical transfer of a single gene from one organism into another creates a product far more predictable than that of the more time-honored and messier gene-transferring procedure we call "mating." For centuries, breeders have mated plants and animals in order to meld specific traits from each parent within a single organism; but mating inevitably leads to some unwanted—or, certainly, unpredictable—as well as desired genetic transfers.

The 1990s will see vital research banned or driven into the waiting embrace of foreign competitors, thousands of research animals freed by absolutist activists, dozens of research projects destroyed, more laboratories burned, careers ruined, and perhaps some poor researcher, in the wrong lab at the wrong time, killed. (In spring 1990, a British researcher's child was injured in a car bombing.) This wave will end when the media tires, victims organize, and public opinion shifts. If animal-rights advocates have the right to burn and destroy to protect mice, parents of cancer or multiple-sclerosis victims have the right to burn and destroy to save their children.

Ultimately, a difficult balance will be struck between an unreasoning fear of technology that restricts its development and, on the other hand, the acknowledgment that biotechnology is going to become intrusive in a way no science has before. There is an old joke: "What do you get when you cross a gorilla with a parrot?" Answer: "I don't know, but when it talks, you'd sure better listen." The real concern, however, is not that a modestly altered organism will get out of control, but rather that we will have too much control. Our mushrooming knowledge of human genetics and biochemistry will permit us to peer through a test tube, darkly, as we scrutinize sperm, eggs, or growing human embryos, rate their genetic potentials, and ponder whether parents should be allowed to select their offspring on the basis of those potentials.

Environmental Engineering: The World as a Garden

By 2020 we will understand in great detail how organisms interact in whole ecosystems. Out of that understanding will grow a lofty field called environmental engineering. Technically we will be able to direct the growth and development of ecosystems; will we want to do it? The whole world can be a garden, if we want it to be.

Right now we depend on a very small number of animals. We call them domesticated, which means they are genetically deficient: they *mind*. By 2020, we'll be able to electronically and genetically control, say, the behavior of herds of buffalo so they don't all decide to trample through a city, which is what wild buffalo would do given half a chance. Huge areas—everybody within a hundred square miles would have to cooperate—can be managed for the quasi-domestication of what we now think of as wild game.

There is no question we'll be able to do it technically in the future. Managing the Great Plains of the northern United States for elk and buffalo would be much more profitable than managing them for cows, as is done now. But for those who love wilderness, genetically altered buffalo are a ghastly thought. Technology will force us to face our own ambivalence.

Another example of environmental technology will be the reclaiming of deserts by planting genetically engineered plants, in conjunction with controlling overuse of grazing lands and overcutting timber. The Gobi Desert in Mongolia was once a partially forested prairie; fragile, overgrazed, and overcut, it never recovered. Desertification, a severe problem in Mexico and on both the northern and southern margins of the Sahara Desert, is also becoming a problem in parts of the western United States.

THE GOOD OLD, SCARY DAYS BEFORE GENETIC ENGINEERING

One chilling example of the benefits of genetic engineering concerns the Salk polio vaccine administered to American schoolchildren in the mid-1950s. Before the vaccine came along, significant numbers of children were killed or crippled by the dread polio virus each summer. Guided by the principles of immunology, Dr. Jonas Salk and his collaborators produced huge volumes of the virus in cultures of monkey kidney cells. (A virus, no more than a mere bit of genetic material sheathed in a protein coat, cannot reproduce by itself; instead, it commandeers the chemical machinery of the cell it has infected.) Then the cells were broken up and viral particles were "harvested"—separated from the cellular debris—and inactivated by chemical means. Thus, they could be injected into a child's arm and serve as "mug shots" for the immune system, which would remain for decades in a state of high alert, ready to destroy the real McCoy should it ever show up in the bloodstream.

The Salk team was well aware of the possibility that one or a few or several of the billions of "inactivated" viruses would remain active and cause an actual polio infection, but the benefits clearly outweighed the risks. Nobody was prepared, however, for the discovery that came later on. Well after the vaccine had reduced the incidence of polio in a spectacular fashion, it was learned that the monkey kidney cells in which Salk's polio virus was being cultured contained another virus as well—one that causes cancer in monkeys, our genetic cousins. Particles of this second virus separated from the cellular debris right along with the polio virus and went along for the ride into the arms of millions of American children, who thus became participants in one of science's greatest inadvertent experiments. Thirty-odd years later, there has been absolutely no upsurge whatsoever in cancer cases attributable to those injections. But who'd want to repeat that experiment?

New vaccines today are typically made through genetic-engineering techniques, such as snapping into bacterial DNA only the genes for the portions of a virus likely to trigger an immune response; the bacteria produce not whole viruses, but merely large volumes of defense-triggering viral material. Not only is there no chance of a "dead" particle turning out to be active; the bacterial host is so simple, and purification techniques are now so advanced, that the resulting product is much more refined than the contaminated mixtures of bygone days.

The Final Frontier: Scientists vs. Space Dreamers

The sky's no limit, but cost is. As the military excuse for space exploration disappears, international ventures to support space exploration will grow in importance. Governments and companies will find international collaboration on space stations increasingly to their advantage, with launch vehicles financed by international coalitions led by the U.S. and the Soviet Union. Given the financial problems and technical prowess of the Soviet Union, space may be the only technical field in which that country is commercially competitive.

Our representatives will undoubtedly be on Mars by 2020. The question is: Will they be humans, or robots? Manned space transportation is a technology looking for a mission. So far, space transportation's only value is for communication satellites, earth-observation satellites, and scientific knowledge, none of which require astronauts. Robots cost a few percent of what humans would cost.

Some new technologies—ground-based rail guns or airplanes in place of rockets as the initial launch stage—may significantly reduce the costs of space by avoiding the waste of burning rocket fuel mostly to lift more rocket fuel. A rail gun accelerates vehicles electromagnetically and can shoot payloads into space at much less cost than huge fuel-burning rockets; however, the acceleration necessary to launch a space vehicle this way is so great that it is beyond the biological limits of live human beings.

The only apparent mission that might justify the expense of sending people to Mars is *terraforming*—creating a livable environment on another planet. This extreme application of environmental engineering will be coming off the drawing boards by 2020. Mars once had a modest atmosphere that was dense enough to sustain life. Existing terrestrial organisms would be unable to survive there now, but a small atmospheric change would permit genetically altered, high-altitude, Antarctic-type organisms to survive; the process could become self-generating. The modified organisms could ultimately transform the Martian atmosphere so that the planet could be settled by humans in self-sustaining settlements. Even foodstuffs could be grown there. That may sound like a pie in the sky now, but with the technologies available twenty or thirty years from now, it will be possible.

CHAPTER

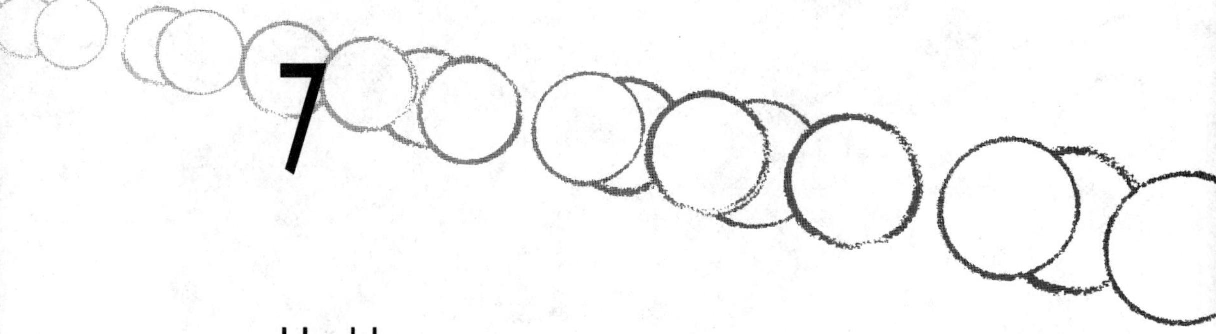

7

Health Care: Rationing Immortality

Another day, another health-care breakthrough. Human growth hormone (HGF), produced naturally in minute amounts in normal human bodies, can now be made in quantity by biotechnology firms using genetically altered bacteria. The newly enhanced supply of HGF allowed University of Wisconsin medical professor Daniel Rudman to run an experiment. For one year between 1989 and 1990, Dr. Rudman administered regular doses of the substance to a score of otherwise healthy men aged 61 to 81 years who shared a deficiency in HGF levels, common among older people. With treatment their muscle mass increased; their fatty tissues shrank. Their skin and their spines grew thicker.

Can HGF reverse the aging process? It's far too early to tell, but perhaps. The trouble is that HGF treatment is expensive—about $14,000 per year per person. For equity's sake, how about spreading the cost through government subsidies or by covering treatments under standard health-insurance policies? You do the arithmetic: More than one in twenty Americans today is over 75 years old. By 2020, it will be closer to one in ten, and climbing.

Meanwhile, fetal alcohol syndrome—incredibly costly to the health-care system and entirely preventable—is now one of the three top causes of birth defects in the United States.

America cannot afford American-style health care, which largely consists of ever more attempts to finance a technological monster—a monster that on a case-by-case basis does help those treated, but is becoming a crushing burden for everyone else. Health care, this nation's largest and fastest-growing industry, is approaching economic disaster. America faces a fundamental challenge: We are daily uncovering more secrets to better health, but for segments of our population, death and illness rates are rising; we are moving toward much better treatment of existing diseases, but new ones are appearing.

Health care, a $600 billion business in the United States, will change more than any other major industry over the next several decades. It will evolve through a series of stages, each bringing a new set of promises and a new distribution of pain. By 2020 the system will be stabilizing in a pattern that will anger many and satisfy few of today's interest groups.

All developed nations face the same challenge, to some degree. Traditional health care has become too expensive for any current health-care system, whether fully nationalized or private, to afford. Health care must evolve in two key directions:

- Preventive behavioral change
- Efficient rationing

The U.S. finds itself in the most difficult position, because it has the most inefficient health-care system in the world. We spend the most—now 12 percent of GNP, heading for 20 percent—and get the highest infant mortality rates and lowest life expectancy of any advanced nation. Because our challenges are the most severe, we will see the greatest structural change in health care.

The actual health status of our population thirty years from now will depend on the interplay of four factors: (1) technology; (2) human behavior; (3) biological evolution; and (4) economics.

The Technical Challenge

We've put enormous investments into advanced medical technology, and those investments are paying off. That's both good news and bad news. Modern technology shows an enormous potential for keeping human beings "alive," by some definition. A question we must face—on a small scale now, but eventually on a large scale—is, What life is worth living?

The future holds an astonishing variety of potential treatment mechanisms. Some of these will be very efficient; at modest cost, they will truly cure disease or infirmity. Other treatment approaches will be absurdly expensive and of questionable effectiveness. These treatments can be categorized roughly as follows (in descending order of relative cost):

- *Transplants.* New drugs will make organ transplants easier, but the donor problem will become overwhelming. Donor black markets will develop, and the system will switch to fetal donors—with all the ethical problems that implies.
- *Artificial organs.* Artificial organs will substitute for the ears, eyes, pancreas, kidney, liver, and heart. Costs will range from high to prohibitive.
- *Advanced surgery.* Microsurgery will increasingly repair blood vessels, fetuses, and the brain. The cost of surgery will remain high.
- *Immune-system intervention.* This will be the principal cure for cancer and such immune-system diseases as multiple sclerosis, but treatment will be expensive because it must be specific to each individual.
- *Genetic intervention.* This will be an early-stage cure for inheritable disease, but it too requires expensive individualized treatment.
- *New drugs.* Drug therapy, with ever-new varieties being developed, will continue to be cheaper than most other treatments.
- *New vaccines.* These will continue to be developed and, as preventive measures, will remain by far the least-expensive medical care.

Much of medical research will concentrate on finding drugs to avoid surgery. Drug profits will still be controversial, but when it comes to high profits, there's no topping the surgeons. Anything that eliminates surgery is a good buy for society. Many of the most promising new drugs will be genetically engi-neered improvements on natural chemicals. Some of the most exciting new drugs, available by 2000, will prevent paralysis due to spinal-cord injury (existing drugs, if given immediately, can already reduce the damage); ultimately, we will be able to repair spinal cords. New paraplegics and quadriplegics will largely disappear by 2020.

We will soon have truly effective artificial organs: combinations of biological and artificial materials that can't be rejected. Success will come first with chemical organs such as the pancreas and the liver, and afterward with sensory organs such as the eye. It will take much longer, though, to develop fully internal artificial hearts and artificial lungs, and these will be very expensive.

The bulk of press coverage and investment has been on the artificial heart, the most troublesome artificial organ. Mechanical organs require an energy source, and there is no good internal energy source on the horizon. An effectively functioning artificial heart awaits both a fantastic battery that is rechargeable through tissue—no mean feat—and materials that both last and do not harm the blood. It is by no means certain that we will achieve useful artificial hearts (except for temporary, external devices for patients awaiting transplants) within thirty years.

Transplant technology is improving rapidly with ever-better antirejection drugs, but there is no easy way to improve availability of donors. The tremendous range of wealth both within the United States and internationally will make it impossible to prevent a black market in organs. A tissue black market does not mean "body snatching." All you need is to tell some poor Peruvian family whose son is brain dead, "We'll give you $50,000 if we can keep this body alive and move it somewhere else." Some nation will certainly allow it, or wink at it; if the United States outlaws the practice, the Swiss will perhaps be more practical.

An alternative, which will become even more controversial, is the use of aborted fetuses for transplant organs. Fetal tissue transplants beautifully and will probably prove useful in curing Parkinson's disease, diabetes, and failed livers. The major mechanical organs—heart, lungs—aren't big enough in a fetus to function in an adult, but they grow quickly. Technically, it will be possible to transplant a fetal heart along with a mechanical heart-assist into an adult; in five years the fetal heart would grow large enough to handle the full load.

The U.S. government has withdrawn its financial support for all experimentation using aborted fetal tissue. Fortunately for the victims of such maladies as Parkinson's disease, other countries are proceeding with this research. Embryology and experimentation with fetal tissue are scarcely an issue in most of Europe, Scandinavia being the leader in that area of research.

A bigger stumbling block for the fetal-tissue approach to transplants, however, is that abortion itself will become technically outmoded. Better birth-control and abortion pills will largely end the abortion of later-term, more "useful" fetuses. By 2010, fetuses will need to be deliberately grown as donors to meet the demand—a prospect that will chill even "pro-choice" groups. By 2020, we will be developing internally regenerated organs to escape the ethical dead end of transplants.

Over the next decade, we will master one of the body's most complex information systems—the immune system. Applying this knowledge means curing virtually all contagious diseases, most arthritis, diabetes, multiple sclerosis, lupus, and amyotrophic lateral sclerosis. By 2020, cancer may no longer be a life-threatening disease.

Thanks to America's concerted efforts—whether through the multibillion-dollar Human Genome Project now underway or otherwise—tremendous progress will be made within the next twenty years in identifying the causes of the 4,000-odd diseases already known to be genetic in origin, as well as many more not yet understood to be inherited. Genetic medicine will allow us to control inherited diseases such as hemophilia, Duchenne's muscular dystrophy, Huntington's syndrome, sickle-cell anemia, some forms of diabetes and Alzheimer's disease, and hundreds of uncommon but still-deadly conditions. We can already detect many genetic abnormalities in the fetus; we will be curing many of them by around 2000, often at the fetal stage.

By 2010 the rate of cure will force us to face the prevention issue—selecting and modifying sperm and eggs so that the defective genes are not passed on to the next generation. By curing genetic disease, we allow those with fatal genetic defects to reproduce, and the defect becomes more common. This has already happened with the heritable form of diabetes. Many other heritable diseases will become much more common in the future, due to successful medical intervention. An increasing proportion of our population, unable to live without advanced medical intervention, will become progressively more reliant on expensive technology. This expense will fuel serious proposals for legitimizing eugenics to protect against the increase of fatal genes in the population.

Reproductive technology will also advance dramatically. While full-scale *in vitro* childbearing—Brave New World gestation of a fetus outside the body—is extremely unlikely during the next thirty years, *in vitro* fertilization will largely banish infertility. The use of surrogate mothers, in combination with cryogenic preservation of sperm and fertilized or unfertilized eggs, will enable people to become genetic parents at a much older age than has been possible, albeit with mind-boggling legal and ethical ramifications.

Genetic research will create angst. The nature/nurture issue will be far from solved. "Nice" genes, as well as those in which a defect leads to a disease, will certainly be identified—for instance, genes influencing height, gregariousness, neural swiftness, body-fat ratios, or even hirsuteness, each of which can arguably affect an individual's chances for social and economic success in our society. Will prospective parents wish to have their embryos genetically screened, then duly modified—or aborted—early in pregnancy on the basis of the screening's results? Will insurance companies have legal access to genetic-screening results? Will they be able to discriminate against individuals with apparent genetic predispositions to heart disease, schizophrenia, breast cancer? Even if insurance companies are denied access to screening records by law, what's to stop those found to have "healthy genes"—i.e. those with the fewest identifiable predispositions to disease—from submitting their results voluntarily in exchange for preferential rates, or shopping around for even cheaper "a la carte" policies that insure only against, say, accidental injury?

Suppose, rather than being squandered in some stupid gambit to create a master race of stereotypical blond musclemen, genetic selection does indeed turn out to be useful in increasing the statistical incidence of healthier, more athletic, or even moderately brighter offspring. Will not any population group failing to take advantage of the technique fall behind within several generations? Perhaps, but there are far surer ways to raise IQs—not the least of which are stable families, good nutrition, good education, and early vaccinations at 3 cents per injection—yet we are already paying a stiff price in the national intelligence quotient for inadequate attention to these needs. It is, at the least, premature to worry that we'll resort en masse to a much more difficult way of making better humans happen. And if some do, it can be argued, so much the better for everyone else.

If the U.S. were to ban genetic screening entirely, the ban would undoubtedly fail. Only a global treaty could, even in theory, prevent the practice entirely; and given the world's record in halting the proliferation of cumbersome, top-secret, ultra-expensive nuclear weapons technologies, what's the probability of enforcing a ban on genetic screening, which requires only a well-stocked lab and trained technicians?

Another ethical issue will be raised by the fact that the organic defects responsible for many specific behavioral disorders will become detectable, predictable, and treatable. By 2020 we will understand the chemistry of the brain, and we will have technologies for controlling behavior. This technical development is the inevitable by-product of our search for the causes of what we now call mental diseases—including Alzheimer's disease, manic-depression, and schizophrenia—many of whose symptoms are produced by chemical malfunctions in the brain when a genetic susceptibility is pushed over the edge by environmental influences. Progress in controlling those disorders with drugs poses a frightening choice. The evidence is overwhelming, for example, that pedophiles—men who are sexually attracted, uncontrollably, to young children—are fundamentally incurable through behavioral means. If, in twenty years, we find a specific spot in the brain that can be altered to reduce that behavioral proclivity, do we have the right to force that alteration on a pedophile?

A growing body of evidence suggests that aggressiveness has genetic components. Until only the past fifty years or so, almost all males in all societies were warriors at some point in their lives. Thus, hundreds of generations of human males were, to some degree, selected for reproduction on the basis of their aggressiveness. The competitive dynamic of the economy and sports now provides some outlets for that aggression. But as we become more and more civilized, the hyperaggressive males among us, once such a crucial element of society, will pose increasing social problems. What shall we do with them? Institutionalize them, monitor their behavior electronically, alter it chemically—or leave them alone and hope they don't kill someone?

Behavior

The United States has excellent birthing facilities, yet the U.S. infant mortality rate is almost double that of Japan, Sweden, and Switzerland.[1] Behind that statistic lurk other statistics that, dark though they may be, throw some light on a national problem. More than 30 percent of babies born in New York City hospitals are addicted to crack, for example.[2] The cost of keeping such a baby alive with state-of-the-art technologies can easily exceed $200,000.

Behavior and nonmedical technologies have always been the keys to widespread good health. For individuals, technology can buy cures, but for a society it buys mostly cost. The society that substitutes behavioral discipline for medical technology—hardly the direction we're headed right now—is ahead 100 to 1, if not 1,000 to 1.

The great breakthroughs in conquering infectious diseases around the turn of this century came primarily through the application of sanitation techniques. That in turn required behavioral change: It was not enough simply to install safe water systems; people had to buy and use them. The whole profession of plumbing had to be created and financed.

Now we face a different set of behavioral problems: "diseases of choice." During the next thirty years, the great majority of diseases of people under age 50 or so will occur as a result of specific behavioral choices. These behavioral choices and their annual death rates for Americans in the 1990s are:

- *Smoking*—300,000
- *Diet*—200,000
- *Alcohol*—100,000
- *High-risk sex*—50,000 to 100,000 from AIDS (some one million Americans are infected)
- *Illicit drugs*—10,000 (primarily from AIDS due to the sharing of dirty needles)

The victims of these behaviors number more than those who indulge in them. Drunk drivers kill others besides themselves. Secondary smoke is a killer. Estimates are that at least 50,000 babies per year in the United States are severely damaged by growing epidemics of both fetal alcohol syndrome and fetal cocaine addiction. Their living status can undoubtedly be improved to some modest degree; but keeping hundreds of thousands of brain-damaged children alive from infancy will become a multibillion-dollar problem. Prevention is clearly preferable, yet may require controversial behavioral intervention: controlling what pregnant women do.

High-quality, after-the-fact medical care can be made cheap to *individuals* through insurance and government subsidies, but it is invariably far more expensive to society than prevention. Ironically, the more faith people have in medical technology, the more health risks they're willing to take. Safety studies indicate that the better the roads and cars are, the more dangerously people drive. In terms of years of productive life lost, automobiles are the great killers of the

THE DEATH-SPORT CAPITAL OF THE WORLD

Chamonix, France, exemplifies the innate human desire for mortal risk. When modern equipment made normal rock climbing too safe, Chamonix turned to totally unprotected solo climbing, where one slip means sure death. Skiing also became too simple, so Chamonix turned to extreme skiing (jumping off vertical cliffs; catching an edge is the end), summer skiing (rocketing down on wheeled skis onto not snow, but rocks), and descente en baulle (rolling down the hill in a giant, inflated ball).

The latest rage is bungee-cord diving, which involves tying a very strong elastic cord around your ankles and then jumping from a height of perhaps 200 feet. If you've calculated everything correctly, you free fall for the first 100 feet; then for the last 100 feet, your descent slows until finally, just before hitting the ground, you bounce back up.

Chamonix's favorite video shows a famous rock climber, Isabelle Patissier, bungee-cord jumping from a balloon. Unfortunately, she cannot get back up to the balloon, and is left hanging helplessly from these giant rubber bands. Her pilot attempts to land, but he entangles Isabelle in a high-voltage power line and her bungee cords catch fire. Somehow she survives.

France's ultimate memorial to risk occurred in the deaths of two famous climbers, Patrick and Marie Jo Vallencant. Marie Jo was dedicating a climbing school as a memorial to Patrick, who had finally slipped and died while solo climbing. As part of the dedication ceremony, the grieving widow elected to pull off a stunt of her own: a reverse bungee-cord dive. A bungee cord was stretched from a crane, attached to her, and released. Unfortunately the calculations were incorrect, and she went up so fast and so hard that she hit the crane and died. Like an Indian widow throwing herself on her husband's funeral pyre, Marie had committed modern suttee.

developed world—although, in the United States, AIDS is quickly catching up. Risky sports such as solo rock climbing, motorcycle racing, and deep-sea diving are growing in popularity among young people who think not only that they are immortal, but that doctors can fix anything. This growth in risk taking is also an apparent reaction to the loss of traditional risks and outlets for aggression.

By 2020, behavioral choices will be the dominant causes of disease. Heart disease is just now entering the "behaviorally induced" category. Moderate behavioral and nutritional discipline, beginning early in life, can probably prevent the majority of pre-age-70 heart disease and, with pharmacological adjuncts, possibly even reverse the formation of arterial plaque. Some behavioral change is already occurring. Age-adjusted death rates from heart disease declined nearly 30 percent from 1960 to 1980, with the decline greatest for men. If this continues, the next century may not be quite the widower's heaven that this one was.

AIDS must be recognized as largely a disease of choice. Since 1981, it has been widely known that exchanging body fluids through shared needles or unsafe sex put you at risk. More than one million Americans have chosen to take the gamble, and have lost. This constitutes a classic example of unfounded faith in technology: "All you have to do is spend more billions and the cure will automatically be there. Therefore, I don't have to change my behavior." Unfortunately, money does not buy miracles, and viruses do not listen to speeches by movie stars or angry demonstrators. Even though medical research has moved astonishingly fast in the case of AIDS, most of those now euphemistically categorized as "showing antibodies to the HIV virus"—meaning "infected"—will die of AIDS. Spending money on research speeds the discovery of the cure—but only up to a point, beyond which money simply can't buy any more time, genius, or serendipity.

As medical care's great victories over infectious organisms turn tragic, the 1990s will see the beginning of the retreat from treatment back to prevention. By 2010, requirements for testing, isolation, and behavioral change will be far stricter, driven by the loss of hundreds of thousands of young Americans to the most easily preventable of all modern epidemics, AIDS.

Nature Strikes Back

A world-famous puppeteer in the prime of life dies suddenly of pneumonia induced by group A streptococcus, an increasingly prevalent, drug-resistant, and virulent bacterial type. A strain of AIDS-causing virus formerly thought to be almost exclusively confined to western Africa begins to pop up in Portugal. A brain disorder known for hundreds of years to occur in sheep begins to spread mysteriously among herds of cattle in England; a cat in Bristol succumbs. France, Germany, Italy, and finally Germany impose bans on imports of British cattle. No human has ever been known to contract it; but after all, if a cow—or a cat—can get it from a sheep, isn't it possible a human can get it, too?

The rapid biological evolution of disease organisms is an under-appreciated threat that will become a serious problem in coming decades. We were fortunate in the period from roughly 1940 to about 1980, when new treatments, especially for bacterial infections, were discovered at a dramatic rate. In the blush of our success with antibiotics and vaccines, we didn't fully appreciate the ability of infectious organisms to evolve. But the race to find cures faster than pathogens can adapt never ends. There are new diseases; minor diseases are becoming more dangerous; and old diseases are returning with new vigor. It's now becoming dangerous to go to some hospitals, where drug-resistant pathogens are increasingly endemic.

International travel, increased population densities, and modern sexual practices are speeding the spread of diseases. The Boeing 747 is one of the most efficient disease-transmission mechanisms in world history; the exchange of body fluids effectively transmits even relatively fragile viruses and is entirely responsible for the AIDS epidemic in the United States, and almost as responsible for the even-worse spread here of hepatitis B, long known to cause fatal liver cancer in Asia. Chlamydia, venereal herpes, and Lyme disease are new. Technology can also create new niches for formerly marginal pathogens; Legionella, the bacteria responsible for Legionnaires' Disease, love air-conditioning systems.

New diseases are not limited to humans; those cattle in England were infected with bovine spongiform encephalopathy, or "mad cow disease," apparently as the result of being fed ground-up remains of sheep afflicted with an analogous disorder. Are humans susceptible? The answer will require patience: The disease is caused by a "slow virus" whose incubation time in the host is 4–8 years.

The most dangerous pathogens are characterized, as is AIDS, by both long incubation times and high rates of genetic change. A slow onset of symptoms makes it difficult to break the chain of transmission; there are at least five asymptomatic carriers of the AIDS virus for every individual showing symptoms. Fast evolution allows a pathogen to quickly become resistant to treatment, vaccine, or even detection. Every time we come up with a new treatment for an infectious disease, we deliver an ultimatum to the invading organism: "Evolve or die." It has been estimated that some viruses evolve more than a billion times as fast as mammals; that poses a challenge for scientists even in an era of molecular biology. A new flu vaccine is required every year; the AIDS virus develops resistance to the drug AZT in a few months. Forms of both hepatitis B and AIDS have developed that are not detectable by existing tests. Several new pathogens, including AIDS and Lyme disease, originally infected nonhuman hosts before evolving to infect humans.

Economics Comes to Medical Care

Ultimately, economics will drive the restructuring of medical care. No sector of the economy can expand its share forever; health care is at 12 percent of GNP now, and will exceed 20 percent by 2020 barring major changes. In 1989, federal expenditures for health care accounted for 17 percent of the budget, Social Security 20 percent, and national defense 26 percent.[3] Medical care will be the federal government's largest expenditure by the turn of the century—bigger than social security, bigger than defense.

All societies have to ration medical care, and they always will, because medical care is an infinite need: Some justification can always be found to provide more care to someone; and, given the difficulty of their work, doctors and nurses will always feel underpaid. This rationing of medical care will become far more difficult as modern care technologies and lifestyle trends hit the limits of economic capacity.

Medical-care economics in the United States has evolved through several stages:

- *Stage 1.* Until the 1950s, medical care was paid for directly by the patient or by charity. Doctors and nurses were poorly paid; hospitals were nonprofit institutions. The problem with this system was that if you were unlucky enough to have a medical emergency when you were short on cash, you would get substandard care—and even so, it could break you financially.

- *Stage 2.* Starting in the 1950s and extending into the 1970s, employer-provided health insurance covered the majority of the population.

- *Stage 3.* From 1964 through about 1975, the government moved enthusiastically into health care. Over 85 percent of the population was covered by some kind of medical insurance. Medical expenditures exploded. Care was somewhat better—

and providers far better off—than before. Those lonely budget analysts who had proposed to retitle Medicare the "Make Every Doctor a Millionaire Act" were proven correct.

- *Stage 4*. Starting in the mid-1970s and accelerating since then, payers have desperately attempted to control medical costs. These cost controls include encouraging fixed-price health maintenance organizations (HMOs), restricting reimbursements to hospitals, and limiting payments to physicians. For every control there is an escape strategy, so medical costs have continued to soar.

- *Stage 5*. In the current stage of cost-control desperation, state and federal governments are attempting to both reduce their own costs and satisfy political constituencies by mandating employer-provided health insurance. These mandates as to the type of care, the extent of coverage, and financing include a variety of anti-discrimination rules that prevent employers from containing health-insurance costs by not hiring high-risk individuals. Massachusetts is just starting to implement a mandatory health-insurance program, and the issue is under discussion in almost every state.

The Death of Health Insurance

No one would consider mandating fire-insurance coverage for known pyromaniacs, but that is the essence of mandating health-insurance coverage today. Health care is no longer a reasonably insurable risk; illness lacks the fundamental characteristics of rarity and randomness that make insurance feasible.

The randomness is gone because we all know who will get sick:

- Age is the foremost indicator of potential for illness.

- Behavior generates much if not most health-care costs for persons between ages 5 and 50.

- Genetic disposition is a major factor in cancer, diabetes, and heart disease. By 2000, genetic markers will allow many such diseases to be predicted far in advance.

- Persons with long-term chronic diseases such as diabetes are easily identified.

Furthermore, health insurance forces consumers to pay for several categories of excessive cost (by averaging those costs into the general rates) that a rational person would probably avoid, including:

- Excessive treatment for the terminally ill.
- High-priced physicians who overprescribe and overcharge.
- Malpractice insurance costs that could be avoided by waiving the right to sue.
- Unnecessary treatment for hypochondriacs.
- Expenses of other people who cannot pay.

Together, these growing and avoidable costs amount to at least 30 percent, and possibly 50 percent to 70 percent, of normal premiums. Both employers and healthy employees will soon find it in their interests to avoid traditional health insurance. Individual coverage is a particularly poor buy; the average healthy, careful worker would probably be much better off taking half of the health-care premium in cash. Minimum-cost catastrophic coverage is the only rational individual option.

Health-care status is becoming one of the most important predictors of whether or not someone can get a good job. Health-care costs are now so large that one of the most important decisions an employer can make is to hire healthy people. Right now, an employer might legally discriminate against smokers, alcoholics, and drug users. As medical detection and prediction systems improve, it will make increasingly good economic sense, from an employer's perspective, to discriminate based on blood pressure, cholesterol levels, infection with HIV or hepatitis B, or incriminating genetic markers. However, a new federal law, the Americans with Disabilities Act (ADA) will make nearly all such health-related discrimination illegal.

Mandatory health insurance is an attempt by providers and government to force individuals and employers to buy an overpriced product—in effect, to turn it into a tax. Proposals to mandate community rating (everyone pays the same price for insurance) or open enrollment (every insurance company must accept every applicant) are merely attempts to make health insurance a more equitable tax.

Proposed antidiscrimination rules have the pernicious effect of rewarding risky behavior. Should you be forced to hire a smoker?

Should you be forced to hire someone who's so overweight that a heart attack is likely? Under ADA, just enacted by Congress under pressure from the handicapped, medical provider, and AIDS lobbies, it is illegal to discriminate against individuals with infectious diseases, alcoholics, or former drug addicts. Five states prohibit employment discrimination against smokers.

Insurance companies will either deny coverage or sharply increase rates. Aggressive insurance companies seek out, and give low rates for, low risks—just as a competitive market says they should. But if everyone adopts that strategy, who will insure the uninsurable? States will be forced to set up funds for employers who can't get insurance from the private sector. Such pools will inevitably have costs far above expectations, and vastly higher government subsidies, because only the companies with the highest risks end up in that pool.

On top of the existing cost conflicts, the inevitable result of mandatory insurance is that all personal-service providers begin to define themselves as a part of medical care. The psychiatrists say medical care must include psychiatric care. The psychologists and clinical social workers climb on the bandwagon, along with marriage counselors and providers of alcohol- and drug-dependency treatment. The list grows and grows until every kind of service that by any stretch of the imagination could be considered associated with health care ends up under that umbrella—which breaks the umbrella.

Health care in the 1990s will be chaotic. Private-sector plans will go bankrupt—several major HMOs have already gone under. State funds will go bankrupt, too. There will also be increased patient dumping: Hospitals will not take in uninsured emergency cases. Without mandates, private-sector health insurance will cover a declining share of the really ill because discrimination is so cost-effective. Small companies will be forced to stay below ADA's magic number—15 employees—in order to discriminate against high-medical-cost employees and thereby retain group health insurance for their people. Individuals with chronic conditions or bad family medical histories will become employable only by government or large companies.

Cost controls will continue to be ineffective. Providers simply shift from newly unprofitable sectors to something else. It used to be profitable to treat patients in hospitals. With the advent of hospital payment restrictions, it became more profitable to treat patients in outpatient clinics, which weren't subject to the controls. The result was hospitals going bankrupt left and right, along with massive construction and organization of outpatient clinics, throughout the United States. Physician reimbursement rules, which impose caps on fees per treatment, will merely raise the frequency of treatment.

Post-2000 Options

By the late 1990s, the nation will be looking at three options, all of which will have been tried by some states:

- *State health insurance* on the Canadian pattern. Doctors would remain private, but local health authorities would have total control over their budgets. Doctors and clinics would receive set dollar amounts based on the size of the population served. Costs would thus be capped, but who gets how much care from whom would be a bureaucratic jungle.
- *Mandatory private health insurance* with government backup. The costs of this option are the most likely to spin out of control; therefore, its popularity will be waning. This is the provider's preferred option.
- *Mandatory catastrophic health insurance* with state backup and discriminatory rates—e.g., smokers pay twice as much as nonsmokers. Coverage would include all preventive services and expenses exceeding 10 percent of income. The remainder, averaging $3,000 to $4,000 per family, would be paid directly by the consumer, creating an effective incentive for cost control. This option will be gaining appeal because its costs will prove to be lowest by far. Providers will hate it.

Of these three options, only one—mandatory catastrophic insurance, combined with discriminatory rates—would be stable, because it would put the brakes on inflation. Mandatory traditional insurance would produce an unsustainable cost spiral.

National health insurance is the most likely option to be chosen by 2010, because both the unions and the Fortune 500 are, ironically, natural allies on this issue and they know it. Large corporations have been stuck with high costs plus nondiscrimination rules, which small companies will be able to escape. Any general tax on corporations would be cheaper than existing insurance premiums for most large corporations. The unions are tired of fighting for health-care increases that just pay doctors more, as opposed to fighting for better wages for their members.

Direct state or national health insurance would turn out to be a political nightmare. U.S. populations are far more diverse and far more unruly than those of Europe or Canada, where national health insurance has been largely successful. National health insurance would force us into formal rationing. For example: "If you're over age 55, you can't get a heart transplant." "If you're a heavy smoker and you've got lung cancer, we won't treat you. You made the choice. We've got more important things to do with our limited resources." "Infant liver transplants are simply not cost-effective." Because many high-risk behaviors are concentrated in impoverished or minority communities, charges of discrimination would be endless. Doctors would migrate to more comfortable practices. Doctor shortages would be even more severe than they are now in isolated rural areas, urban ghettos, and among AIDS patients.

Governments are unique in that they can regulate, by statute, people's and organizations' conduct. If the government is paying the bills, it can be expected to take an increasing interest in matters of advertising or product content. For example, simply adding tasteless, colorless, odorless vitamins to alcoholic beverages or junk food would have a significant health impact on some sectors of the population in the United States. The government's position has been that to do so would be seen as "encouraging junk-food eating." But given the job of paying the medical costs of people who subsist largely on the stuff and suffer the nutritional consequences, the government might begin to see things quite differently.

Once the government becomes the safety net for health care, it also becomes very much in the government's interest to legally regulate people's behavioral patterns—to become a national nanny. Some aspects of this may be a civil libertarian's nightmare. For a preview, take a look at the current tough anti-smoking and anti-drunk-driving campaigns in Scandinavian countries. It has now become socially and politically acceptable in most of the United States to discriminate against smokers. In the future, smokers will be just one of the many groups, along with reckless drivers and alcoholics, whose behavior will be under attack. Certain treatment regimens might be mandated. For example, there is a drug that makes you violently ill if you touch alcohol. If, having legislated national health insurance, you can spend $50 million a year giving that drug to alcoholics or $50 *billion* a year treating the results of alcoholism, the incentive to do the former is obvious.

Ultimately national health care insurance would be destined to evolve into explicit two-tier medicine. England's nationalized system, for example, provides a modest, minimal level of medical care. If you don't like that—and if you have the money—you can buy significantly better care. Employer health insurance would return to buy this better level of care for its workers.

One impact of these medical changes will be to accelerate the loss of control by the individual physician. By 2010, a great majority of physicians will have become employees. They will not be partners or owners. An elite of nonemployee physicians will provide specialized care. Physicians' real (inflation-adjusted) net earnings, which have been declining since the mid-1970s, will continue to do so.

The Ultimate Health Question

We all want to know: Come 2020, how long can people reasonably expect to live in good health? The answer depends more on a person's ability to lead a disciplined life than on that person's ability to pay for increasingly exotic technologies, both preventive and therapeutic. The keys to longevity are better diet, moderate exercise, lucky genes, and avoidance of high-risk behavior. Young people who obey the known rules will, on average, remain active and healthy until well into their eighties. There's already a test group of such individuals; they're called Mormons.

Can technology get you much beyond the energetic eighties? There will certainly be individuals who will live longer as a result of novel medical interventions. Estimates of the over-age-85 population range between 20 and 50 million by 2050. The boost of active lifespans into the 80-to-90 range will be reached mainly through disciplined behavior and self-monitoring. Accurate, convenient, inexpensive home-diagnostic kits to assess pregnancy status, cholesterol levels, blood chemistry, and infection will proliferate. Administering human growth hormone to healthy 70-year-olds may get much of the population into their nineties in good health—at an annual cost of $14,000 apiece. Simply shelling out for costly, after-the-fact medical care, instead of being careful to begin with, barely gets people to a comfortable 65.

However much exotic life-preserving technologies—or more down-home novelties such as fat substitutes (several food companies have them now) in your cheesecake—may seem to allow having your cake and eating it too, there is an apparent ceiling to the human lifespan. Collagen, the basic structural protein in your joints, simply wears out. Blood vessels, skin, and tendons lose their elasticity. At some point it becomes impossible to repair the damage.

Will more people hit 100? No question about it. Right now centenarians are one in a million. When a population begins to approach an average lifespan of 85 years, that statistically translates into millions of people living beyond 100. Technically, millions more could be kept alive in states of vegetative misery; the only limit is cost.

CHAPTER

8

The Environment: A Question of Priorities

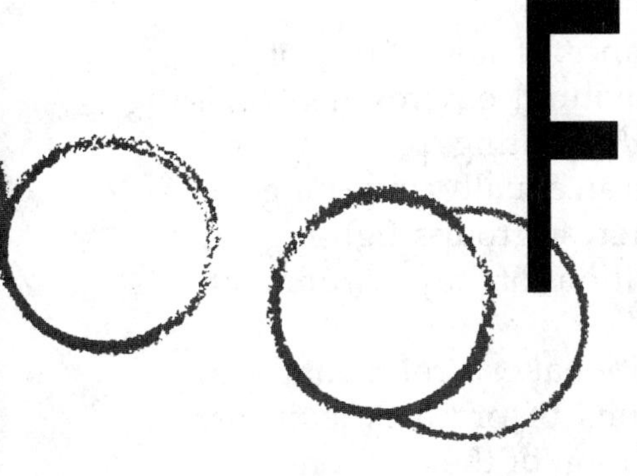

For the first time, the global environment is threatened by human action. Several aspects of the environment are likely to deteriorate over the next few decades. Slowly but surely, the climate will get warmer, the sea level will rise, the once-vast herds of African wildlife will disappear, and the rainforests will shrink.

But the key environmental impact of the future will be political, not physical or biological. The growing battle over environmental issues will prove to be one of the most disruptive and politically explosive controversies of the next few decades.

- The environment is becoming a political battleground, with a variety of groups fighting for the commitment (along with contributions) of the environmentally concerned public.

- Environmental issues are culturally divisive, with priority on environment valued primarily by wealthier European-Americans.

- The American environment is improving by most definitions, but the global environment isn't doing as well.

- The two largest causes of U.S. environmental problems—farmers and government—receive little attention.

- Too little environmental improvement is being bought at too great a cost. By 2020 we will have adopted cost-benefit analysis to minimize the economic disruption caused by environmental controls, and *global environmental management*—economic, biological, and physical engineering—on a worldwide scale.

The Players

Much confusion arises from the abundance of definitions of the environment and environmentalism. The natural environment is a wide range of poorly understood and fluctuating physical and biological phenomena. Environmentalism is an equally wide range of quasi-religious, political, and economic interest groups fighting for contributions, influence, and different definitions of the environment.

- *Wildlife lovers*—This is the core of traditional environmentalism: a sometimes shaky coalition of millions of ordinary citizens, hunters, and naturalists. By their definition of the environment, wildlife survival, much progress has been made. There are serious new concerns about lost wetlands and rainforests, but the recovery of species ranging from bison to bald eagles has been dramatic. The wildlife enthusiasts offer an enormous reservoir of money, votes, and influence.

- *Eco-industry*—This group includes scientists, lawyers, lobbyists, and corporations. Their participation is vital and their criticisms often on the mark, but their economic interests influence their environmental concerns.

- *Eco-religion*—For many Americans and Europeans, the environment is increasingly providing a substitute for the lost religions of Christianity, patriotism, and Marxism. The environment—life on earth in all its forms—is a new god. This religious viewpoint inspires fierce commitment, up to and including violence.

- *Eco-media*—Cursed by peace and prosperity, the media have turned to the environment for salvation in their eternal search for the sensational. Since media coverage is a source of votes and contributions, the media have great influence in defining the environmental issues. Media biases are eternal, but straightforward: the bigger the headlines, the more awful the projected disaster, the better.

- *Eco-Marx*—This wing of environmentalism is attempting to radicalize traditional environmentalism and redirect its enormous wealth and numbers. Marxism's widely admitted failure to outproduce capitalism has been followed by a seamless shift in leftists' attention to the environment as the new excuse for centralized government control of the economy. The Eco-Marxist definition of environmentalism is simple: any issue that can be used to criticize Corporate America.

Environmental Trends

A number of environmental threats are serious. Others are more media hype than reality. Some are well known; others receive little coverage. To combat both accidental and politically motivated media confusion, environmental issues need to be sorted out into those of little consequence and those that matter:

- *Intractable long-range problems*
  - Global warming
  - Loss of high-altitude ozone
  - Loss of tropical rainforests
  - Loss of coastal wetlands

- *Solvable, but politically difficult, issues*
  - Acid rain
  - Water shortages
  - Loss of habitat

- *Overlooked major issues*
  - Desertification

- *Issues receiving politically motivated overemphasis*
  - Nuclear power
  - Toxic wastes
  - Garbage
  - Local air pollution
  - Energy shortages

- *Environmental hustles*
  Farmland shortages
  Growth controls

THE GREENHOUSE EFFECT

Two trends are mingling in the atmosphere: global climatic warming caused by increases in carbon dioxide (CO_2) and other gases, and a loss of high-altitude ozone leading to an increase in ultraviolet radiation. Both of these related trends are complex, uncertain, and subject to technically difficult, controversial, and imperfect controls.

The so-called greenhouse effect refers to CO_2, chlorofluorocarbons, methane, and nitrogen oxides in the atmosphere. These gases trap heat at the surface of the earth by preventing it from radiating back into space, just as closing the windows heats the interior of a car on a cold, sunny day. The greenhouse effect is absolutely vital to life on earth. Without it, the average temperature of the planet would be below freezing. But a rapid rise in world atmospheric temperatures could be catastrophic.

No climatic theory completely explains actual world temperature trends. The greenhouse effect should have led to accelerated warming throughout this century. Instead, average global temperatures declined from about 1940 to the mid-1960s, and resumed a slight warming trend after that time. A recent Agriculture Department study of nearly 1,000 weather-station records found that, contrary to prevailing prejudice, most U.S. cities have cooled slightly since 1920. Conversely, observed declines in solar radiation and increases in volcanic activity since 1980 should have led to a cooling of the climate, but temperatures increased.

Significant climatic warming, *were it to occur,* would be by far the most important environmental impact in history. Global warming would produce slow but inexorable rises in sea level and altered rainfall patterns. These impacts are far from all negative. The world is better off warmer than colder. A reoccurrence of the "Little Ice Age" of the 1400s through the 1600s would be more disruptive than the currently projected level of greenhouse warming.

The commonly discussed projected warming of 4° to 10° F. is a long-run estimate that would not be reached until well after 2100. The "best-guess" overall temperature rise between now and 2020 is in the range of 2° to 4° F., with temperatures nearer the poles increasing by two to three times as much, primarily on winter evenings—to the lasting delight of Minnesotans, Alaskans, Canadians, Scandinavians, and Russians, who would also benefit from the longer growing season. A United Nations panel has estimated that a 3.5° F. rise in worldwide atmospheric temperatures would lead to increases of 40 percent in the Soviet Union's agricultural output and 20 percent in China's.[1]

Global warming would certainly lead to longer growing seasons and rising sea levels. Longer growing seasons are beneficial, but the sea-level rise could prove disastrous for some parts of the world. The predicted sea-level rise is about six inches by 2025 and one to two feet by 2075. (The widely publicized projection of a four- to five-foot sea-level rise over the next century is an extreme and unlikely scenario.)

Humanity has dealt with shifting sea levels throughout history, but the projected rise would be much more rapid than in past experience. Rising sea levels have flooded many ancient ports in the Mediterranean, while rising land has left some former English and Scandinavian ports high and dry. The main impact of sea-level rise comes in the form of more coastal flooding during storms. The most severely affected areas will be those that are already flooded and should not have been developed, such as the coastal-barrier beaches of the eastern United States. Rising sea levels will also cause destructive saltwater intrusion into coastal freshwater supplies and into brackish (partially fresh) coastal marshes.

More uncertain, yet possibly more severe, are the effects of shifting rainfall patterns. Rainfall is much more important to agriculture, forests, and wildlife than is temperature. Higher temperatures mean more rainfall in total; but timing and location are uncertain. Over centuries, whole forests, deserts, and patterns of vegetation could change. Some climate models predict less-reliable rainfall in the Great Plains of the U.S., which means more frequent droughts, but the actual impact would probably be detected only over decades of experience. The *normal* drought cycle is far more severe than the likely greenhouse impact. The 1988 Midwest drought, for example, was just a normal cycle, possibly strengthened in a minuscule way by the greenhouse effect.

The potential for limiting or slowing the greenhouse warming depends on the relative contributions of the different greenhouse gases. Exact details of which gas contributes how much to future warming constitute a key scientific uncertainty, but their estimated contributions are as follows: carbon dioxide, 50 percent; methane,10 percent; nitrous oxide, 5 percent; ozone, 10 percent; and chlorofluorocarbons, 25 percent.

The contribution of carbon dioxide, the original greenhouse gas, is decreasing, because its impact saturates as concentrations grow above the current 350 parts per million. This saturation effect is fortunate, since CO_2 emissions are nearly impossible to limit—physically, economically, or politically. The immediate shifting of all U.S. electricity production from coal to nuclear power, for example, would reduce the CO_2 level in 2020 by less than 2 percent. Most growth in CO_2 emissions is coming from developing countries, many of which, by virtue of their equatorial geography, are themselves little affected by climatic warming. India and Brazil are unlikely to agree to stop industrializing to avoid flooding luxury condos on Miami Beach.

Many headline-grabbing schemes to sharply limit CO_2 levels are environmentalist hustles. A possible exception is a proposal by the National Research Council, an arm of the National Academies of Sciences and Engineering, to seed the world's oceans with slow-release, floating pellets of iron, thereby spurring giant blooms of marine algae that would soak up massive amounts of CO_2. Fertilizing the oceans this way would create more marine life all the way up the food chain, at a cost of only a few billion dollars per year, and allow us to set the world's CO_2 concentrations and temperature at whatever level we wanted. (The problem, of course, is, Who gets to decide?)

Failing such an admittedly experimental measure, only general energy conservation, reforestation, and protection of the rainforests—desirable for many other reasons—now seem to have prospects for modest success for reducing CO_2 levels. Methane, which traps heat twenty to thirty times more efficiently than CO_2, is similarly uncontrollable, but for quite nonindustrial reasons; it is produced by cows, rice paddies, and termites.

Of the greenhouse gases, nitrous oxide and the chlorofluorocarbons are the most easily controlled. The former are produced by fertilizer use, cars, and power plants. Widespread use of such technologies as catalytic converters on cars and scrubbers on power plants—already mandated in the United States—can reduce nitrous oxide emissions. Western Europe, Eastern Europe, and the Soviet Union are the largest current polluters that can afford these technologies. Controlling nitrogen oxides would also help solve acid rain and ozone problems.

The most realistic way to slow climatic warming is to eliminate chlorofluorocarbons. Molecule for molecule, they are at least 10,000 times more powerful than carbon dioxide in raising the earth's temperature. Fortunately, they are produced in small volumes, mostly in the developed world, and many substitutes are available. An international treaty already calls for the phaseout of chlorofluorocarbon production by the end of this century.

Whatever is done, the world can expect to experience some degree of atmospheric warming over the next century, although realistic human action might retard the trend. In the end, the actual degree of global warming, and of the accompanying sea-level rise and climatic change, will be largely determined by still poorly understood natural cycles and climatic interactions. Human activity accounts for the annual release of 7 billion tons of CO_2 into the atmosphere; natural processes such as plant decay and volcanism, about 200 billion tons.[2]

The greenhouse effect may actually deliver the world from disaster sometime within the next few thousand years. The present, unusually warm century may have marked the peak of the interglacial period. Interglacial periods are relatively short, lasting 10,000 to 12,000 years, and this one is already over 10,000 years old. Our knowledge is insufficient to predict when the time for a new ice age will come, but when it does, the greenhouse effect may be strong and permanent enough to prevent or stall the glacial advance.

OZONE

At low altitudes ozone is both a health problem and the main culprit in modern smog. High-altitude ozone, however, is beneficial, because it limits the level of dangerous ultraviolet radiation that reaches the earth's surface.

Chlorofluorocarbons (CFCs) are the chief cause of high-altitude ozone destruction. (Volcanic eruptions, which also destroy ozone, lead to natural fluctuations in ozone levels.) CFCs are used as refrigerants, foaming agents, and aerosol propellants. Once released, they persist for as long as a century in the upper atmosphere, where they serve as chemical catalysts that destroy high-altitude ozone. Springtime "ozone holes" with sharply reduced ozone levels have been discovered in both the Arctic and Antarctic. There has as yet, however, been no observed increase in ultraviolet light in populated regions of the earth's surface.

The significance of increased ultraviolet radiation reaching the earth's surface, should that occur, is difficult to assess. The health risk depends primarily on skin exposure, which is a matter of style and taste. Americans already overexpose themselves to sunlight, resulting in hundreds of thousands of cases of skin cancer per year—generally easily curable. On the other hand, if sunbathing habits remain constant, the reduction in ozone will mean tens of thousands more cases of skin cancer in the U.S. alone. The problem is real, but it is easily avoidable and pales in comparison to other health risks.

A more serious health impact of reduced high-altitude ozone may be an *increase* in *low*-altitude ozone—down where it can be breathed as the principal irritant in local smog. Ultraviolet light initiates chemical reactions between hydrocarbons and nitrogen oxides to produce ozone smog. More ultraviolet light reaching lower altitudes means more smog. (Ironically, smog also protects against exposure to ultraviolet light.) Another charge against ozone loss—that it reduces the productivity of plankton—is highly speculative.

The long-lived, multiple impacts of the key chlorofluorocarbons—CFCs 11, 12, and 113—are so severe that an international phaseout of production has been arranged. The political difficulties in obtaining a CFC ban were extreme. Only the U.S. and a few European nations ban use of CFCs in spray cans, and Japan and most of Europe resisted any significant controls until recently. India insisted on receiving an international bribe to stop using CFCs. Substitutes are available, but they are costly, often dangerous in their own right, and less efficient. (CFCs were originally introduced as substitutes for deadly and less effective ammonia.) According to a study at Oak Ridge National Laboratory, using substitutes for CFCs may raise America's electricity consumption by 3 percent—enough to drive a dozen full-sized power plants at 100 percent capacity. The fact that it took over a decade to agree on a solution to this acknowledged worldwide environmental problem, costing a few billion dollars per year, underscores the futility of attempting trillion-dollar, draconian solutions to the greenhouse-gas problem.

By 2000, production of the most troublesome CFCs will end, thus putting a cap on the ozone problem and slowing climatic warming. But the CFCs already emitted will guarantee further ozone loss until well into the next century. Atmospheric warming will also still be with us, and the world will learn to live with both a warmer climate and (temporarily) more ultraviolet radiation.

TROPICAL RAINFORESTS: PARADISE BURNING

If you love tropical wilderness, see it now. The endless rainforests of Brazil and the teeming herds of African wildlife will be shadows of themselves in thirty years.

Some 30 to 40 million acres of rainforest—an area equivalent in size to the state of Washington—are being lost each year to deforestation, whose most ardent practitioners are Brazil, India, Indonesia, and Burma. The loss of tropical rainforests contributes to greenhouse warming, threatens wildlife, creates new semi-deserts, and increases large-scale flooding. Tree burning accounts for about 30 percent of worldwide total CO_2 emissions. In 1987, Brazil—whose annual rainforest losses run to between 12.5 million and 20.5 million acres—released as much carbon into the atmosphere by burning trees as the United States did by burning fossil fuels. The clearing of rainforests removes not only reservoirs but absorbers of carbon, destroys their wondrously diverse indigenous wildlife, and threatens migratory species—for example, the majority of North American land birds, who winter in Central and South American rainforests.

The local climatic impacts of cutting rainforests are even more complex. Rainforests have basically poor soils; the nutrients are recycled on the forest floor. When the trees are cut, the nutrients wash away in about a decade, leaving sterile, hard, laterite soils that have little agricultural potential. The land ultimately becomes a semi-desert, horribly eroded in the rainy season with massive downstream flooding, and baked to brick in the dry season. Recovery of the forest takes centuries.

Rainforest destruction is largely a matter of national policy. Faced with overpopulation and political turmoil in the cities, along with competing claims for frontier regions, the governments of Latin America and Indonesia are using their rainforest frontiers as an escape valve. The United States encouraged settling of its own frontiers for similar reasons. These policies may even produce short-term economic benefits from logging and the immediate (and, generally, unsustainable) agricultural output.

In the long run, rainforest destruction is a bad investment, much of which is being financed, directly or indirectly, by loans from the World Bank as well as private U.S. and European lenders. U.S. political pressure is already reducing World Bank loans for environmentally destructive projects; refusing federal guarantees for private loans to

Brazil would have the same effect. Ultimately, the developed world will also need to simply buy rainforest to save it. Even with these efforts, significant further loss of rainforest is inevitable.

The recent activist campaign to "Boycott Burger King and McDonald's to Save the Rainforests" is an excellent example of the political use of environmentalism. The proportion of U.S. hamburger that comes from cattle grazing on former rainforest acreage is a few percent, at best, and most rainforest clearing has little to do with cattle. The true purpose of the campaign is to find some new environmental excuse to bash big corporations and grab headlines. The real villains—foreign governments and poor farmers—don't fit the script.

COASTAL WETLANDS

Coastal wetlands are an unusually productive and dynamic environment, vital to both ocean life and waterfowl. Always threatened by development, they will now be caught between continued development pressure, reduced siltation, and rising sea levels.

When sea levels are constant, wetlands extend themselves by capturing silt. They grow on one side, extending out into the water, and die on the other, as marsh slowly becomes dry land. If sea levels rise, the process reverses; marsh is lost to the sea, but reclaimed from once-dry land. Rivers are vital to marshes. They bring not only fresh water and silt, but also sand to replenish the barrier beaches that protect the marshes. These beaches are ever-shifting creations of storms and sand. They guard the Atlantic and Gulf Coasts from Boston to Brownsville. They look wonderfully attractive to beach lovers, who do not realize that most major barrier-beach islands are flooded several times a century.

Now we have both dammed the rivers, cutting the flow of silt and sand, and heated the atmosphere to raise the sea level. The result will be accelerating flooding and loss of both barrier beaches and coastal marshes. The U.S. is already losing 30,000 acres of coastal marsh per year in Louisiana alone.

The long-run health of coastal marshes rests with a choice to be made in the next century. The sea-level rise is a dream come true for the construction industry and the Corps of Engineers—fighting the sea would be a massive, endless source of money and jobs—but the marshes would be wiped out between the protective dikes and the rising sea. Such a fight would also be hopeless and impossibly expensive. The current federal flood-insurance guarantee program alone would suffer losses of hundreds of billions of dollars to sea-level rise.

This is one of many examples where economics and the environment will be allied against traditional politics. The sensible policy would be to abandon the barrier-beach developments to the sea, and to let the beaches and the marshes recreate themselves inland. This means abandoning the great majority of coastal beach developments, defending only a few cities, and investing in resettlement. The major cities at greatest risk are probably New Orleans, Miami, and Galveston. Such a choice should be made as soon as possible, allowing decades for the transition; but the politics border on the impossible. What politician dares tell constituents that their homes must be abandoned? The most likely scenario is the wasting of tens of billions of dollars on fighting the inevitable until well into the next century.

ACID RAIN

Acid rain is a difficult, but more localized and solvable environmental problem. Rainfall is naturally acidic to begin with, but its acidity is increased by the burning of fuels containing sulfur (mostly coal), which produces sulfur dioxide, or by high-temperature combustion (mostly in cars and trucks), which creates nitrogen oxides. Acid rain can be as acidic as tomato juice.

The chemical reactions that produce acid rain are so slow that the acid rain can fall hundreds of miles from its source. Most of the damaging acid rain in the U.S. is caused by emissions in the Midwest. The most harm occurs when acidic rain falls in regions that are already naturally acidic, such as southern Canada, the Adirondacks, or Scandinavia. Acid rain primarily affects lakes, killing most fish and many invertebrates. Affected lakes are crystal clear and sterile. Fish eaters, such as loons, starve. Acidic mists are also killing high-altitude coniferous forests in both the U.S. and Europe.

Controlling acid rain is already underway, but it is expensive, costing billions of dollars. The issue is how to control it at minimum cost. Sulfur emissions have already been cut by about 25 percent, although they need to be cut more. Even doing so, however, may not save small lakes located in areas where soils are naturally acidic; a more effective and far cheaper method would be simply to treat those lakes with lime to neutralize the acidity. On the other hand, nitrogen oxide emissions—which also contribute to the greenhouse effect, smog, water pollution, and ozone depletion—have only been held constant. New laws will cut both sulfur and nitrogen oxide emissions.

Other inexpensive options include repowering older electric generating plants with new clean-coal technologies, turning from high- to low-sulfur coal, tightening nitrogen oxide emission standards for cars and trucks, and encouraging the replacement of high-pollution older vehicles with cleaner new ones. A tax on emissions in sensitive regions would encourage technical innovation and a wide range of solutions.

The main obstacles to reducing acid rain have been political. Any efficient solution would damage the Eastern (high-sulfur) coal industry, the economically weak Midwest, and the automobile industry in particular. Existing rules protect Eastern coal and Midwestern power producers by requiring few controls on old (pre-1975) power plants, even while requiring all new power plants (not just those causing the damage) to install expensive control technology. Thus older, dirtier plants are kept in operation well past the time when they would ordinarily have been retired.

Actions in both the U.S. and Canada are likely to largely solve the North American acid-rain problem by 2020. A few highly sensitive lakes will require active rehabilitation. The great majority will slowly recover by themselves, as they already have in parts of southern Canada, where sulfur emissions have been sharply reduced.

WATER SHORTAGES

The supposed water shortage is bad economic policy masquerading as an environmental problem. In dry years, there is not enough water to meet the competing demands of cities and farms. Prices are the ideal mechanism to allocate such scarcity, but the price system is not allowed to operate freely in the case of water.

Water shortages exist, primarily in the West, because water is underpriced—mainly to farmers. City dwellers generally pay over $100 per acre foot (enough water for the average family for a year) while many Western farmers pay as little as $10 dollars per acre foot. Most Western farmers pay far less than the cost of storing and delivering their water. When droughts occur, city dwellers are asked to let their lawns die so that farmers can keep growing surplus rice and cotton to earn more subsidies.

The economics of the case against current water policy are overwhelming; the nation will ultimately move to water marketing, which will redistribute water from farmers to cities. This program is well under way in Arizona and Colorado; other states are following. Other proposed solutions to the water problem, such as desalinization or massive water-transfer projects, are far too costly. Rather than finance such projects, the United States should pay farmers to stop farming—or at least stop paying them to turn scarce water into surplus crops.

Significant economic dislocation will ensue as realistic water prices force Western farmers to switch crops, conserve water, and, in some cases, stop farming. Most farmers will be paid handsomely for their water rights, but many farming communities will suffer. The most severe dislocation will be felt on the Great Plains, from South Dakota to West Texas. This area is farmed by pumping from the Ogallala Aquifer, an Ice Age relic. The Ogallala, a one-time resource, will be essentially dry in Texas, Colorado, Kansas, and New Mexico by about 2020. (The remaining water will be so deep that pumping costs will be prohibitive.) The Great Plains area depends on farming, but continued intensive farming will create another Dust Bowl. For this region, less pumping, less farming, and less population are the only realistic long-run solutions.

WATER MONGERING

Ninety percent of the water in the western U.S. is used by the agriculture industry, which gets the water at giveaway prices. About 7 percent of California's water supply—more than the entire Los Angeles area consumes—is used to grow rice, a crop made profitable only by taxpayer subsidies. The West's chronic water shortage could be resolved with a single wave of the legislative wand, in what might be called the "Farmers' Paid Vacation Act." It would be far cheaper, in many cases, to pay a rice farmer simply to not plant; the amount saved in subsidies would more than pay for the "vacation"; huge amounts of water would become available for other, more productive uses.

While more than 80 percent of California's water goes to farmers, the media relentlessly pit Northern and Southern California cities against one another in a battle for this or that drop of the precious fluid. Coincidentally, two of the biggest agricultural landholders in the state of California are major stockholders of the San Francisco Examiner and the Los Angeles Times.

WILDLIFE AND HABITAT LOSS

Wildlife protection is a great, untold environmental success story. Publicizing success would threaten contributions, headlines, and votes.

The big game animals that were nearly extinct at the turn of the century—buffalo, elk, antelope, and moose—now number in the tens to hundreds of thousands. There are more deer in the U.S. today than when Columbus landed. Canadian geese have become an abundant delight to many and a nuisance to many others. Whooping cranes, bald eagles, peregrine falcons, mountain lions, and wolves are all back from the edge of extinction.

Although the success is real, so are some new threats. The fundamental determinant of wildlife survival is habitat. We are adding millions of acres of wildlife refuges, but we are losing millions of acres to dams and farms. (Hunters, environmentalists' original foes, now save more wildlife through habitat protection than they kill.)

Among the threatened habitats are coastal marshes (already discussed), freshwater marshes, riverside forests, and Western forests. The loss of prairie pothole marshes is particularly severe, leading to decimation of some duck populations. These habitats are threatened primarily by government subsidies of farming, water development, and forestry. Without federal subsidies to build uneconomic dams, erect cities on floodplains, drain marshes at outrageous expense, cultivate land that is too poor to be farmed, and build unaffordable roads into the wilderness, habitat loss would not merely diminish but reverse.

Agriculture is even reducing the once countless numbers of American songbirds. Modern farms plant every square inch, leaving no cover for the birds. These farms are biological deserts, with only one or two species of plants and animals living on thousands of acres. Simple grazing of cattle is also taking a toll by creating niches, particularly on marginal farms throughout the East, for the deadly (to other birds) cowbird. Cowbirds are nest parasites: They lay their eggs in other birds' nests, and their offspring destroy the young of the host species. Once relatively rare, cowbird parasitism has become so common as to threaten songbird populations in several states. Trapping and killing cowbirds is the only solution—to the horror of animal-rights activists.

Saving habitat is economical; in many cases it pays for itself. For example, if hunting regulations and agricultural subsidies were revised, many Western farmers could earn higher incomes raising antelope and elk than raising cattle. The expense is political; habitat progress would require breaking the current truce between environmentalists and the pork barrel politicians who now happen to be their political allies. The environmental-activist coalition instead focuses on toxics and nuclear power, which have minuscule wildlife impacts but make for great media coverage, higher contributions, and easier political alliances.

DESERTIFICATION

Desertification is mankind's oldest environmental problem, but still the least publicized. Deforestation, overgrazing, irrigation, and plowing fragile soils have destroyed more of the world's productivity than have all forms of pollution combined. A desert grows slowly as salts poison the soil, wind blows it away, and erosion cuts the land. The warming climate will make the world, including parts of the western U.S., even more susceptible to desertification. Only careful management can prevent it.

Why does this known, severe environmental problem receive such little attention? First, the process is too gradual to interest the media. Desertification takes place over decades, not years. Only its most dramatic manifestation—dust storms—makes for good TV. Second, the villains are ordinary farmers and misguided government policies. Good corporate villains are hard to find. Third, whole regions are at risk, and no smart politician dares admit it. Several parts of the American West are overgrazed, overfarmed, and overpopulated.

This problem will be solved either by policy or by tragedy. If land is not to be lost for good, there must be much more stringent grazing rules for federal land (not set by the grazers), more water conservation, and less irrigation. These policies will be in place one way or another by 2000, but it would be preferable to begin immediately.

NUCLEAR POWER

We are spending billions of dollars to try to achieve the impossible dream of absolute, eternal safety from nuclear power plants and commercial radioactive waste, while other environmental, health, and safety programs starve for funds. We spend thousands of times more on nuclear safety, per potential casualty, than we do on other risks. Our most severe radioactive-waste problem, defense-plant contamination, went largely unnoticed for years because of the focus on commercial nuclear power. (The political script has become so dominant in environmentalism that monitoring efforts overlooked government as a potential environmental villain. One mustn't criticize the government, because government's role in the script is saving us from the evil corporations.)

Every human technology, from the taming of fire to the invention of the wheel, has some health impacts. Why has the environmental movement spent so much effort on commercial nuclear power, which has little impact on wildlife and no demonstrable human victims in the U.S.? This newest technology was so connected to nuclear weapons, and therefore so frightening to the public, that focusing on it brought forth an abundance of the three C's: contributions, converts, and coalitions.

The volume of commercial nuclear waste in the U.S. is small—only a few thousand tons of high-level waste per year, compared to millions of tons of equally toxic chemical waste. The commercial nuclear-waste problem can be solved through recycling in ultrasafe new breeder reactors, vitrification (encasing the waste in glass), and deep burial. A program of treating and disposing of waste from nuclear power is already underway in France. The U.S. continues to waste billions trying to improve on this approach, just to be absolutely certain that infinitesimal amounts of waste do not escape into the groundwater thousands of feet underground, centuries into the future.

Nuclear power in the U.S. started as oversold, overbuilt, and under-designed. Today it is the reverse: In the U.S., garbage power has killed more people than nuclear power (a garbage-fueled power plant in Ohio exploded in the 1970s and killed four persons). Only the most outrageously incompetent and risky use of nuclear technology, as at Chernobyl and the U.S. weapons plants, runs significant environmental risks. New nuclear technologies, safer than the existing ones, represent America's best hope of weaning itself from dependence on CO_2-producing Mideast oil imports; but chances are that by the time the public wakes up to this fact, the Japanese will be miles ahead with standardized, tested designs, and will dominate the nuclear power industry.

TOXIC WASTE

There are three categories of toxics: a small volume of dangerous toxics released in dangerous concentrations (mostly illegally), a larger volume of dangerous toxics released in barely detectable concentrations, and a very large volume of minor toxics. The focus ought to be on the first category, of which such widely publicized disasters as the cadmium poisoning of seafood in Japan (Minimata disease) in the 1950s are examples. Holding producers responsible for the costs of close monitoring and permanent disposal (preferably by incineration) of dangerous, concentrated toxics will discourage their use and prevent dangerous release. Pre-release screening will prevent widespread contamination with new chemicals. Sites containing high concentrations of dangerous substances will have to be cleaned up, at great expense.

More controversial environmentally, politically, and economically is the issue of widely dispersed and less dangerous toxics. Modern instruments can detect parts per trillion—one drop in a football field covered with 50 feet of water. There is no solid evidence that anything is dangerous at such low concentrations. Low-level toxicity evidence is weak, even for such widely criticized chemicals as PCBs and dioxins. Even where chemical concentrations are much higher, such as at toxic-disaster sites like Love Canal, scientists are still arguing whether there were any casualties.

Clean-up should concentrate on real dangers. Most toxic clean-up sites do not even contain dangerous toxics. According leaky gasoline tanks the same priority as Love Canal disrupts the economy, with minimal environmental benefit. The gasoline-tank regulation alone is coming close to destroying the independent gas-station industry in the U.S.

If the toxic waste problem is so terrible, where are the casualties? A major reason for the emphasis on the toxics issue is its political appeal. Relatively few people are concerned about wildlife, but nearly everyone is concerned about health—particularly if the national hypochondria, cancer, is involved. The nation is convinced a cancer epidemic exists, despite the fact that most cancers—except smoking-related lung cancer—are declining in incidence, as are stroke and heart disease. If age-adjusted rates of death from all causes were the same in 1988 as they were in 1940, 4 million people would have died; only 2.2 million actually did.[3]

There is now overwhelming evidence that the pesticide and food-additive cancer scare of the last three decades—from cranberries in the 1950s to apples in the 1980s—was a vast scientific error and media hustle.[4] A former environmentalist divinity—biochemist Bruce Ames of the University of California, who years ago invented the test that is today a standard for screening potential carcinogens—has been excluded from the environmentalist pantheon since the mid-1980s, when Ames began to point out that many typical foods are far more "carcinogenic," by the lights of *that same test*, than the industrial chemicals we have come to fear.

LOCAL AIR POLLUTION

Air quality has improved dramatically from its worst in the 1970s, but further progress will be very expensive. How much improvement is enough? Future air quality will be better than it is today, and much better than it was in the 1960s and 1970s. The U.S. spends more on controlling air pollution—in the range of $40 billion per year, and projected annual costs could easily exceed $100 billion—than on any other environmental issue.

The great majority of the nation is already in compliance with federal standards for lead, nitrogen dioxide, sulfur dioxide, and particulates. Twelve cities had carbon monoxide problems and 57 major cities violated the ozone standard for more than five days during 1988; nearly all cities were in compliance of the standards for both pollutants for the great majority of the year. The costs of improvement run in the hundreds of millions of dollars per each day shaved off the violation tally. Because of local geography, much of the Sunbelt, particularly Los Angeles, is unlikely to ever meet federal ozone standards.

Significant further improvements in air quality are possible, but by the year 2000, questions of cost will lead to the relaxation of standards in some regions. In most cities, current health impacts of air pollution are so small as to be difficult to measure, and concentrated in a few sensitive groups. For decades, Los Angeles has been a terrible place to live for someone with emphysema; how many billions of dollars is it worth to solve that problem?

GARBAGE

The garbage issue is a minor toxic-waste problem and a major political problem. Everyone uses the dump, but no one wants to live near one. Some faction can be counted on to oppose every solution to waste disposal—every landfill, incinerator, recycling station, and ocean dumping scheme. The result is paralysis. Since no perfect new solution is available, we continue the bad old practices. Environmental degradation and economic disruption are both maximized.

The garbage problem will be solved by a combination of siting new landfills, recycling, and incineration. Too many toxic wastes are being buried instead of burned. Anything concentrated enough to be poisonous, if it is slow to break down chemically, should be burned in special, high-temperature incinerators. Incineration does involve potentially toxic ash and emissions, so it is far from perfect. Recycling is expensive: Most products are cheaper to produce new than to recycle, and recycling involves sorting trash. Japan has achieved 40 percent recycling and 33 percent incineration, but of a smaller waste stream. It is unlikely that the U.S. could reach more than 25 percent recycling and 25 percent incineration, up from about 10 percent each today. Even with these levels of recycling and incineration, landfill will continue to dominate waste disposal, and new landfills will have to be sited. Landfills must be equipped with liners, and leachate (water that drains through the dump) continually monitored and treated. Much higher charges for garbage disposal will be necessary.

ENERGY SHORTAGE

U.S. energy is both underpriced and overregulated. A gasoline tax would do more for the environment than any conceivable set of regulations. Electricity is also underpriced. Users should pay at rates reflecting the cost of new power plants, rather than a blend of new and old costs. Price problems combined with complex regulations discourage energy conservation in general, along with efficient new energy techniques such as co-generation, whereby industrial plants can turn excess steam into electricity and use it for their own needs or sell it to utilities.

There is no fundamental shortage of energy. As we exhaust sources of cheap energy, technology "creates" new oil and gas by making existing resources easier to find and exploit, and makes potential resources such as solar energy usable. Energy-conservation technologies also stretch resources. With continued technical improvement, centuries worth of coal, natural gas, and oil will fuel the long-run transition to improved nuclear and solar technologies. (The notion that cheap solar power would be magically available if the government would only spend enough money on solar research is one of environmentalism's religious myths.)

FARMLAND SHORTAGES

The farmland-shortage issue is an appeal to emotion rather than logic. The acreage of U.S. cropland is slowly declining, but production continues to grow, mostly because farmers are subsidized to grow more than consumers want to buy. Except during years of extraordinary drought, such as 1988, the system produces enormous surpluses—at a subsidy cost of tens of billions of dollars per year.

Modern, intensive agriculture is far from benign, and leaves no room for wildlife. Today, farming is the chief contributor to habitat loss, toxic chemical exposure, and water pollution. The average suburb has more wildlife per acre than the modern farm. The nation needs less farmland, not more.

GROWTH CONTROLS

Environmentally based controls on housing are in full force in California and the Northeast, and are spreading throughout the nation. Growth controls began with opposition to industrial plants, extended to fighting highways, and now concentrate on stopping new housing developments. The controls have produced disastrous housing shortages, economic disruption, and traffic problems in many places.

Under current environmental rules, combined with the U.S. legal system, anyone who can afford a lawyer can stop anything. The result is the substitution of proceduralism for planning. Suburbs increasingly use zoning controls not to benefit the environment but to fight the construction of anything except large, expensive homes on large lots.

Residential growth controls have the effect of creating all-white, middle- or old-aged, high-income enclaves, protected against the encroachment of nonwhites and the 21st century. Modern industry and offices increasingly locate near these high-income suburbs (where the owners live), which often encourage (clean) industry, yet oppose higher-density, lower-cost housing, thus generating local shortages. The shortage of housing near employment centers forces longer commutes, more air pollution, more exurban sprawl, and higher housing prices. The net result is environmental and economic degradation, all justified under the environmental banner.

A dangerously divisive political conflict is brewing. An increasingly nonwhite younger generation now faces the first large-scale peacetime housing shortage in the nation's history, much of it due to zoning controls that create massive monopoly profits for existing homeowners—nearly all of them European-Americans. The image of a nearly all-white environmental movement supporting exclusionary zoning to maintain lily-white suburbs is long-run political suicide.

Can the environmental movement break out of its nearly all-white base? Asian, black, and Hispanic cultures have few environmental traditions, and these groups are the principal victims of environmentalism's current anti-growth direction. In the long run, education and economic progress may erase this gap; but current, effectively anti-minority, anti-growth policies could make the gap permanent.

CHAPTER

9

Housing and Infrastructure

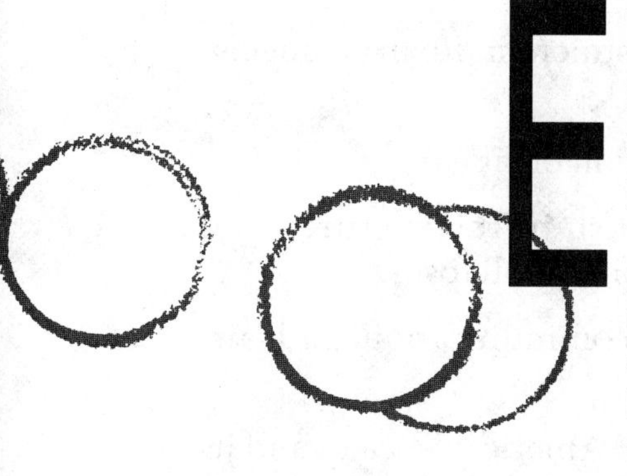

Easy money. In May 1984 a couple and their two children moved out of their three-bedroom home in Marin County, California, into a bigger place on a one-acre lot that cost just under $500,000. The couple held on to the old house for eight months after the purchase of the new one, without even trying to rent it. "We just didn't like the idea of being landlords," shrugs the wife. No harm done, though. By January 1985, when the laid-back family finally got around to putting it up for sale, the first house—for which they'd paid $57,000 in May 1976—sold almost instantly at $140,000, having appreciated far more than enough during its eight-month vacancy to cover their $362/month mortgage payments.

Housing plays a huge role in American society. In fact, one of the chief reasons the United States has such a dismal personal-savings rate is that American homeowners look at their accumulated equity as savings. Here, a house is more than a physical place where people live; for the majority of American home-owners, their home represents their principal source of accumulated wealth. Why salt away cash when your suburban split-level or urban condo is doing it for you?

Booms in real estate are fun while they last—if you own some. But the great upward trend in house prices throughout the past two decades is over. Meanwhile, as our government's tax policies, under the influence of a growing housing lobby, were leading Americans to build bigger and bigger houses, other countries were building factories, roads, airports, and bridges. To provide a better quality of life to its citizens and regain its position of economic leadership, the U.S. must now revisit its attitude toward housing and infrastructure, with an eye toward:

- Increasing the stock of affordable housing.
- Ending subsidies on unnecessary investment in luxury housing, offices, and retail centers.
- Adjusting to the ongoing decentralization of cities.
- Rebuilding the urban and transport infrastructure, and maintaining the existing stock—before it all collapses.
- Accelerating investment in the telecommunication and air-travel infrastructure.

For over 100 years, the spatial structure of American society and its resulting infrastructure needs have been driven by one key factor: the desire for individual home ownership. The United States is by far the best-housed society in the world. The proportion of homes that are owner-occupied is higher in the United States than anywhere else. And, next to the United States, Australia, and Canada, everybody else is in the minor leagues in terms of per capita square feet of living space. What's more, houses in the United States have been getting bigger and a lot better. The average new home built is 30 percent larger, and of higher quality, than what passed for a home twenty years ago. The American houses built in the 1950s were cracker boxes by today's standards.

Several things drove American housing towards the single-family, owner-occupied pattern. First, right from the beginnings of our social history, Americans have been independent. Many came from Europe to escape hated landlords, who in some countries still retained semi-feudal powers. Second, land was plentiful and cheap, even in settled areas; with horses and railroads (modern transportation at the time), population could be dispersed much more here than in Europe.

Still, restrained by the technical limitations of the horse and buggy and the train, urban populations remained concentrated, and multiple-family housing predominated. The rich lived in rowhouses; the rest of the inhabitants occupied apartment buildings. Around the beginning of this century—early in our history, but very late in European history—the electrical trolley car came along, a major innovation followed in short order by the automobile. Our newer cities were thus designed around a more modern transportation technology than were their European counterparts, and an urban population that wanted to spread out began to do so.

A series of financial innovations created tremendous incentive for these outward-bound urbanites to buy their own homes. The level-payment mortgage of this century permitted a mortgage to be paid off over many years rather than in a lump sum. Another 20th-century innovation, the income tax, created an incentive to own a home. The flip side of the tax was the deductibility of personal interest, including mortgage interest. This in effect encouraged individuals to seek large loans and pay them off slowly. Finally, in the 1930s federal mortgage insurance and federal chartering and guarantee of deposits at savings-and-loan institutions generated a huge, dedicated pool of funds for lending to homebuyers at interest rates below what a pure free market would have demanded.

The trend toward home-ownership, continually assisted by the federal government since the 1930s, has accelerated as Americans' wealth has grown. This, along with increasing automobile ownership, has produced several long-run consequences.

First and most obvious, our cities are much more spread out than cities anywhere else in the world except Canada and Australia, which both have histories and geographies similar to ours. And more and more, instead of people commuting to jobs in city centers, the jobs are moving outward to the people. The factories, offices, and research centers of the modern era don't have to be either on the river or next to the railroad. They can locate wherever people want to live, because the resources of a modern economy are overwhelmingly human.

Second, every homeowner is not only his or her own landlord, but also a capitalist. The great majority of U.S. citizens end up owning homes at some point in their lives. Over 60 percent of housing is owner-occupied, and over 70 percent of the population lives in their own homes. Moreover, that statistic includes both young, single people who haven't bought their first house yet and elderly people who have sold their homes and moved into an apartment or nursing home. The proportion of 40- to 50-year-olds living in owner-occupied dwellings is in the 80 percent range.

Homeowners have a dual stake in their government, both as users of services and as payers of the property tax, which until very recently was the principal tax collected in this country. (The income tax wasn't even invented until early in this century; the sales tax came even later.) Broad ownership of property is one of the factors that have made the United States much more conservative than the European countries. We were considered a radical nation a century ago; now we are the most politically conservative nation in the world.

There has been another, unintended, impact. Because America, with a large but fixed amount of land, has grown constantly in population, land and property have generally gone up in value. Real-estate speculation has been the foundation of many, if not most, of the fortunes in the United States. The constant rise in U.S. real-estate values, combined with broad ownership—a markedly different pattern from that of Europe—has meant broad participation in the American real-estate wealth machine. Owner-occupied housing was an escalator that almost everybody could hope to ride eventually.

Indeed, perhaps one of the larger economic disadvantages of racial minorities in the United States, especially African-Americans, is that they have not been equal participants in this real-estate boom. Two American families with the same incomes, both paying the same price for houses—one in the black area of town, where the property values are at best stable, and the other in a suburb or white area of town, where property values are going up—will occupy vastly different financial positions within a decade or two. Only recently, with significant housing integration, have African-Americans gained access to the real-estate wealth-making machinery of the United States.

Future Trends in Housing

Averages are misleading. A significant proportion of America's population is now overhoused, while another group is underhoused. Tax subsidies have, in effect, encouraged the wealthier members of our population to sink as much money as they can into housing. Mortgage interest and property taxes are tax deductible—even on a second home.

Reductions in tax welfare for the rich and overhoused are a certainty over the next few decades. The tax benefits of owning a large home, or a second home, will be significantly reduced. The next tax reform will include a limit on the deductibility of state and local income taxes—a limit that will ultimately be extended to the property tax deduction for large homes. The 1986 Tax Reform Act imposed the first major limitation on the tax advantages of owning housing, a $1 million mortgage-deduction ceiling. That ceiling, at ten times the average home price, affects only a couple hundredths of a percent of homeowners. It will surely be reduced to three to five times the average home price, or the tax-deductibility of mortgage interest limited to something in the range of a flat $30,000 per year.

It is not only subsidized demand that has been pushing housing costs higher; supply restrictions have proliferated. Local communities used to play an aggressive role in encouraging housing production. They surveyed the land, put down roads and sewers, built schools. But in some parts of the country, community governments have turned from midwives of housing construction to its greatest obstacles. Growth-control restrictions, which began in a few very-high-income locations in the West and the Northeast early in the 1970s, have spread elsewhere. In California and the Northeast, developing a piece of raw land into buildable homesites takes a skillful lawyer, a lot of money, and near-infinite patience—and it helps to be politically well connected. In some parts of the country (California is the extreme), land by itself has no value; only permits have value.

The combination of subsidized demand, restricted supply, and the coming of age of the baby boomers created the great housing-price escalation of the 1970s and early 1980s. The baby boomers, all trying to buy a house at the same time, bid prices up to unsustainable levels, well beyond what most buyers could afford. Inevitably, housing prices have topped out. Nationally, the average housing price has been declining in inflation-adjusted dollars. Once again, averages are misleading. In some locations—Texas, Arizona, parts of the Northeast—the market has collapsed. Housing prices are stable in most of the nation and rising significantly in only a few locations such as Seattle and inland California.

One of the myths of U.S. housing is that housing availability is determined by three things: interest rates, interest rates, and interest rates. This is no longer true. In a tight market, buyers bid prices up to whatever level their incomes will support; if interest rates go down, prices go up, and monthly payments remain constant. The chief beneficiaries of artificially low interest rates are not homebuyers, but land speculators. The reason markets have been so tight is supply shortages, induced by growth controls.

In many localities, the availability of housing is determined by three new factors: permits, permits, and permits. Where constraints on construction—primarily public-policy decisions made at the local level—are severe, competition is essentially eliminated, and housing prices will stay very high. If localities make it easier to build more housing, prices will go down.

The lack of low-priced rental housing for low-income Americans is a local phenomenon. In the past, the so-called filtering effect has generally worked well: Higher-income residents move out of lower-cost housing in the older part of the community to something nicer; low-income residents move in. Supply remains in equilibrium with demand, and rents are low. Some people are so poor that they're going to be underhoused, as well as underfed; but this is primarily an income problem, not a housing problem.

But when a population with reasonable incomes lives in a community with restricted housing markets and, therefore, *un*reasonable housing prices, it's a housing problem. In the San Francisco Bay Area, New York City, the Boston area, and the central slums of many cities, it is possible to work full-time at average American incomes and not be able to afford decent rental housing. This phenomenon is mainly a product of restrictive local housing policies.

While skyrocketing housing prices have driven some to the streets, there are important noneconomic factors behind homelessness in the United States. A significant proportion of today's homeless individuals would have been institutionalized in the 1950s and the 1960s. Since the 1970s, many psychotic patients have been released from mental institutions without being given adequate outpatient services. In addition, the number of homeless individuals with substance-abuse problems has increased. America has always had men with alcohol problems; every city had its skid row. What's new are the growing numbers of women and of those addicted to drugs other than alcohol. Unable to care for themselves, they're on the streets. Still other homeless people are the victims of the decline of the nuclear and extended family, once willing and able to take in any relative who stumbled into dire financial or emotional straits.

At least some homelessness, however, must be attributed to the sheer economic burden imposed by artificially constrained housing supplies. To live in a housing-short area is to participate in a game of musical chairs. Everybody is underhoused relative to their desires; but the lowest-income sector of the population is not housed at all.

It is questionable whether massive government programs to help people afford housing do any good—in fact, aren't fundamentally destructive—in areas where local government policies are severely restricting the production of new housing. If more living units can't be built because of local zoning laws, density controls, or permit snags, providing added financial resources to buyers simply bids up prices.

On a national basis, our housing affordability problems will diminish, because the coming slowdown in total population growth—especially significant in those segments of the population likely to form households—is about to cause housing demand to drop sharply relative to supply. The construction industry is capable of building 1.5 million to 1.8 million units per year. That's roughly in line with today's household formation rate; and it will be above the household formation rate by the second half of this decade.

Some analysts have used this demographic projection to predict large inflation-adjusted declines—close to 50 percent—in housing prices by early next century.[1] Those predictions are extreme; income growth as well as population increases determine the price of houses. The key to prices is policy. By restricting demand for the housing we *don't* need through the reduction of tax and fiscal subsidies for expensive homes, and by encouraging supply of housing we *do* need through the relaxation of growth controls, federal and local government can ease America's housing situation significantly by the end of this decade and well into the next century. On the other hand, if local restrictions on housing spread, America will have a housing disaster on its hands.

Growth control, one of the big issues of the environmental movement and also one of the big sources of intergenerational conflict, will play out differently in each area of the country. It will spread in faster-growing regions, especially along the two coasts, where the prospect of new arrivals—in particular non-English-speaking or nonwhite arrivals—makes growth control look very attractive to the existing population. Growth control will be less appealing elsewhere, so that the present geographical divergence in housing prices may become even more extreme.

The median resale value of a house in the San Francisco Bay Area in the third quarter of 1989 was about $270,000; in Peoria, under $50,000. The housing market of the 1990s will remain a composite of several local/regional markets that operate very differently. Most of the country has already returned to a normal, competitive condition, which means prices go up roughly with inflation, or a little less, and people with ordinary incomes can buy a house. The average sale price for existing homes in the U.S. is about $95,000, almost exactly three times the national average family income. This ratio reflects both the basic mortgage-financing mechanism and the rough cost of producing and selling a house.

The House of the Future

During the next thirty years, there will be subtle but important innovations in the physical structure of housing. Homes won't look much different; consumers are very, very conservative in this area. A massive increase in the cost of energy could, in the long run, force drastic changes in the number of windows, the thickness of walls, or even the proportion of the house that's underground. But don't hold your breath; the real price of energy is little different from what it was in the 1950s.

While plastics are clearly taking the place of ceramics in kitchens and bathrooms, houses will continue to be built mostly out of wood. No one has come up with a good substitute for wood and concrete so far, because they're strong and cheap. What *will* change is the way houses are built. Twenty to thirty years from now, the predominant mode of housing construction will be bolting together modules. Houses will be completed in a few weeks rather than the few months it takes now. The foundation will go in; the modules will come to the site and be bolted in; there'll be a little bit of finishing carpentry; then the roof will be dropped on and bolted in.

The use of modular sections in the home—whole bathrooms or whole sections of a kitchen, some of the more expensive parts of the home to build, dropped into place and connected—is now restricted more by building codes and tradition than anything else. Factory-built wall panels that could be put together in an infinite number of combinations, with every panel connectable to all other panels, may be feasible, although the cost of shipping will be high. The problem is not one of technology so much as of standardization. The housing industry is composed of numerous small producers; nobody can make enough of an investment to become the dominant manufacturer and set a standard so that all the wall panels fit together. There's no IBM of housing—yet.

But the factory-built modular mode of production is the way of the future, for two reasons: First, modules produced in a highly mechanized factory can be assembled into a high-quality house by unskilled, non-English-speaking laborers—the keys to cost control in a labor-short country. Second, in many locations, borrowing expenses represent the largest single cost to a homebuilder, who must buy the land, spend months getting all the permits, and then put up a dwelling on it before any profits can be realized. If that process takes a year, the carrying cost on a $100,000 lot will be at least $15,000. Knocking two to three months off the construction process through the modular approach translates to a $5,000 saving—in some cases, the difference between profit and loss.

Houses will continue to get larger and better-appointed. The communication systems will be much better: Networks of homes will be tied together, and to central data banks, with fiber-optic cable. The computer-appointed, telecommunication-ready offsite office will be of growing importance for knowledge-industry workers. A very small part of the population—larger than today, but still small—will work entirely at home, but a much larger proportion will work partly at home, as opposed to commuting daily into a centralized place of work.

The Return of the Neighborhood

The sheer expense of relocating (especially in the case of two-income families and large distances), combined with the slowing of cross-regional job-hopping and retirement, is fostering a tendency to stay put. This in turn may be catalyzing the return of the neighborhood identity through the advent of neighborhood-level community centers. If a way could be found to control liability and organizational costs, these centers could supply, organize, and maintain boats, skis, Ping-Pong tables, specialized vehicles, and woodworking, art, and mechanical tools, allowing for more efficient use of the home.

Strengthened neighborhoods will reduce the capital costs of the modern family. For example, kids love home swimming pools, but parents soon come to hate their maintenance and cost. The community swimming pool is a wonderful compromise. More and more Americans also find they're spending too much money on needed but rarely used pieces of recreational equipment or full sets of tools. When you need them, you *really* need them; but how often are they used?

Tomorrow's all-purpose neighborhood center, encompassing services like daycare and rental of needed but rarely used pieces of equipment, will go far beyond the community recreation center. High-income, time-short homeowners will be attracted to the broadened community-center concept, entailing not just a swimming pool but a full recreation program integrated with daycare and the school system. The concept could be expanded to include basic home and landscape maintenance.

The City

What's the future of major downtown cities, especially financial downtowns such as Manhattan? Electronics allows decision makers to interact as well as they do now without having to be physically adjacent to each other. Corporate headquarters are dispersing. Low cost is more important than the ability of the president of Texaco to have lunch with the president of Chase Manhattan Bank. You pay a lot for that privilege.

The New York Stock Exchange floor is an anachronism; so are the Chicago Board of Trade and all other nonelectronic trading systems. Financial markets will disperse dramatically in the coming decades. Actual trading will be entirely electronic rather than physical. Tradition is slow to change, but any information-intensive industry now concentrated in the cities is ready to move.

High-income people are moving *into* residential areas of such culturally vibrant, reasonably well-kept-up cities as San Francisco and small parts of other cities: Capitol Hill, Georgetown, and Kalorama in Washington, D.C.; Beacon Hill and Back Bay in Boston. But no such trend is occurring in Chicago, St. Louis, or Atlanta, much less Detroit.

In the longer run, many cities will find themselves obsolescent as new technologies change the basic pattern of where and how people live. The information sector allows its employees to inhabit areas that are now primarily recreational. If you want the best software engineers, locate near the best beach or the best ski area. The only locational requirement for those industries is having an airport within driving distance of an hour or two.

Regional Patterns of Growth

The modern economy is more amenable to dispersal than ever. While it may be intellectually popular to hate the automobile and the single-family home, there are no substitutes on the horizon. For a high-income population, time is the scarcest commodity; and no means of transportation is as efficient as a private automobile. Other methods may cost a few dollars less, but people value their time far more than any other possible savings.

Although decentralization is accelerating, the 1970s marked a peak in Americans'—especially homeowners'—propensity to move. It's expensive for a two-income couple to change locations, because the income at risk is far greater than it was for the traditional one-income family. In addition, the cost of moving a modern family's numerous possessions has increased. Most important, the sheer cost of trading houses—commissions on both ends, plus refinancing costs—has become more expensive as house prices have soared. The mere front-end financing fee paid to a bank for an average house today inflicts on the buyer a one-time loss that exceeds the total cost of moving in the 1960s.

America is at last approaching regional equilibrium. The wholesale spatial rearrangement of the United States—the dramatic relative growth of one region at the expense of another—that took place in the mid-20th century is winding down. The post–World War II baby boom came along at about the same time that the South was finally recovering economically from the Civil War and becoming a place where a well-educated Northerner might choose to live. The baby boom is over, and the South has been repopulated with well-educated professionals, who are now reproducing themselves at replacement levels. The "Flight of the Snowbirds"—a mass migration of Northern retirees who discovered in the 1960s and 1970s that with their generous Social Security benefits, they could afford to relocate to Florida, California, Texas, and Arizona—has also peaked. We're in the final stages of settling the West. Florida still is underpopulated, but will reach equilibrium before 2020.

Our national growth pattern will be affected by our economy's steady integration with Canada's. The free-trade agreement will boost the population of the northern United States as well as that of southern Canada. For both countries, north/south trade is much more efficient than east/west trading.

Since the late 1960s, the population of the United States, driven by international trade and communications, has been polarizing toward the two coasts. The Midwest was a victim of a backdoor disinvestment in some industrial sectors, much of that the product of our government's foolish handling of the dollar in the early and mid-1980s, when our interest rates and, consequently, the exchange rate of our currency went far too high. The entire community of Peoria, Illinois, depends on Caterpillar Tractor, one of the nation's biggest exporters. At 200 yen to the dollar, Caterpillar's Japanese competitor, Komatsu, destroyed Caterpillar's overseas markets, although probably not one person in fifty in Peoria understood what was happening at the time. Recently, though, the Midwestern heartland has begun to revive. Some parts of the Midwest are now doing very well, building on their efficient governments, good public service, and good education systems. Housing costs are less than half their corresponding levels on either coast.

California's population will keep on growing, even though the influx will be from overseas instead of the Midwest. While California's smog is getting better, its congestion is getting worse, and housing costs are horrendous. But if you're living on some dirt-poor farm in Mexico or being shot at in El Salvador, California is paradise. Double the congestion, double the pollution—it's still paradise. It's where your uncle and your grandfather went, and you're going to give paradise a try, too, if you can get there.

Commercial Property

The U.S. is mortally overbuilt in terms of its commercial offices and stores—by far the biggest in the world. Investments were misdirected for several reasons:

- The great inflation made all real estate look like a good buy.

- Localities encouraged commercial development and discouraged housing.

- Threats of rent control made apartment building risky.

- Unbelievable federal tax subsidies to commercial development made money-losing buildings profitable after taxes.

- Given the money, developers will always build, and the banks and S&Ls cranked out hundreds of billions of dollars of uneconomic loans.

All this is over. In most places, commercial construction is a money-losing proposition. We will spend years working off the surplus. Markets will be highly localized. Tax subsidies will not return.

Large-Scale Civil Infrastructure

The United States has stumbled badly in both new construction and maintenance of its civil infrastructure. Our especially serious upkeep problem reflects the working of our federal government, which subsidizes building new roads, new sewers, and new pollution treatment plants. Maintenance, however, goes unrewarded; everyone is tempted to skimp on it.

The strange workings of the system are exemplified by the federal government's financing, since the 1960s, of the construction of the country's sewage treatment facilities. To receive federal help to build one, all a municipality had to do was to get on the priority list and wait until it reached the top. The overwhelming—and unintended, if predictable—result was that municipalities that would have otherwise gone ahead and built decided instead to wait for assistance. Moreover, because these grants were merely for capital construction, nobody paid much attention to how well the plants would actually work, or how easy they would be to maintain; so in many places they wound up not working well at all.

We're now finding out that the design and maintenance have been so bad that we have to completely rebuild numerous sewage-treatment plants. Roads, bridges, water systems, transit systems, and other public facilities are in the same state of disrepair. The hundred-billion-dollar bill for improperly designed, built, or maintained public facilities will have to be paid by the next generation. The long-run solution would be a capital-facilities budget that includes plans not only for initial construction but for cost-effective, long-term operation and maintenance.

But no government sector in the U.S.—federal, state, or local—has anything close; the reason is, in a word, politics. Every politician knows that nobody will notice, in the short run, if the government skimps on maintenance. Hopefully, the problem won't be seen until the politician has retired; meanwhile, let's use the money to keep somebody happy right now. But time passes, politicians retire, and bridges and dams collapse—as they have in New York, Connecticut, Ohio, Pennsylvania, and West Virginia, with more to come.

In addition to rescuing existing pieces of our infrastructure, we must build many new ones. In many places, road construction has fallen behind. In some places, school construction is way behind. Everyone agrees that we need a lot of new airports, but nobody wants one built next door.

A major limit to our future economic growth is how quickly we reorganize air transport. By failing to build airports or market take-off and landing slots, the federal government has produced near-market failure in air travel. There is no premium for taking off at peak times, so every airline tries to leave at once. Some airports in the country—San Diego, Boston's Logan Field—are so badly situated and so outmoded that they're downright dangerous. Since 1974 commercial air traffic has doubled, but no new commercial airports have been built. We are going to see air travel continue to grow; yet our air-traffic control problem is already deficient, while billions of dollars sit frozen in a federal trust fund created specifically to pay for a better system. The inevitable American way of doing business dictates that some horrible headline-grabbing air crash must occur before we finally take action.

High-speed conventional rail systems, featuring trains that travel at speeds of about 150 miles per hour, are forging downtown-to-downtown links between East Coast cities a few hundred miles apart. From a businessman's standpoint, the Metro Line is a cost-efficient competitor to air travel for the Washington-to-Philadelphia, Philadelphia-to-New York, and Washington-to-New York runs.

To compete with airplanes along corridors in the 400-mile range, an even-faster, futuristic rail-like form of transportation called *maglev,* which has reached speeds on the order of 370 miles per hour on experimental test tracks, has been proposed. A maglev vehicle does not have wheels, but is instead *mag*netically *lev*itated above and propelled along metal guideways.

Right-of-way is a stumbling block to the development of either conventional high-speed rail or maglev systems. Existing railroad rights-of-way have too many curves for such fast-moving vehicles to negotiate. (Air traffic enjoys the advantage of free right of way.) Friction makes maintenance of conventional high-speed rail systems particularly significant. Japan's 200-mile-per-hour Shinkansen trains require massive nightly rebuilding of the tracks.

Maglev's operational costs are a bit lower than a conventional system's, but those costs are comparatively trivial in any case. The cost of obtaining new rights-of-way dwarfs both construction and maintenance costs. There is, at best, a narrow range of intermediate distances where a maglev system might, in theory, outcompete both conventional high-speed rail and air traffic.

The unpublicized problem of all ground-level high-speed transit in this country is vandalism. Japanese kids don't throw rocks, and for the most part European kids don't, either. However, vandalism is a reality in the United States. A rock thrown at a 200-mile-an-hour train does 16 times the damage of a rock thrown at a 50-mile-an-hour train; at a 300-mile-an-hour train, 36 times as much. There are other dangers, as well. An unshielded, 300-mile-an-hour maglev would kill birds in significant numbers.

The Politics of Urban Mass Transit

Our transportation policies are cursed by two facts: Too many politicians remember playing with electric trains, and too many voters hope the other guy will take the bus. We are not building 19th-century cities, easily served by mass transit, but 21st-century cities—which are inherently decentralized. It is at the outskirts of our metropolitan areas, not downtown, that millions of jobs are being created. Twice as many people now commute from suburb to suburb as from suburb to city center. Mass transit is more a political than a real infrastructure need. Unless we change the form of our cities, traditional, high-volume mass transit will never work.

Current American policies discourage high-density buildings in most residential locations. Attempts to conjure up mass transit without changing our land-use regulations to allow more density will, by definition, fail. In addition, the United States has probably done the worst job in the world of integrating its transit systems.

An efficient subway system must be tied into the long-distance rail, the airport, and the buses. Travelers, who automatically come off the train or airplane without a car, represent a natural market for urban mass transit. Moreover, a mass-transit system connection to an airport is not peak-hour loaded, as are commuter runs; it is instead used uniformly throughout the day. But very few airports in the United States are tied to subway systems. When they are, it's usually a long, unpleasant, cold walk to a subway people aren't quite sure they can trust, and once they're on it, there are relatively few places they can get to.

Successful transit must follow the pattern of Toronto, Paris, and Stockholm, where the location of stations was linked to new residential and commercial development. The Toronto metropolitan-area government planned its mass-transit system, condemned the land around the new stations, and rezoned it for high-density commercial or residential use; so that, by design, several thousand people live or work within easy walking distance of each station.

Toronto didn't need hundreds of millions of dollars from a federal government. The difference between the pre-station market price paid for the condemned land and the post-station price received for the rezoned land paid for almost the entire system. The Toronto experience demonstrates the virtue of a more powerful regional government than most U.S. cities have.

HOW NOT TO DO IT

San Jose, California, built a nearly $500 million, now mostly empty light-rail system because the federal government was willing to pay for most of it. The system was designed not to serve concentrations of population, but to touch as many supervisorial districts as possible. The train goes past the airport; but the distance between the air terminal and the light-rail line is about three-quarters of a mile, with no shuttle connection. Nor does the subway connect with the rail line. A system that was supposed to serve 40,000 people a day serves fewer than 11,000. Operating losses are over $10 million a year.

The subway system in Buffalo, New York, built in 1985 at a cost of $600 million—almost entirely with federal and state tax dollars—hooks up neither with the football stadium nor the main campus of the state university, the largest employer in the area. In April 1990 the system shut down, flat broke, to be rescued two days later by the imposition of a real-estate sales tax. Empty buses and empty transit cars don't save energy; they don't save pollution; they just cost money.

What's the American method? Conflicting decisions made at different levels of government. And it so happens (just by accident!) that developer friends of the politicians on the transit board find out before anybody else does where the stations are going to be, so they're the ones who are able to buy the land at $5,000 an acre and sell it at $50,000.

At the stations, we put not homes or offices but parking lots. Parking lots are, obviously, for people who have cars. *Operating* a car costs about a penny a mile, less than the fare of any transit system in the country. *Owning* the car, at 10 to 20 cents a mile, is the expensive part; if you already own a car, you may as well use it, unless road conditions make driving an impossible nightmare.

After the San Francisco Bay Area's earthquake of October 1989 knocked out a key bridge for several weeks, a natural experiment took place in which tens of thousands of people were forced to try mass transit. But now the earthquake is forgotten. And what are people doing? Led to the water of mass transit, they sipped it for a while, decided they didn't like the taste, and spit it out. They're back in their cars. They find that the savings in time and convenience to them is worth fighting the traffic on one of the worst commutes in the United States.

How will America's growing traffic congestion be reversed? Just plain building roads, with carpool lanes and electronic controls, will help a great deal, as will outfitting cars with internal electronic traffic monitors to route them away from jams. Another approach (very controversial in most American communities) is more high-density construction. Raising parking-meter rates in crowded urban areas in the direction of market rates would work wonders for both mass transit and city coffers. An additional solution resides in the adoption of flexible working hours.

A final, and inevitable, alternative is telecommuting. The trend toward dispersion away from city centers, and the prospect of fiber-optic hook-ups permitting massive amounts of two-way data flow, feed naturally into workstyles that replace transportation with telecommunication. Today's office workstyle will evolve into a continuum: sometimes at home, independently; sometimes at home, connected to the office; and sometimes at the office.

The proliferation of telecommunications options in the coming decades will spawn a need for far more communications channels than are available today. Even though digital electronic techniques confer an amazing ability to pack information onto the airwaves, there just isn't enough spectrum to go around to communicate through the radio waves. What we should have is a single fiber-optic cable, with its huge carrying capacity. A large portion of that capacity should be common carriers, open to all users and information suppliers at a uniform price, to ensure open access instead of a new monopoly.

Right now, as a result of the terms of of the AT&T breakup, we have two independent point-to-point transmission systems—a telephone line and a separate cable TV line—and we're paying for each one. We will be forced to let the phone companies put fiber-optic cable into every house in the country to integrate cable TV with all the other information services we need.

While telecommunication is surely going to affect our workstyles, it will never entirely alleviate the need for cars and roads. The case against full-time telecommuting is that it is too lonely; the isolated worker misses the important social interaction of the white-collar workplace. However, part-time telecommuting is going to become commonplace. Human beings may innately require physical proximity to maintain social relationships over the long haul; but that proximity may be attainable to a degree through daily, several-hour-long, low-key, interactive videoconferencing sessions among networks of home offices, each with its own huge, high-resolution video wall panel. The simulated office environment would be enhanced by frequent large-scale staff meetings at a central location.

Not only the office, but the school system will be affected by the decentralizing character of modern telecommunications. Educational computer systems, installed both in the school and in homes and connected through cable, will permit instruction to be not only decentralized, but more individualized than is now the case. Students will be able to access their instructional network from diverse locations—from the home, from a school near the office where one of the parents is working that day, from a work site itself or even from a remote spot where the family is vacationing. The changing American home will be reflected in the changing character of the American school.

Housing and Infrastructure

CHAPTER

10

The Education Gap

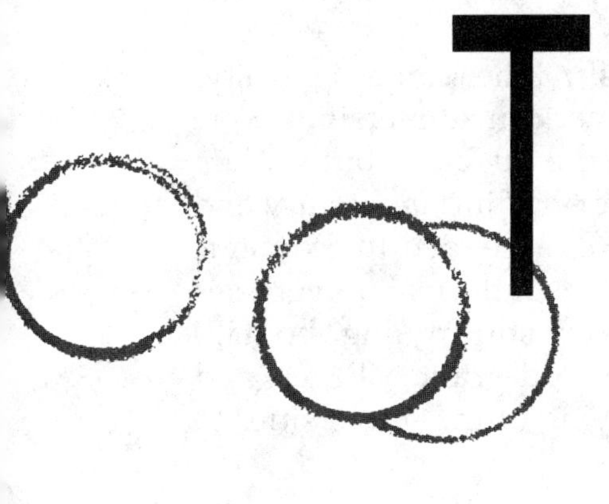

The ammunition of World War IV is education, and the condition of America's armory is mixed. The United States has both the greatest higher-education system and the most troubled K–12 school system in the developed world. Although we spend about 25 percent more per school-age child on education than our nearest rival, West Germany,[1] the average American student graduating from high school is academically two years behind his or her counterpart in Germany or Japan.

Nor do American schools, generally speaking, provide decent vocational training—especially by the standards of Germany, which has by far the strongest vocational training system in the world, including the world's best apprenticeship program. Sometimes-scandalous private-sector trade schools in the United States are ripe for reform. Shady operators have taken advantage of easily available student loans to open trade schools, guarantee jobs, collect tuition, then provide a near-worthless education or, worse, lock up and make off with the money. Even at its best, vocational education here is a complex mix of public and private, secondary and college programs, united in only one aspect: a uniquely distant and unproductive relationship with employers. As labor shortages grow in the 1990s, links between schools and employers in the U.S. will be forged, with state and federal support.

Germany led the world in creating an education system with an economic mission. The modern university—not a monastery-like arts, religion-, and literature-oriented retreat, but a technical, business-oriented institution—developed in the late 19th century shortly after Germany's unification under Bismarck. Germany likewise designed its lower-level education system to produce workers and entrants into the university system.

This model stands in contrast to our English/American community-based educational system. English and American universities were founded not to produce better science to serve business, but to train preachers and to provide places of refuge for traditional literary and artistic scholars. One reason the United States ascended to economic leadership is that the U.S. shifted to the German pattern of universities long before England did. (In fact, the English are still arguing about it.) That shift originated in the 1860s with the land-grant colleges, and accelerated during World War II with the tying of the universities to the war effort and the economy.

Higher Education: Stronghold in Transition

In the 1990s and beyond, economic pressures will force American universities into a wide range of nontraditional solutions that will change them dramatically. The monastic university is dying; we will see its end in the next century. In its place will emerge the full-blown, Bismarckian educational enterprise.

The university is becoming a key player in the American economy, evolving into an independent, quasi-profit-making organization with a reach equal to that of large international corporations. This evolution is weakening community ties, as the public's willingness to voluntarily transfer public or private funds to institutions once considered charitable erodes.

American higher education is successful because it is competitive. In recent years private colleges, with not quite one-third of total U.S. enrollments, have played a role beyond their numbers at the innovative end of higher education. Both the adult-retraining movement and the establishment of ties with industry and business were led by private colleges and universities responding to economic pressures. When Stanford University was having financial problems in the 1950s, it found a way to turn near-worthless land into the Stanford Research

Park and developed strong relationships with local industry. At the University of California at Berkeley, then probably the best-funded and the highest-quality public university in the United States, that didn't happen.

Private colleges have boosted their enrollments, despite the baby bust, by substituting master's-degree candidates for undergraduates, part-timers for full-timers, night students for daytime students. But simply keeping enrollment up doesn't solve financial problems. Private colleges sell a very valuable commodity, undergraduate education, at perhaps 80 percent of cost. The public schools sell, at 20 to 25 percent of cost, what is on average not quite as good an education.

So far the elite colleges have found no limit to the tuitions they can charge; Harvard and Stanford would fill their thousand-some-odd annual undergraduate openings with qualified students, even if they doubled their tuition. But that's not true of second- and third-tier private schools. Thus, private schools are hurting financially. The pain will inevitably grow, because professors' salary demands will rise while their productivity, as measured by their ability to serve more students, won't.

The modern university competes with the private sector for talent. Corporations are increasing their productivity all the time and, therefore, can keep on paying more money. If a university wants to hire the same people, it must pay private-sector salaries—directly or indirectly. Universities, especially private universities, have finessed this requirement by giving faculty members not only a job but also a "hunting license"—often more valuable than their salary—whereby they are permitted to seek lucrative consulting contracts.

To maintain the quality of its education, a university may limit the amount of time its faculty spends consulting; but then it must raise salaries in the specialties where it's competing directly with the private sector—notably science, engineering, business, and economics. It takes a $100,000-plus salary to hold onto a highly regarded professor in economics or the sciences, but an elite university can get all the teachers of French literature it wants—the top in the field—for $50,000. A decade from now, the French-literature expert will still be at $50,000, adjusted for inflation; but experts in economics and the sciences will cost twice as much. Traditional arts-and-sciences university communities will inevitably be torn apart by the growing economic disparities among departments.

To pay their bills, private universities increasingly accept—and often solicit—support from private industry in the form of chaired professorships, equipment, and new research facilities. Several years ago, Harvard rejected support from a German drug company because the company wanted to get first crack at research results before they were published. Now similar arrangements are routine, though informal. The sponsoring company still gets first crack at research results, not by formal agreement but because the company's researchers, who are based in the university labs, automatically find out about it first.

Universities are looking to earn money directly through patents, direct business services, and research parks. Research is a major source of wealth in a modern economy. More and more, universities have been demanding a piece of the action in the form of patents on new technologies, which they then license to industry. The temptation for the university is to take this logic to its limit; that is, to:

- Perform research for the government and the private sector on contract.
- Follow up patents with aggressive investments and marketing approaches that maximize their value.
- Take equity positions rather than straight cash for research. Why give all the profits to the public, the corporations, or professors? The university's alternative is to organize its own company: Throw a market forecaster from the economics department and a business-organization expert from the business school into the same cage with a Nobel laureate in biotech who has a great idea; provide start-up capital, and share in the profits. Some of these ventures will fail, but enough will succeed to allow universities to capture a much greater share of the value of their innovations.

Universities are also generating funds by becoming large-scale, global enterprises. The university as an international organization evolved from humble origins: campuses abroad to which students were shipped for a semester to learn French. But the international branch campuses of the future will educate not only American students of Japanese design and French architecture, but also Japanese and French students of engineering and molecular-biology. Only tradition now holds back our top-tier schools; solid, second-tier American schools—San Francisco State, Clemson, Indiana, and Tulane, to name a few—are getting their feet wet by offering business-education programs overseas. The international college industry could become one of America's faster-growing and most profitable business sectors.

Back home, higher education is already an important export, with a significant positive impact on America's balance of payments. A large proportion of graduate students in the United States are from foreign countries. This is particularly true in critical technical fields. Yet crazy U.S. immigration rules force any foreign national who has come to the United States on a student visa to get a degree in, say, electrical engineering to leave after graduating. The intention, of course, is to limit immigration. But these are exactly the people America should be encouraging to stay; they pay their own way from the start. As labor shortages grow, we will point our controls elsewhere and make it easier for foreign graduates to linger in our laboratories for as long as they like.

Public and private elite universities' evolution into fundamentally self-supporting organizations, driven by economic rather than academic considerations, represents a major departure from tradition—and presents a dilemma for society. Knowledge has greatest value to its owner if the owner can restrict access to that knowledge; but to hinder the exchange of information is to slow technical innovation. (On the other hand, it could be argued, American universities' open dissemination of research results chiefly benefits Japanese corporations, who are superb at quickly turning those results into proprietary products.)

Government will initially discourage this evolution. Right now, public as well as private universities are cryptically supported by federal scholarship programs and "overhead" payments tacked on to federal research grants. If universities become profit centers, the federal government can be expected to let its support lapse. The reconstituted elite research schools will receive fat fees for research and business services. Not just the Stanfords but the Berkeleys, too, will adapt by charging high tuitions for all students.

Initial state-government dismay will eventually turn to encouragement. Among all the groups competing for public funds, universities appear to be among the most well-off. Their faculties, in particular, have high average incomes and limited workloads; at least it looks that way to a typical government employee. State legislatures will ask, especially of the top-tier institutions: "Why should the general taxpayer subsidize such a valuable product as a college education for individuals who predominantly come from—and certainly wind up in—the highest-income segments of society?" This question could take a radical form: "Why don't we get out of higher education entirely and simply offer need-based scholarships and let the kids go wherever they want?" In a lot of states, about the only thing impeding that change will be sentimental attachment to the college football teams.

Community Schools and Winged Pigs

Unlike its higher-education system, America's K–12 school system is by and large neither competitive nor successful. The American school is a troubled institution, with both more difficult challenges and more constraints on the horizon. This is not just a question of expenditures per student, however much more money may be needed. By every measure, throughout the country, we spend far more per student than ever before. Inflation-adjusted expenditures per student have nearly doubled since 1970. Japan's class size averages greater than 35, but their children learn far more than ours do with 21 students per classroom.

A school has two official central purposes: (1) socializing young monsters, and (2) training them specifically to fit into the modern economy. Today's schools have a third effective purpose: They are the largest childcare institutions in society, by far.

Universities don't need to worry about socialization (18-year-olds are presumably socialized), but lower-level schools do. An isolated institution—a school that is not part of a web of adult influence on children—can't really succeed at socialization. And those other great socializing institutions, the family and the church, are floundering.

Public elementary and secondary schools once were the central institutions of the community. This is no longer the case today, for several reasons:

- Most American households don't have school-age children. Aging, mobile, often childless people have increasingly distant connections to local schools; indeed, many American communities lack central institutions of any kind.

- Almost throughout the United States, schools are no longer financed by communities, but by the state. Most policies of any consequence are set at the state level. The local school board chooses the superintendent, but the superintendent is paid by and works for a state bureaucracy. The board has vastly less influence today than it had twenty years ago.

- Schools have become much more rule-bound. The courts have intervened in school discipline; and the teacher, who was once queen or king in the classroom, is now just a hired hand. The modern image of the teacher is not of a person from the community working in a human-relations-intensive institution, but of a bureaucrat who escapes daily to a distant, usually white, enclave.

MONEY VS. MOTIVATION

The educational power of a community was demonstrated by a 1979 study in which a number of school districts were identified as statistical outliers: All the standard socioeconomic measures—low incomes, high unemployment rates—said kids in these schools should be doing very poorly; yet their performance was excellent. They did not fit the theory of the time, which held that parents' economic circumstances were all that mattered.

One such district, Ironwood, was on the upper peninsula of Michigan, the Midwestern equivalent of Appalachia. The community's abandoned homes reflected its deserted factories and mines. Some neighborhoods resembled junkyards; rusting equipment littered the streets. The town had as many families on welfare as an urban ghetto. A massive school building, built near the turn of the century, stood glowering over the town. The area's citizens had been forced to close many of their local schools; this was the last.

But Ironwood High had spirit. The hallways were old, but so clean you could eat off the floor. The students were noisy but orderly. Everything was painted and well kept-up. Although class sizes were far above average, students' test scores were terrific.

Asked by researchers for an explanation, the assistant principal responded, "It's simple. Last week a young freshman came to my office, almost weeping over a bad test grade. I told him one test wasn't a disaster, but he said I didn't understand: His father had told him he would break the kid's arm if he flunked his class, and his father meant it. There's no economic future in this town. Education is the only way out. Parents know it; kids know it. They ask us to assign more homework. Everything we want the parents to do, they do. The kids know we're trying as hard as we can with what money we have. With that attitude, who cares if there are 35 kids in a class? Without it, even if we had 20 kids in a class it would be hopeless."

This trend may not matter much in elite suburban public schools, where students are well prepared by the time they begin classes and where whatever the school is teaching is continually reinforced in the home. But it matters a great deal in precisely those places where the school's role is most critical—namely, in low-income urban neighborhoods, where both community and family life have broken down. Schools once were fortresses of stability, however chaotic the conditions outside; now many of them are just as hellish and chaotic as the communities that surround them; so much so, sadly, that the community views them only as sources of jobs and money for adults.

Current budget trends symbolize the school/community gap: When the schools are squeezed financially, where do they save money? While the traditional, community-based school was often criticized for spending too much money on the band and on the football team, the modern, bureaucratic school has gone to the other extreme; it cuts out the entire sports and music programs, the two main connections to the community.

Demographic and Other Pressures

The nation will see a peak of elementary- and secondary-student enrollment between 1995 and 2000. After rising by about 4 million—or by about 10 percent from today's figure—enrollment will drop back to its present level by 2010.

Meanwhile, the United States is fast becoming more demographically diverse. Differences in ethnic composition among states, and within them, will grow. Differences between urban cores and the areas surrounding them (Seattle vs. Washington state, for example) will be particularly stark. In 2010, adult America will still be more than 70 percent European; high-income, suburban America, at least 80 percent. The northern rural United States, from east to west, will continue to be essentially all-white. In contrast, school-age populations in much of the nation will be increasingly nonwhite.

Most Midwestern and Northeastern big-city school-age populations will be less than one-half European, with the largest minority African-American, but with growing Hispanic and Asian representation. Nationwide, the school-age African-American population will grow steadily, but slowly—by about 15 percent between now and 2010 nationwide—remaining concentrated in central cities in the Northeast and parts of the Midwest, and spread more evenly throughout the

Southeast. Three out of ten schoolchildren in much of the Southeast, both rural and urban, will be African-Americans.

The Hispanic population will become the largest minority in the United States sometime in the next century. By 2010, the school-age Hispanic population will be almost as large as the school-age African-American population, and far larger in the Southwest—California through Texas. Three of every five Southern Californian school-age children will be Hispanics, Asians, and African-Americans, in that order. In many California school districts the Hispanic proportion alone will be over 40 percent; African- and Asian-Americans will number roughly 10 percent each, with the Asian proportion growing over time.

This means increasing language problems in the schools. The portion of the school population whose native language is not English will approach 20 percent by 2020. The trouble isn't that this number is so big, but that it's so concentrated. There are some school districts today, and there will be more in the future, where more than half of the students entering school are non-English speaking.

Only in California is the problem truly multilingual. The Southwest has a bilingual problem, with significant Spanish-speaking minorities in the school systems in Texas, Colorado, New Mexico, and Arizona, as well as California. Chicago and New York City have a similar situation, but the rest of the nation is hardly touched; in most states not thousands of kids, but ten here and twenty there, will have difficulty speaking English.

Schools can deal with language barriers, if society cooperates. Given half a chance, children learn English very quickly. In the 1920s, America had just as large a proportion of non-English-speaking children—20 to 25 percent, and greater than 50 percent in some school districts; then it was New York City; this time it will be Los Angeles. One might expect it to be easier this time, because the range of languages spoken by the students is smaller. The hordes of immigrant children of the 1920s spoke Italian, German, Swedish, Russian, and a dozen other languages. This time about 70 percent are Spanish-speaking.

A far more difficult problem for the schools is that of family status. While enhancing low-income families' material welfare, the exceptionally low unemployment rates of the coming decades—a simple demographic phenomenon—will further rupture the connections between the community and the school system. More and more mothers work. The school-supporting mom—not just the volunteer helping out during the day, but the mother that a teacher can call during school hours—is an endangered species, because the teacher leaves at 3:30 and mom doesn't get home until 5 or 6 p.m. Since both mom and dad are working full-time, neither has the time or energy to go to evening school meetings. This description will increasingly apply even to low-income populations, because, where things haven't broken down completely, everybody's going to have a job.

But two-income families are the least of the problem. Today, over one-half of all African-American children are growing up with no father around. For the nation as a whole, that number is pushing 20 percent. More than 60 percent of all children born today, writes Karl Zinsmeister in the June 1990 *Atlantic Monthly*, will spend at least some time in a single-parent household before their eighteenth birthday.[2]

Schools are not islands. When violence rages outside, it tends to reach within the schoolhouse walls, as well. According to Zinsmeister, nearly 300,000 high-school students are physically attacked *every month*; in many American inner cities, homicide is the leading cause of death among children. Combine a language problem with a community in chaos and drug-addicted parents: What you get is a 5-year-old child essentially dropped at the doorstep of an ill-equipped school system. The schools have never seen anything like this before. It's an epidemic.

If a child from an intact family is blind or deaf, or has cerebral palsy, the school can educate that child—at a cost of two to three times that of educating an average student. One of our schools' great successes has been in dealing with physical disabilities. We've put enormous resources into it. Whereas education budgets have been inching up on a real, per student basis, expenditures on physically handicapped students have soared.

But no technology exists for teaching the "new handicapped." By the mid-1990s more than one of every five elementary-school youngsters will be bringing multiple problems to the schools: a language barrier; an absentee father; a severe drug habit on the part of the child and/or parent; a crime-ridden community. If these troubled children were spread out evenly, perhaps the school system would be able to handle it. But 20 to 40 percent of the student body in some districts will be composed of multiple-problem kids. Many will be burdened with at least minor brain damage—the legacy of parental drug abuse or alcoholism, as well as malnutrition and neglect or even child abuse, all of which will manifest as severe behavioral problems.

Judges as School Administrators

The 1990s will see the peak, and then the decline, of what has become a dominant and increasingly destructive force in many school systems—the courts. Encouraged by their initial success in ending legally segregated schools, courts have attempted to enforce judicially created rights ranging from racial integration to equality of women's sports. These attempts have not only failed, but have done far more harm than good. Court-enforced busing, for example, has spent tens if not hundreds of millions of dollars, torn apart community/school relations, and ultimately increased the level of racial segregation in most major cities. (You can't integrate children who aren't there; and families have reacted to busing by pulling children out of the public schools into private schools, or by leaving the cities.)

Courts can't create economic resources; they can only redistribute them. Mandating a series of costly absolute rights for some groups—e.g., the handicapped—routes money away from other groups. A series of laws and court decisions have mandated that, no matter how broke a school system is, it must install elevators and/or wheelchair ramps, achieve specified numerical guidelines of integration by busing, and so forth. The court doesn't say: "And, to do this, fire the following teachers." But that's the effect. Near-bankrupt school systems are spending tens of millions of dollars busing kids around, educating no one; or building perfect wheelchair ramps that are never used.

Courts have also attempted to mandate absolute equalization of expenditures per student, and this too has failed. Equality turns out to be nearly impossible to define. School costs differ sharply across a state. Furthermore, equalization removes the incentive for parents who value education to fight for more local funding. There has to be a way to give people who want their children to receive outstanding educations a means of doing it without shifting to private schools.

Another egregious example of court intervention is in the area of discipline. The same proceduralism that has undermined criminal-law enforcement has introduced chaos into the school system, where day-to-day, immediate decisions have to be made. If there's anything we know about child psychology, it's that nothing matters more than immediate reinforcement. Yet a school cannot discipline somebody who commits an act not expressly forbidden by written school rules. Thus, schools face the task of precisely defining all proscribed behaviors without limiting behavior in unintended ways. Moreover, a school must hold formal hearings before taking serious action. Expelling a student takes weeks, not minutes.

The legislators and judges creating these policies live in ordinary, middle-class areas where assaults do not occur in school, much less rapes, murders, or gang shootouts. Such incidents do occur—and with increasing frequency—in central-city schools. According to a 1987 survey of 11,000 8th- and 10th-graders in twenty states, one in 150 students carried a handgun to school *daily*.[3] (Knives are much more common.) The courts have spent years deciding whether or not schools could search students and their lockers for guns. Meanwhile, dozens of children are gunned down every year in American schools.

No other nation could conceive of such legalisms in schools. To the contrary: The Japanese *sensei* (teacher) and the German Frau Doktor or Herr Doktor are in absolute control of their classrooms. In 1990, a Japanese school official accidentally killed a student by slamming the gate on her when she was 30 seconds late to school! The school gamely declared that it would consider gentler means of enforcing the tardiness code.

Movements for Reform

A growing number of low-income, multilingual students with severe social handicaps are entering schools torn apart by the loss of community support. At the same time, parents and the business community demand that everybody get far better academic and vocational training than ever.

A range of mechanisms for reform is on the table. One suggestion is simply to put more money into the existing system, but America has been no skinflint in education expenditures to begin with. In 1986, American industry directly spent nearly $100 billion a year on training, a figure comparable to total public expenditures of about $162 billion in 1986 for the entire K–12 system. The difference used to be overwhelming. Even figures uncorrected for purchasing-power distortions show that in 1985, America outspent any other country except Switzerland, on a per student basis, for elementary and secondary education and devoted a significantly larger fraction of GNP to education than either South Korea or Spain, both of whose students outperform ours academically.[4] Our schools need more than money.

A second approach—Chicago is moving in this direction—is to foster more local control over the existing system, especially in large cities, by breaking districts down so that each small group of schools has its own school board, with real power. But with jobs the key currency of urban politics, the potential for corruption—political dogfights over which political faction, which ethnic group or coalition, can gain control of the board and give maintenance and teacher's assistant jobs to its own adherents—is overwhelming.

The third mechanism, open enrollment, is more extreme. The heart of the American school system is geography. If you're on this side of the street, you go to this school; if you're on the other side of the street, you go to that one. You have no choice. Open enrollment breaks this geographic monopoly: The money follows the child. Schools that lose students lose public funds and have to drop workers and teachers.

At least five states have been moving modestly toward open enrollment within the public schools; twenty more are considering the idea. In California, you can move your child from a school in the community where you live to one in the community where you work, if there's room. Minnesota has tried it for purposes of solving rural school consolidation problems; instead of ordering schools to merge, the state is letting the students vote with their feet.

The most extreme version of open enrollment is the voucher system, whereby parents can choose among not only public but private systems. A voucher is a piece of paper given to the parent, who hands it to the school; the school returns it to the government; and the government gives the school money. Vouchers will gain political support over the coming decades, for several reasons. First, an increasing proportion of America's student population will be Catholic. Without a voucher system, the majority of Catholic schools in the United States will close in the next twenty years. However, popular pressure to break the geographic monopoly of public schools will come not just from Catholics but from a much wider range of parents. The American housing markets of the 1950s and 1960s made it very easy for most families to escape a bad school system; you just moved. Now, home-price disparities between communities with good schools and those with bad schools are so great that, if you're not wealthy, you're stuck.

In early 1990, Wisconsin's state legislature passed a law initiating this country's first experiment in school vouchers for low-income children. The law specified that 1,000 students from low-income Milwaukee families were to be selected by lottery for state scholarships of up to $2,500 per year, which would be diverted from the public school system's budget to private, nonsectarian schools of the students' choice. Since the state's public schools save the $5,000 they would have spent annually on each of these students, no money is drained from the public coffers.

That the state's Republican governor signed the Wisconsin initiative into law was not surprising in and of itself. In the early 1970s President Richard Nixon supported the voucher idea. What *was* surprising was the originator of the bill—not a fellow conservative, but black Democratic state legislator Polly Williams, a Milwaukee inner-city resident and two-time state chairwoman of Jesse Jackson's presidential campaigns. The city's main black newspaper supported the plan. But teachers' unions filed a lawsuit challenging the bombshell's constitutionality, and editorials in both of Milwaukee's major newspapers inveighed against it. Officials of the NAACP, an organization whose constituency is more middle class than inner-city poor, sided with the teachers' unions.

Why? An expanded voucher system would cause money to flow to the schools that parents deem to be doing the best job of teaching their children; bolstered by voucher funds, those schools could add more staff and space. Obvious beneficiaries would be private schools, whose enrollment has decreased since 1965 (although private elementary-school enrollment has increased slightly since 1979). Inner-city public schools—and the tenured teachers and administrators who staff them—could be big losers.

In August 1990 a judge gave the Wisconsin voucher plan a green light, and similar proposals have been floated elsewhere—notably Oregon, where a statewide voucher initiative was placed on the November 1990 ballot. But the troubled urban school systems will get much worse before they get better. Big-city school systems are the closest thing we have to Stalinist economic management—vast bureaucracies spending huge sums and accomplishing little beyond roll call. Free choice of public schools will be common nationwide by the late 1990s; eventually, voucher systems will prevail in most large cities.

In the rest of the country the retreat of the judiciary branch from classroom micromanagement, combined with a wave of new technology, will create 21st-century schools. New telecommunications technology will make possible two-way video hook-ups between students and distant classrooms, further deepening the chasm that separates good and mediocre teaching environments—and yanking yet another nail from the tattered frame of the Little Red Schoolhouse.

CHAPTER II

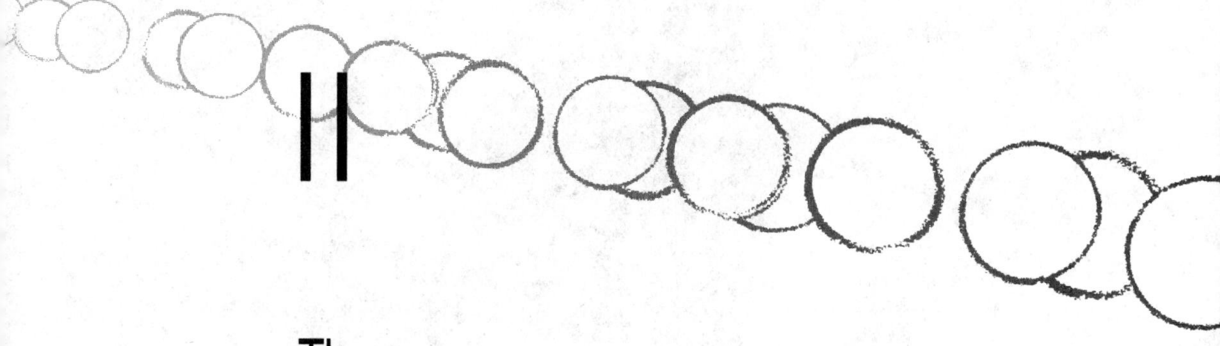

The Community under Assault

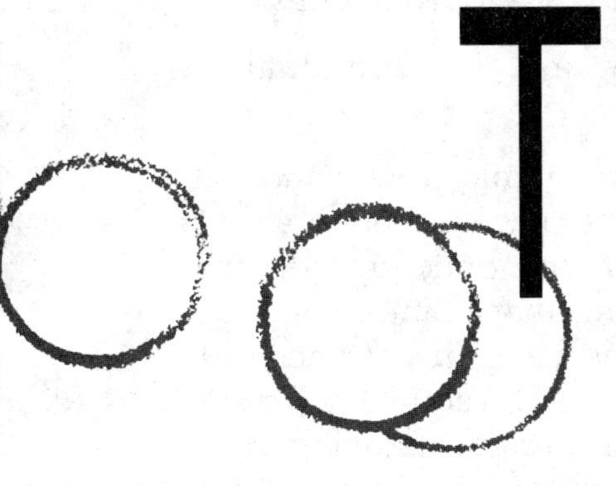

The United States is the world's fastest-changing society. Rapid change has contributed to a wholesale collapse of community institutions; and, in parallel, to upsurges in drug abuse, teenage pregnancies, child neglect, crime. In some communities, there's no community left—no information transmission across generations, no maintenance of even minimal order.

Violence rules the American city. The U.S. Senate Judiciary Committee predicts that there will be at least 23,000 homicides in the United States in 1990—a ten-year record. Children are especially vulnerable. In a survey of urban 11th- and 12th-graders, 13 percent reported having been attacked on school property or in a school bus within the past 12 months. In a four-month period in 1987, 102 Detroit youngsters were shot, nearly all by other children.[1]

The American nuclear family, as an institution, is beginning to resemble a nuclear catastrophe. Half of all marriages end in divorce. About one in ten American women 18 years old or over—some 9.6 million—is raising a child in a home where the father is absent. Child neglect begins in the womb. A House subcommittee report estimates that more than 100,000 cocaine-exposed babies were born in 1988—a figure that could rise to anywhere between 500,000 and one million annually.

A fundamental conflict exists between how a modern economy works and how human beings work. Human beings need stability in their family lives as children, within their community as they are growing up, and in their adult business relationships. But stability within American communities is threatened by two conflicts:

- The conflict between the needs of the economy and the needs of the community, a conflict shared by all developed nations.
- The conflict between the community and the individual, a uniquely American problem.

There comes a point where full-throttled economic growth and the championing of individual over community rights generate social dissonance so severe as to undermine both economic growth and individual freedom. America is fast reaching that point. Economic disincentives and demographic dislocations have disenfranchised families, created disorderly schools, and spawned an entrenched drug culture. The national political pendulum will continue its swing from an advocacy of pure tolerance to one more supportive of community needs, accompanied by a surprising assortment of pragmatic policies, ranging from decriminalization of now-illicit drugs, in combination with enhanced mechanisms for stigmatizing drug abusers, to greater attention to the financial plight of young families.

Portrait of the U.S. as a Young Quick-Change Artist: Economy vs. Community

During the last third of the 20th century, a way of thinking and living that may be called economic pragmatism has spread throughout the world. Its tenets are these:

- Purchasable goods and services are the key measure of living standards.
- A high standard of living is best achieved by creating and exploiting ever-more-sophisticated levels of technology.
- Decisions should be made on the basis, not of ideology, but of cost-benefit analysis—a pragmatic assessment of the measurable economic trade-offs between competing alternatives.
- Economic progress, by its nature, requires change and, therefore, great human flexibility.

Traditional barriers to economic growth are disappearing. Political barriers have fallen with the erosion of living standards in countries foundering under such ideologies as Marxism or Islamic fundamentalism, which are antagonistic to economic pragmatism. Another traditional barrier to the ideal of a continually expanding economy—a supposed scarcity of resources—has faded from public consciousness since 1986, when the energy "crisis" magically disappeared. Today's environmental concerns are precisely the opposite of our pre-1986 worries: The worry is about too much, not too little.

Nor is today's most-popular apparent limit on economic growth—the fear of environmental degradation—an encircling wall, although environmental preservation will loom increasingly larger in advanced nations' economic planning. The greatest environmental problems in the developed world are not in the United States or West Germany, but in Eastern Europe and the Soviet Union. These Marxist regimes eschewed such modern pragmatic tools as independent regulation and efficient pricing, leading to environmental disasters like the Chernobyl nuclear plant explosion in the Soviet Union, metal-eating water in Poland's Vistula River, and 5- to 8-year shorter life expectancies of those who live near the center of East Germany's chemical industry. According to Hungary's state news agency, MTI, a one-hour stroll in the streets of Budapest is the equivalent, in lung damage, of smoking a pack of cigarettes.

There are, however, social and cultural limits to the speed of economic change even in free-market democracies. The United States is the first to bump up against those limits, for two reasons. First of all, we are far more culturally and ethnically diverse than any other nation. Our chief competitors in developed-world economic growth and prosperity—Switzerland and the Scandinavian countries, with near-equivalent living standards; and Japan and West Germany, both rapidly closing in on the U.S. economically—are, overwhelmingly, culturally homogeneous and socially structured societies. Second, ours is the nation that has been forcing the pace of economic and technical change. American society, by virtue of its cultural pluralism and unconstrained personal freedom, is uniquely suited to invent and exploit new technologies and new ways of organizing the economy. That dynamic generates overall economic growth, higher overall standards of living, global integration—and local instability.

The United States is consumer heaven—there's no place like it except, perhaps, Hong Kong—but the economic power of mass merchandising has eroded the structure of traditional neighborhoods. One of the great engines for social and economic change in the United States has been the humble discount store, the first institution to offer lower prices through less service, the convenience of longer hours—and foreign imports. The small, independent shops that helped define and unify communities have been destroyed in the U.S., but they have been deliberately (and expensively) preserved in Japan and Europe. Retail employees have had to juggle their home lives in order to adapt to round-the-clock work schedules. Mass merchandising's emphasis on price-competitive imports, while a boon to shoppers, has doomed U.S. manufactures of many categories of consumer goods. The American consumer is king (or queen)—if only he or she can find a job.

Meanwhile, our competitors have deliberately slowed the pace of economic change within their own borders. The internal economies of West Germany and Japan are quite rigid by American standards. Most developed countries have compartmentalized economies, consisting of an efficient export sector and a hobbled domestic sector. Germany has Sunday closing hours for retail shops that the United States jettisoned thirty years ago. It is nearly impossible to start a large, modern store in Japan; as a result, Japanese retail prices are the highest in the developed world.

The Dissolving Community

The fast-changing American economy has created four sources of domestic community pressure. First of all, there has been pressure on families. Since the mid- to late 1960s, a combination of stagnating wages and radical rises in house prices and rents in many parts of the United States—both, perhaps, exacerbated by the baby boom—has driven men to second jobs and pushed into the work force women who would otherwise have stayed home. In 1988, 72 percent of American women aged 25–54 were in the labor force, in contrast to 62 percent and 61 percent, respectively, of their Japanese and West German counterparts. (A robust 90 percent of Swedish women in the same age bracket are in the work force, but working mothers get plenty of help from the Swedish government.)

The majority of American families have barely held their own since the 1970s, despite the proliferation of two-income couples and working mothers. The chief constraint on American families, even more than dollars, has become time. A 1989 study by Louis Harris and Associates showed that the average American works almost 49 hours per week, up some 20 percent from 1973.[2] Japanese men work even longer hours, but their wives are home with the kids.

Participation of women with young children in the labor force is wildly socially disruptive. Women have always worked, but never before have the majority of women worked the majority of the time away from their young children. What we do know is that, in country after country, as women gain full economic parity with men, they stop having babies. Declining population is now a serious problem in West Germany and Scandinavia. Only Eastern Europe, whose labor force also has high female-participation rates, is experiencing steeper declines in births.

The Scandinavian countries—ultra-homogeneous societies with such low birthrates they're desperate for babies—have pro-natalist policies. Their governments have substituted for traditional families by creating a help network so extensive that being a single mother is not the economic disaster it is here. Swedish family allowances, their substitute for welfare, provide a modestly comfortable standard of living for single mothers. In addition, Swedes receive 15 months parental leave—the first year at full pay, or very close to it. Maternal leave is widespread throughout the world, though nowhere as generous as in Sweden: West German parents get 14 weeks at full pay; French parents, 16 weeks at 90 percent; Japanese, 12 weeks at 60 percent pay. Chile gives 18 weeks at full pay; Poland, 26 weeks.[3] The United States federal government provides no such safety net, although several states have now taken steps toward creating one. A federal bill mandating maternal leaves of 13 weeks without pay was vetoed in May 1990 by President George Bush.

Women raising children alone have a far harder time of it than do those sharing the responsibility with a mate. Divorce was once uncommon. Social restrictions of old wouldn't allow the breakup even of awful marriages. Now marriages break up, taking a toll on children and spouses, for no compelling reason. Ironically, climbing divorce rates may well be more the effects than the causes of the influx of women into the labor market.

Scandinavia has found a new substitute for absent fathers: the government. Denmark and Sweden have rates of unwed motherhood comparable to those of our African-American community. Because of our ethnic diversity and our economic traditions, we're unwilling to spend, as the Scandinavians do, the enormous amounts of money necessary to substitute a bureaucracy for the family. And anyway, we don't know if that bureaucratic substitution will work, because the Scandinavians haven't been trying it for very long. What we do know is that intact families are a lot cheaper: More than 80 percent of never-married mothers in the U.S. are receiving some kind of federal, state, or local government assistance; still, a full 38 percent of single-parent homes, but only 6 percent of husband-wife families, are below the poverty line.[4] Poverty in the United States has become almost entirely the province of single mothers and their children.

The fact is that, for all its opportunities and temptations, nobody knows how to integrate the modern economy with families; it's a new pattern of human culture.

A second challenge to the community created by the modern economy is geographic mobility. IBM was once said to stand for I've Been Moved. Americans move more than anyone else, and that disrupts communities, which are no more than sets of long-term relationships. In traditional human communities, those relationships, chiefly familial, had power across generations. When the typical household moves every five to seven years, those relationships disappear. Geographic mobility leaves the extended family a thousand miles away. Modern communication allows us to communicate more easily, but can't compensate for that loss. Moving is all the more wrenching when both husband and wife are employed.

Beyond the nuclear and extended family is a web of community ties. Child-oriented institutions such as the Boy Scouts and the YMCA are desperate for volunteers. The dearth of volunteer help is especially daunting for those community organizations that have relied on nonworking women. Large proportions of the men in a typical community were once members of voluntary membership organizations: the Lions, the Elks, the Rotary, the Eagles, the American Legion, the Masons. Despite the male-exclusive character of these organizations, they did knit communities together. If something went wrong, there was somebody there to help. The decline in traditional fraternal organizations has been balanced by a surge in ad hoc, interest-focused groups.

The neighborhood church played a major role in American life until about twenty years ago. Religious organizations in the U.S. traditionally helped to unite the community by serving as a meeting place across income lines. There may have been stratification between groups—Episcopalians had the highest income, Baptists the lowest—but within

PATHOLOGICAL COMMUNITIES

Some American communities border on the pathological, imparting ruthlessness, dependency, and despair to their impressionable young instead of skills and values useful to the surrounding society. No single ethnic group has a monopoly on community dysfunction. But inner-city African-American enclaves, victimized not merely by poverty per se but also by rapid economic change, have proceeded farther and faster down the road toward breakdown than any other easily identified communities. The African-American community, although impoverished, was tightly knit—intact families, low divorce rates, unifying community institutions—until the middle of this century, when an enormous, disrupting wave of geographic movement from the South to Chicago or New York was followed by dispersal to other communities. Unusually high unemployment rates became endemic among black men, who possessed only the old, rural skills and were denied entry into Northern labor markets by racism. Just as racial barriers began to fall and African-American men were breaking through into decent-paying industrial jobs, the first wave of Japanese imports hit, and industrial employment collapsed.

While black men were losing their jobs, black women were experiencing a great upsurge in employment opportunity. The interaction between economic change and family structure was extreme. Inner-city communities disrupted by mobility and male unemployment were further eroded, inadvertently, by civil-rights reforms of the 1960s and 1970s. These reforms made it easier for successful African-Americans to move into middle-class communities previously restricted to European-Americans. The gain for these successful individuals, ironically, was a loss for the inner-city neighborhoods in terms of community leaders and role models.

African-Americans have the shortest life expectancies, the highest rates of teenage pregnancy, and the highest rates of children growing up with only one parent. While African-Americans constitute 12 percent of the population of the United States, they account for more than a quarter of all cases of AIDS reported to date in the U.S—a fact for which a higher incidence of intravenous illicit-drug use is chiefly responsible.

One in four American black men in their twenties—as contrasted with less than one in fifteen young white men—is either in prison, out on bail, on parole, or on probation. Blacks are likewise much more likely than whites to be victimized by violent crime. In 1988, more than 1,000 black children were murdered—50 percent more than in 1985.[5] The probability of violent death is a significant reason why the life expectancy of men in Harlem is lower than that of men in Bangladesh.

each individual church there was, and still is, a substantial range of incomes and social classes.

Membership in religious organizations peaked in the 1950s at nearly 75 percent, dropped in the 1960s, and has stabilized since 1975 at about 60 percent of the total population. Between 1957 and 1987 the proportion of the population actually attending church or synagogue dropped from 47 percent to 40 percent—a modest decline in membership, but a greater decline in influence.

Traditional religious organizations face a generational watershed. Protestants born between 1900 and 1920—who, as a group, have been the membership-, volunteer-, and dollar-mainstay for the church—are now retiring and moving away. Over the next ten to twenty years they are going to die off. Who will replace them? The Catholic community has similar problems, most apparent in two areas: a lack of lifetime volunteers (i.e., nuns and priests), and a lack of dollars, resulting in the closing of parishes and schools.

On the other hand, Hispanic-American population growth and normal economic progress will increase Catholic attendance and donations. Nontraditional religions, too, are on the rise. Evangelical Protestantism, a growing force in Latin America, appears to be gaining strength in the United States among Hispanics. Islam has acquired a foothold among poor African-Americans. Environmentalism as a nascent quasi-religion has so far been confined almost entirely to wealthy European-Americans, but it is gaining momentum.

One effect of the unraveling of traditional community structures has been a dramatic increase in tolerance in the United States across religious and cultural groups—we are much more integrated than we were. The waning of the close-knit community has also brought an increase in perceived personal freedom. Anonymity and privacy are close cousins.

But there's a trade-off. For lower- and middle-income communities undergoing tremendous economic change and never-ending social turmoil, the loss of powerful community organizations, which can communicate with the government but aren't bound by bureaucratic rules, has been catastrophic.

A third problem of rapid economic change is lack of job security. The workplace as a stable social entity is disappearing. The modern economy forces frequent changes both in the type of work you do and in the organization you work for. The average U.S. job lasts only 6.6 years. Many new jobs are available, but they demand new skills. Long-term relationships with employers and employees are vanishing, even at the middle-management level. Global capital flows make even the largest corporations fair game for acquisitions, often followed by waves of involuntary layoffs.

The fourth problem generated by the modern economy is, perhaps, counterintuitive. An advanced information economy is regimented in its own way, although far more subtly than in the low-tech industrial economy that preceded it. In many ways, that old form of regimentation was probably easier for integrating diverse ethnic groups. The training and communication required were fairly simple: You got to work on time, punched in, did a single task repeatedly, took a half-hour lunch break, worked some more, and punched out. That old industrial economy could easily integrate Italians, Poles, and Swedes; the new one cannot.

Nowadays, a language barrier constitutes a serious problem. Modern workers—especially in the fast-growing information sector but in industrial jobs, too—must perform complex tasks that require accurate communication, familiarity with technology, and self-discipline. A computer doesn't care what color you are or what god you pray to, but is demanding in other matters. If you aren't literate, are uncommunicative, don't value organized ways of thinking and acting, or are unwilling to participate in an orderly society, you do not fit easily into today's economy. Someone with a 1920 level of training, let loose in a modern steel mill, might well do $10 million worth of damage on the first day.

Individuals vs. Community

America has a unique problem: The glorification of individual rights has cost communities the ability to protect themselves from destructive individuals. There can be too much of the good thing of freedom, and the U.S. has found it.

Holden Hollom is a San Francisco cabdriver, sometime Hollywood stuntman, recent hero, and defendant in a lawsuit. On May 2, 1989, Hollom witnessed the mugging of a diminutive Japanese tourist by a 210-pound man who knocked her down, kicked her stomach, grabbed her purse, and ran for it. Wheeling his cab into action, Hollom managed to maneuver the fleeing assailant into a cul-de-sac and pin him against the wall of a building. The young victim, her purse restored, was treated for a head injury. The mugger pleaded guilty to a robbery charge, but is now suing Hollom and his employer, a small taxi company, for $5 million in damages, contending that Hollom used excess force in making his citizen's arrest.

A February 1990 U.S. Supreme Court case involved a mother who had severely abused her young child. The child was taken away, the mother counseled, and the baby returned to the mother under a social worker's supervision. Some time later the baby disappeared. The mother refused to tell the social worker where the child was or what had happened to her. The case dragged on for months, while somewhere out there was a severely injured—or, perhaps, dead—child. Eventually, the Supreme Court ordered the mother to tell the authorities where the child was. But Justice Sandra Day O'Connor added that, if the child were indeed dead and the mother were to lead authorities to the body, this evidence could not be used against the mother in court.

Uncounted numbers of psychologically unstable people, released en masse from mental institutions during the past 25 years in a national sacrifice to the gods of individual rights and tight budgets, roam confused, hungry, and miserable through the streets of our cities. Unable to take care of themselves, they deteriorate before the very eyes of passers-by who, inured by sheer overexposure to these poor, ubiquitous souls, no longer look.

The U.S. homicide rate is almost nine times that of West Germany and more than ten times Japan's. The coming drop in the number of Americans in the most violence-prone age bracket is unlikely to help much. Even though the number of 12- to 17-year-olds declined by 8 percent between 1983 and 1988, the number of minors arrested for murder rose 31 percent.

In the United States, almost 150,000 full-blown AIDS cases have been reported as of September 1990; there are over a million HIV carriers. Yet only eleven states now have procedures for tracing sexual partners of people infected with the AIDS virus. In contrast, when the Japanese were confronted with AIDS, they identified carriers, contacted their sexual partners, and stopped the epidemic. The total number of AIDS cases in Japan as of mid-1990 was less than 300, with the number of HIV-infected carriers totaling only about 1,200.

Interestingly, it is illegal to discriminate in housing by race, by sex, and in some states by sexual preference, but you can discriminate against children. A trend toward private, gated, restricted-access communities, mostly for senior citizens attempting to isolate themselves from disorderly communities, is picking up steam. ("Senior citizen," in this case, is defined as someone aged 45 or older.)

The willingness of the American political/legal system to sacrifice the innocent to protect the rights of the guilty surpasses that of any other society. In the name of protecting individuals against the coercive power of the state, America's legal and political establishments have favored policies that have catalyzed the process of community breakdown and the rise of violent crime, whose greatest victims are the long-suffering, law-abiding inhabitants of America's inner cities:

- The right to privacy has been extended to protect drug abuse and criminal records. It is difficult, if not impossible, for an employer to dismiss drug abusers, alcoholics, criminals, or the mentally unstable. The 1990 Americans with Disabilities Act will make such dismissals more difficult than ever.
- Legal requirements are so complex and so endless that it is virtually impossible to cut off drug dealers' government benefits or to throw them out of their taxpayer-supported housing projects, which have become hotbeds of drugs and crime.
- The American criminal-justice system is so tied up with endless proceduralism that dangerous individuals are routinely released earlier than scheduled, or never incarcerated, even while serious crime is exploding; abusive parents and pregnant drug addicts are allowed to retain custody of their children, dooming these youngsters to deprivation, pain, and, far too often, death.
- School systems, paralyzed by bureaucratic due-process requirements, are unable to protect their young wards by taking effective disciplinary actions against violent offenders.
- It is politically and socially unacceptable to appear intolerant regarding sensitized subcultures whose behavior spreads lethal infectious diseases. San Francisco spent years of bitter debate on closing the gay bathhouses while thousands were being infected. California prohibited doctors from telling women that their husbands were infected with AIDS. The next wave of AIDS will be in low-income African-American neighborhoods. More than 10 percent of the babies born in the South Bronx are "HIV-antibody positive"—a euphemism for "infected with the virus that causes AIDS, and likely to die slowly over the next few years." We use that euphemism only for political reasons.

Additional cultural ingredients, blended with our cumbersome criminal-justice procedures, push crime rates in our country higher:

- *Television*. This medium exaggerates huge and growing wealth disparities in the United States, inciting invidious comparisons. Television also glorifies violence in general and gunplay in particular.
- *Guns*. Most countries have strict regulations regarding the purchase and possession of firearms. The average police chief will be glad to tell you that easily available guns contribute to high violent-crime rates. But, owing to an ambiguously worded Constitutional Amendment, the United States probably won't banish guns anytime soon. Growing arsenals of assault rifles in the hands of drug dealers and gang members suggest that the worst lies ahead.
- *Drugs*. Illegal drugs are not necessarily unobtainable—far from it; nearly one in 100 Americans use cocaine at least once a week—but they are typically expensive and frequently addictive. Getting them, selling them, and keeping them lead to much more crime than using them does. Drug profits are so enormous that a frightening political potential is turning into a waking nightmare: Drug dealers not only are better armed than police, but are able to buy the police force and the legal system. In the U.S., several city neighborhoods are already drug-controlled. Anything is buyable when you have billions of dollars behind you. Whole nations have been utterly corrupted by the immensely lucrative cocaine trade; the head of Colombia's Medellin cocaine cartel is a multibillionaire.

A Modest Proposal: Decriminalize Drugs

The only certainty in the war on drugs is that current efforts will fail. Procedural constraints on the U.S. criminal-justice system effectively doom criminal-enforcement procedures against well-financed drug groups. Massive government eradication and interdiction campaigns in Peru, Bolivia, Texas, and California make headlines, but little headway. Tiny quantities of illegal drugs are so profitable that cutting off the supply is physically impossible.

The relationship between illicit drugs and crime is, first and foremost, one of definition. If illicit drugs were decriminalized, those who procured, possessed, and consumed them would no longer be outlaws, assuming they harmed nobody else. Between 28 million and 40 million Americans committed crimes in 1988, simply by virtue of having used illegal drugs. A paltry 839,000 of those users—2 or 3 percent—were arrested that year, but it was enough to clog our criminal-justice system.[6]

In 1988, drug-use and -trafficking cases accounted for 23 percent of all felony convictions in state courts, as well as 40 percent of all felony indictments in New York City and more than 50 percent of those in Washington, D.C. Drug-law violators composed one-fifth of New York State's prison population and one-fourth of all new admissions to Florida's prisons in 1987.[7]

Radical as it sounds, the decriminalization of currently illicit drugs in combination with other control methods represents the most cost-effective anti-crime measure the United States can take. Total government expenditures on drug-law enforcement in 1987 exceeded $10 billion. Yet there is no particular rationality behind our present scheme of selective prohibition. Marijuana is not addictive; of the 60 million Americans who have smoked it, not one has ever died of an overdose. Only some 3,500 deaths in 1985 were attributed directly to the use of all illegal drugs combined.[8] Contrast this with the 50,000 to 200,000 yearly deaths directly or indirectly attributable to alcohol, including 10,000 from overdose (as well as 40 percent of all 1983 traffic deaths); or the 320,000 deaths each year traceable, in the aggregate, to smoking cigarettes. Tobacco's key substance, nicotine, is as addictive as heroin.[9]

Heroin is not particularly physically damaging to the body; nor, being a sedative, does it induce a violent state. Any relationship between violent behavior and heroin results from the desperate search for more heroin, or for the money to pay for it. On the other hand, according to Justice Department statistics, 54 percent of all inmates convicted of violent crimes in 1983 reported having used alcohol just prior to committing their offense.[10] There are about 18 million alcoholics in the United States.

Only their illegality makes marijuana, cocaine, and heroin expensive. The foreign-export price of cocaine is 4 percent of its retail price; that of heroin, 1 percent. The markup is everything. A Rand Corporation study of 11,430 Washington, D.C., residents charged with drug selling between 1985 and 1988 found that the typical small-time dealer made $30 an hour selling cocaine part-time.[11] What legal job could compete with that? Only 36 percent of these dealers had high-school diplomas.

If drugs were legal and relatively cheap, users wouldn't have any reason to steal, kill, become dealers themselves, or consort with the criminal elements that traffic in these drugs; and pushers would lose their profits, with which they corrupt law officials and purchase assault rifles to outfit their private armies. The criminal-justice approach is worse than a failure; it is destroying American cities.

The case against decriminalization holds that, with easier access to drugs, current addicts would kill themselves by overdose and overuse; and many now deterred from drug use by legal sanctions would become addicts. Even if this were true, the victims would at least be voluntary, not innocent bystanders. Nor is it a foregone conclusion that decriminalization leads to increased use; there is evidence to the contrary. The Dutch, who not only have legalized marijuana but don't enforce their laws against heroin and cocaine (except against international shipments), have a small and declining number of cocaine and heroin users.

Even in a worst-case scenario, given a choice between stepping over a few more nodding users and having your children shot at by a swarm of Uzi-toting gang warriors or getting mugged by crazed addicts foraging for drug money, many people who actually have to live in drug-infested neighborhoods would choose the former. Decriminalization's biggest beneficiaries would, in fact, be those in inner cities, where deterrence through criminal sanctions is a proven failure. Legalizing drugs is the quickest way to end violence and put a halt to the current epidemics of AIDS and hepatitis B now spreading like wildfire in urban ghettoes through the sharing of needles used to inject drugs intravenously.

Decriminalization would render moot the argument that arbitrary police sweeps of black communities violate the civil liberties of young African-Americans and preferentially criminalize them. The higher criminalization rate of young black males compared to young white males reflects, in part, the ease of busting a drug user on a street corner (where many young blacks buy their drugs) as opposed to inside a plush high rise (where many young whites buy theirs). Inner-city residents would likewise benefit from the redirecting of police attention to crimes involving victims, and from the rechanneling of anti-drug funds into treatment programs.

To decriminalize drug use by no means implies tolerance of behavior destructive to others; rather, community controls are vastly more efficient than criminal-law controls, which work only when a very small minority of the community is breaking away. Our objective, rather than reducing aggregate drug use by some arbitrary fraction, ought to be creating drug-free schools, neighborhoods, and workplaces—without evolving into a police state in order to do it.

A New Synthesis: Alternatives to Laissez-Faire

There exists a wide range of options, many of which will undoubtedly become policies in the next decade, for restoring order to troubled communities and reducing drug use:

- Shift to school vouchers, permitting parents to choose from among schools anywhere along the continuum from permissive to hypervigilant and, thereby, allowing them to keep their kids as drug-free—and violence-free—as they'd like. Expedite expulsions from school for anti-social behavior.
- Substitute housing vouchers for public housing, allowing poor families now concentrated in public housing projects to escape concentrated subcultures of poverty/welfare/drugs/violence and relocate in neighborhoods with better role models for young, poor children. Sell the housing projects to their occupants.
- Establish an absolute legal right for employers, schools, insurers, landlords, and government agencies to discriminate against drug abusers in any way they see fit, as well as a legal-defense fund to defend all private parties who discriminate against drug users. Prohibit contingency fees for attorneys representing drug users in discrimination lawsuits.
- Heavily tax newly legalized drugs. Marijuana is the largest cash crop in several states. Organized crime is estimated to net $50 billion a year from the sale of illicit drugs. If price drops due to legalization were to cut the profits by a factor of ten, a 200 percent sales tax would yield $10 billion annually—five times the amount spent by state governments to jail drug users in 1988.
- Divert portions of those taxes into drug-treatment programs and anti-drug educational campaigns. Ban drug vending machines, advertisements, or sales to minors. License restricted-

access drug-use areas (read: bars). Negative advertisements, public education, packaging requirements, and advertising prohibitions have led to a reduction in the percentage of American adult smokers from 40 percent in 1964 to 29 percent today.

- Deny public benefits—including public housing, welfare, and driver's licenses—to those whose use of drugs has incapacitated them. Mandate treatment programs for incapacitated addicts. Enforce strict penalties on those whose children are found in violation of weapon or drug laws.
- Socially and economically stigmatize those whose behavior threatens others. Allow drug testing of employees, and protect employers who fire suspected drug abusers. Levy severe penalties on drug use by drivers and by those in law- or safety-related occupations. Establish closer monitoring of diseases spread through sexual contact or intravenous use of illicit drugs.
- Hold parents responsible for children's health and behavior. American society can't tolerate more abused, fetal-alcohol-syndrome, cocaine-addicted, or "HIV-antibody-positive" babies. Under no conditions should crack- or alchohol-addicted babies born to mothers who have sought no prenatal assistance—despite a widespread proliferation of well-advertised, free programs—be raised by those mothers.

Cases of communities and individuals near total breakdown—from ordinary property crime and drug use to violent, inexplicable, multiple murders—are the extreme manifestations of the trade-off of economic growth and individual rights vs. quality of communal life. But the lesser pressure felt by larger numbers—not social breakdown, but a quality of life that, while prosperous, is unpleasant—is equally significant. The United States has far and away the greatest pace of economic and technical change of anyone. We are the innovation leaders of the world. How much pressure is it worth just to keep this economic machine moving faster all the time?

Investing in families and community coherence, and retarding the rate of economic change and geographic mobility, will spread the benefits of our economic and technical knowledge more broadly. Over the next few decades, America will adopt powerful taxation and subsidy mechanisms for doing this:

- Making the school-to-work transition easier. Nearly all Americans go to school, get a job, and then find out how little they know. Germany has an elaborate apprenticeship system, with clear gradations. It's less flexible than our system, but during their last couple of years of school, students are being trained directly for specific jobs; they then move into those jobs without any wild thrashing around.

- Making it easier to build more housing, especially lower-cost housing, through eased zoning rules and density restrictions. We have backed into a policy of subsidizing high-end housing through our tax laws while restricting housing opportunity, to the detriment of young families.

- Building more transportation facilities, primarily highways. The transportation problem clobbers the young, who are forced into a choice between 70-mile commutes and paying jacked-up housing prices. Short of a radical change in density patterns of American industry and residences, new highways are a must. Subsidizing mass-transit systems to serve low-density areas doesn't work.

- Supporting childcare through family allowances, paid maternity leave, and childcare tax credits, which would give mothers equal subsidy whether they want to stay home or purchase childcare.

- Reforming childcare-liability insurance, which is a mess. Current government policies are restricting supply when they should be expanding it. It's almost impossible to meet all the rules, so most childcare providers end up being illegal to some degree.

Helping young families to raise their children, supporting community cohesion, offering more choice in schools and housing, redirecting law-enforcement efforts toward crimes with victims—all of these are fine ideas. Exactly when local, state, or federal policies will be enacted to achieve those goals cannot be predicted, but changes will come faster if our political system, now in many respects paralyzed, can be revitalized.

CHAPTER

12

Breaking the Political Logjam

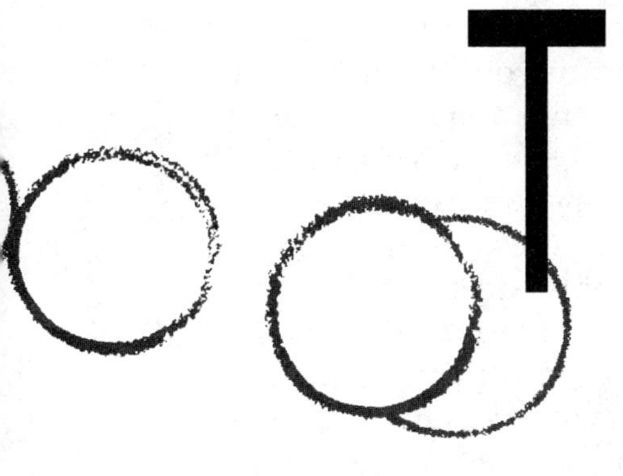

There is an old saying that if you drop a frog in boiling water, it'll jump out so fast it'll live. If you just put it in cold water and slowly turn up the heat, it'll boil to death.

The American political system has been very froglike: It responds well to clear, immediate crises, but it generally lets slow but serious problems heat up to the near deadly boiling point. Examples abound in our history. The divisions that led to the Civil War, the financial scandals that preceded the 1929 crash, the diplomatic errors and military weakness that brought on World War II, the mistakes that caused our disastrous involvement in the unwinnable war in Vietnam; all these problems were allowed to fester to near-disaster while American politicians concentrated on their real goals: making money for themselves and a few of their supporters.

This ability to march serenely into disaster is not a uniquely American trait. England politely destroyed its economy after World War II. Britain's decline was sedate, slow, and more destructive than World War II. It took somebody really nasty like Prime Minister Maggie Thatcher to start turning things around. Brutal though some of her policies may have been, her basic economics were correct.

Americans have prided themselves on the superiority of their political system, but that superiority is gone. In World War IV, an economic conflict, the social and political structures of countries like Japan and West Germany will win out. In pure economic terms, their systems are more workable. That's why they were smart enough to skip World War III.

The essence of political efficiency is the swift formulation of nonideological policies that work. Efficiency means using human and financial resources wisely. It means operating within realistic budgetary constraints, rather than promising the impossible and producing the inferior. American politics are inefficient because our politicians, and the interests they serve, have become *too* efficient. Modern polling and media techniques, given enough money, virtually guarantee the election of any incumbent. Modern political staffs and bureaucracies forge unbreakable links with their corresponding interest groups. Modern lobbyists, armed with sophisticated computer models and up-to-date polls, know more about government than the government.

The politicians themselves have much less power than in the past. Issues are so complex that influence has devolved to the staff level. Voters are really electing corporations, not individuals; Ronald Reagan was a figurehead on most issues. Similar corporations are ascending to governorships, the House of Representatives, and the Senate.

The 1990s will see the continued advance of media-oriented, single-issue politics. There will be two levels of politics: The electoral decisions that *don't* count will be made by poll-driven media manipulation. The decisions that *really* count will be made by the iron triangle of the permanent bureaucracy, the permanent congresspersons, and the best and brightest lobbyists that money can buy.

The modus operandi of the people behind the thrones—the ones who really understand what's going on, who play interest-group politics like an organ, who are an inherent part of interest-group politics, who move in and out between the decision-making side and the decision-influencing side—is to work on a congressional staff for a while, then get a job with one of the leading public-relations or legal-consulting firms. These people don't work merely because they love politics (although most of them do), but also to gain technical knowledge and contacts—the staff job is just a stepping stone to the outside where the big money is. The congressperson or president they work for is just a temporary figurehead.

The recipe for political chaos is single-issue politics—proof that the American political system doesn't work very well except in crisis. World War IV is a technical and economic horse race, with America's lead no longer insurmountable. Yet while we're being overtaken, Congress and the state legislatures are fighting over minor ideological issues like abortion, which have taken on an importance of their own. In the next thirty years, several political developments will unfold:

- The continued weakening of the presidency, and bankruptcy of the federal government.
- The rise of political groupings based more on age and race than the traditional divisions by economic class.
- The recoalescing of the two major political parties, with both at risk.
- A re-orientation of issues away from defense and economic redistribution and toward economic efficiency, the environment, and growth controls.
- A shift in political power from federal and local levels to the states.
- Political retreat from judicial activism.
- The peaking in the 1990s and reversal in the next century of the country's experiment with government by referendum, which confers great power on well-organized single-interest groups able to devote massive amounts of time and money to their cause.
- The continued evolution and growth of environmentalism into a quasi-religious movement equivalent to the anti-slavery movement of the 1840s and 1850s.

Who's President? Who Cares?

There's been a warp in the formation of political consciousness over the baby-boom generation. Those of us born before 1945 were trained to look at the president as a hero, especially if we read our history books. The baby boomers and later generations have been trained to look on the president variously as a crook, an incompetent, and a media creation. The next generation will learn to look on the president as a welsher—breaking the unkeepable promises of his predecessors.

Both the presidency and the influence of the federal government are being weakened and will continue to ebb for at least another decade, owing to three factors:

- Congress and the presidency are nearly permanently split. Congress will remain far more liberal, and more subject to the control of special interests, than any electable president of either party.

- The federal government is financially bankrupt. The next decade will be spent deciding what promises to break, with no room in the budget for anything new.

- Major traditional military challenges, the stuff of national consensus and great presidencies, will increasingly be replaced by remote, bloody, ambiguous regional conflicts with divisive political potential at home.

Four factors have played a role in creating a near-permanent split between the president and the Congress: (1) the voters' requirement that a president project a strong image abroad and be good for business at home; (2) Democratic control of state legislatures, which in turn gerrymander political districts to maximize the number of seats Democrats hold nationally; (3) the still-strong Southern tradition of voting Democratic in local elections; and (4) the power of incumbency. The first three of those factors, taken together, ensure weak presidencies; the latter, weak political parties. The combination makes it almost impossible to establish priorities and generate consistent policies.

The weakening of the president's power is a relatively recent phenomenon. It began in the 1960s and accelerated with the election, in 1968, of a Republican president hated by the bureaucracy and Congress. A Republican majority in the Congress and a Democratic president would have provided the same dynamic, a function of split-party government. The classic "liberal vs. conservative" distinction does not apply, either. What matters is not ideology, but efficiency. Germany is much more "socialist" than the U.S., but it is an efficient socialism; the German government has never produced anything like the vast losses of our S&L disaster.

The essence of efficiency is establishing priorities. A weak presidency and a weak set of parties can't afford to say no to anybody. The result is a series of pork-barrel policies; billions of dollars are spent doing things everybody knows are silly in order to buy votes. Initially sensible legislative drafts end up as "Christmas tree" bills: something for everyone.

To maximize the likelihood of their re-election, individual congressional officeholders have to satisfy specific constituencies; and to do that, they need a weak president who can't overrule their projects. The conservative/liberal distinction starts to break down in this logic. Business plays this game just like everyone else.

Question: Why does a "peace Democrat" like Senator Alan Cranston become one of the main supporters of the B-1 bomber? Answer: California defense jobs. Our military system has evolved into an enormous pork barrel, as have such sectors as construction, traditional rivers and harbors, agriculture, welfare and social services, and, last but not least, the tax code.

WEAK DOMESTIC PARTIES MAKE FOR STRONG FOREIGN LOBBIES

Foreign influence in our politics is on the increase. The Japanese have the most efficient system of money politics in the world. Japanese corporations' payments to the politicians are essentially automatic: a monthly check. As part of their World War IV strategy, foreign powers have had an astonishing impact on our economic policies. A revealing case in point was the government's decision some years back to impose quotas on automobile imports.

There are two ways to restrict imports: quotas and tariffs. If you establish a quota, prices for cars rise, and the Japanese manufacturer pockets extra profits amounting to tens of billions of dollars. If you establish a tariff with an equivalent effect, those tens of billions of dollars go into the U.S. Treasury. The consumer pays more in either case. What did we do? We went with the quota, and gave the profits to the Japanese.

Those quotas played a big role in creating the huge capital pool Japanese car manufacturers needed to get a technical jump on the United States. Billions of dollars per year have aggregated to an extra $75 billion to $100 billion or more, which the Japanese companies have reinvested—profitably, and much of it within the United States.

The Japanese auto manufacturers have a brilliant lobby, an association of automobile importers. Even though it looks like it's from the U.S., it gets its money from Japan. There are other importer associations: one for textiles, one for consumer products, one for steel—and all well financed.

The Democratic Congress does its utmost to weaken the Republican president by maintaining congressional oversight on everything the president does, rejecting presidential appointments, and attempting to jail presidential lieutenants. (The U.S. may yet inadvertently back into a parliamentary system, in the generic sense of a legislator-dominated government, through impeachment of another president.) The attack continues even when a Democrat is president, because any chief executive will be more economically prudent than a Congress of permanent pork-barrel incumbents. Finally we end up as the only developed nation that has, instead of a budget, an essentially nonbinding resolution that specifies how much different committees are *supposed* to spend—and then those committees do what they want anyway.

In the past the federal budget was so small that such an abdication of fiscal responsibility wouldn't have mattered much. The Budget Bureau brought together the requests from all agencies, and the president sent in a unified budget; because he was from the same party as the majority in Congress, he'd cut a deal with the Speaker of the House. Lobbyists would peck away at the edges, but the president's decision pretty much stood.

Without a strong president or even a strong party to watch over them, triumvirates of lobbyists, agency bureaucrats, and congressional committee staffers now effectively run Washington. And instead of a billion here and a billion there, they're now dealing with tens of billions and hundreds of billions of dollars. Nobody cares how the whole thing fits together. So it *doesn't* fit together—fiscally or operationally.

The premier example of bipartisan disaster is the savings-and-loan fiasco. The U.S. Savings League was in complete control of both key committees in Congress and of the bureaucracy. Everyone did exactly what the S&Ls wanted, accepted enormous contributions (many of which have been hastily returned under the glare of the investigative spotlight), and helped create the greatest financial scandal in human history.

Many agencies are totally beyond presidential control. The Federal Bureau of Reclamation is an excellent example. Jimmy Carter prepared a hit list of water projects he intended to kill, and got cut to pieces. Everyone knew Carter's position was right, both financially and environmentally; but the bipartisan coalition on the congressional committee made mincemeat out of him, and he lost the support of the Western politicians.

Further tarred by the hostage-as-photo-opportunity crisis in Iran, Carter lost the 1980 election. The environmental movement has since moved from that important, but politically unwinnable, issue to issues that are politically much sexier; away from rivers and harbors, land use, and water policy and toward panicking people about toxic apples and playing on a national cancer scare.

The upshot of all this is a flow of power from the federal government to state governments. The federal government is so broke and so tied up in special-interest politics that states have had to take on leadership in some areas. States must use real budgets. Because their borrowing capabilities are limited and they can't print money, they are forced to make efficient, constrained decisions and to pay up front for implementing those decisions. In 1960, state governments accounted for 16 percent of all taxes collected; by 1988, the figure had grown to 26.5 percent.

The Case for Regional Government

Excess financial speculation in the past decade, most egregiously in real estate but in other areas as well, has resulted in the doing of many things that should not have been done. Equally great harm can come from not doing things that should be done. An example of government paralysis is our airports. As was mentioned in Chapter 9, commercial air traffic has boomed in the last two decades, but not a single new commercial airport has been built. The absence of dominating regional governments makes it difficult to agree on where physically to put new airports or to expand existing ones. At the state and local levels, land-use planning will be a politically explosive issue for the next few decades. Over the next thirty years, we will add 40 million to 50 million people. Most cities don't want them; that would mean supplying housing and roads and factories, which would all have to be put somewhere.

If you want to look at the future of American politics under current trends, look at Italy, a political entity with a weak presidency and weak political parties. The bureaucracy and lobbyists run the country. Immense power, relative to anywhere else in Europe (although not as much as here), resides in individual cities.

Land-use change is always unpopular, to some degree, among people who are already settled. But in Europe, at some point the federal government says, "You're going to build the houses here. The highway is going to go there, and the factories are going to go over here." The locals may complain a bit, but it happens. In the United

States, citizens not only complain; they have virtual veto power. The United States has far and away the most localized land-use planning powers of any nation. Our individual cities have powers that, virtually everywhere else, are wielded at either the national or state level.

The San Francisco Bay Area is an example of local dominance over land-use planning. A major highway, Interstate Highway 80, comes west from Sacramento in central California and crosses the Bay Bridge into San Francisco. The traffic jams are horrendous. Everybody knows that Highway 80 has to be widened. California is willing to pay for it. But the city of Berkeley doesn't want to do it. Why not?

DEATH OF VENICE

The Italians have known since the late 1950s that Venice was sinking, due to the digging of deepwater channels to the mainland through a lagoon, the prevention of silt deposition as a result of upstream damming of rivers, and the pumping of natural gas and water—all approved by government. The nation was unable to respond to experts' predictions that if these actions continued, Venice would sink into the sea.

Here we are in 1990, thirty years later. Venice is sinking, and for the last decade the Italians have been arguing about whether or not to put up some tidal barriers so that even if Venice sinks some more, it won't be flooded. Years have been spent building the first experimental gate. There the delay is not from litigation, but from bureaucracy. No consistent set of policies has been established at the national or at least the regional level mandating that Venice is going to be saved and how this is to be accomplished. Italy is very close to losing an entire city.

In thirty years the United States may lose New Orleans to sea-level rise and loss of protective marshes; but our political decision-making processes are just as frozen as the Italians'.

First, highways are noisy. Second, Berkeley residents don't think it would help them much. The road serves mostly San Francisco and Oakland. Third, the environmental movement has great power in Berkeley. Among environmentalists, the fashion is to hate cars. Environmentalists all *drive* cars; they love them in specific but hate them in general. A good way to exercise that hatred is to block the widening of that freeway.

Berkeley has veto power—unless the state legislature takes over, which would be opposed by all the other cities, because they want to retain *their* veto powers. So that freeway can't be widened. And even if the city doesn't veto it, any small group of individuals that can afford to hire a lawyer can effectively veto things through our legal process. In many key decision areas, we've handed out almost universal vetoes.

The ease with which litigation can be launched in our political system is unrivaled anyplace else on earth; still more unparalleled is the ease with which that litigation can be used to at least delay—and in many cases stop—major public- and private-sector decisions. The state legislature can say, "For the interest of the entire Bay Area and the California economy, let's widen this road." Anywhere else in the world (except, perhaps, for Italy), as soon as a decision was made, the bulldozers would start to roll. In the United States, if there's any controversy about the decision, the bulldozers stand still. First, years are spent on paper justifications called environmental-impact statements; then additional years are spent in court.

Wherever you have population growth, you need economic growth to pay the bills. But in precisely those places where the economy wants to grow, the local communities are saying no.

The San Francisco Bay Area's notorious housing inflation was a strictly local creation. On average, factories bring in lots of property-tax dollars and few service needs. People bring in few dollars and many service needs—schools, roads, parks, police. So the Bay Area's constituent city governments each made it as easy as possible to build factories and as difficult as possible to build housing. Local governments' housing policies ended up choking the growth of what is probably the single most important industrial region in the United States. This kind of problem is something that the Japanese or the Germans couldn't imagine. While their engineers are spending night and day trying to catch up with us technically, our engineers are still looking for a place to live.

The payoffs to realistic regional planning are both environmental and economic. If you plan regionally, your transportation system will work because you can integrate your transportation and land-use decisions. Planners in Paris designed the city's transportation system around satellite quasi-cities on the periphery, with high-speed trains coming into each concentrated mini-city. The heart of Paris is still the architectural wonder it was, but the city works economically too, because land-use and transportation decisions were made in parallel.

Somewhere around the turn of the century, the pendulum will start to swing back in the U.S., in the form of intervention either at the state level or by powerful regional governments encompassing entire metropolitan areas. A few municipalities are already moving in that direction: Minneapolis, Atlanta, Indianapolis, San Diego, Seattle, Sacramento. By 2020, major metropolitan-area governments will prevail throughout the country. We'll see the return of the city-state.

Generational Politics

Sometime in the 1990s, the $100-billion-per-year influx of European and Japanese capital now propping up our debt-addicted economy is going to stop. U.S. debtors in general, and the federal government in particular, will have to start paying their debts in real goods and services instead of paper. When foreign demand for U.S. assets drops off, there will be a sharp decline in the value of the dollar. The decline will make our exports cheaper and discourage imports of foreign products. The consumer boom will be over.

It is a safe bet that foreigners will pull back within the next decade, because, at 10 percent interest compounded annually, $100 billion per year for ten years yields a net increase in total foreign ownership of U.S. assets of well over $1.5 trillion—on the order of 4 percent of America's total worth. What foreign owners gain in productive capacity, we lose. Interest payment outflows will exceed $150 billion annually just for debt acquired during the 1990s.

A standard objection raised to the above argument is that, unlike Brazil, we print the money in which our debts are denominated; we can always run the presses, if need be, to pay off foreign creditors in devalued dollars. That's valid only for as long as the Germans and Japanese are foolish enough to accept dollar-denominated debt and OPEC is willing to denominate payment for oil deliveries in terms of dollars. The world is rapidly moving towards yen- and mark-denominated debt and oil settlements.

A second, more substantial, objection is that it's okay to borrow virtually any amount, as long as the money we borrow is used to finance productive investment into the United States. That's true, but the influx of foreign capital is being used mainly to finance consumption. Our investment rate lags behind that of other developed countries; worse, our investments have been disproportionally in unproductive areas such as real estate.

As foreign investment in the U.S. dries up, American politics will become increasingly defined by age and race rather than region and traditional economic class. Older white Americans are by far the wealthiest population in the world, on average, but the U.S. has the developed world's poorest young families. At some point the young, including the young minorities, especially Hispanics, will start to vote their pocketbooks. Between 2000 and 2010, this unstoppable demographic force will collide with the unbreakable barrier of political domination by the elderly, to whom wealth has been transferred through housing inflation and Social Security payouts that far exceed anything recipients have put into the system.

One way the baby boom generation will pay off the debt America accumulated during the 1980s is by receiving reduced Social Security benefits. Social Security has been a bonanza for all recipients to date—the best investment you could have made except for California real estate. Somewhere around the turn of the century the government will say, "Whoops, we were wrong. We miscalculated. We promised you too much."

The current generation is experiencing the earliest retirement in history, a phenomenon that will accelerate for a while; but the younger generation is going to find themselves working much longer and getting less. The average retiree in the year 2000 will be much better off than the average retiree in 2010 or 2020.

The Politics of Growth Control

Growth controls are helping to break up traditional political coalitions. The future of local politics in the United States was foreshadowed in the late 1980s when Tom Bradley, the black mayor of Los Angeles, aligned himself with conservative, Republican, white business leaders in a most controversial proposal: working with an oil company to develop city-owned oil lands offshore of one of the highest-income white areas in the community. The city would make money off of the deal. Those fighting it hardest were environmentalists, who are mostly white, and residents of a nearby community, which was very high-income, mostly Democratic, and disproportionately Jewish. Here was one of the core groups in the Democratic coalition fighting another Democratic core group; and the issue was growth and development.

In the Northeast, on the West Coast, and in parts of the Midwest, growth controls are the dominant local and state issue, the issue by which state legislatures are won or lost. Swinging the legislature determines the composition of Congress, because the legislature and its computers gerrymander the district. Whoever controls the computers in California determines which party has the majority of California's congressional delegation.

The Democratic Party can't live with growth controls. It can't maintain its younger, minority membership and be the party of growth control at the same time. This issue tears apart Republicans too, because it puts the business community, one core group, in conflict with older, white voters. Many successful business proprietors live in wealthy, conservative enclaves where growth and land-use controls are overwhelmingly tight; those same people complain about the problems that growth controls bring to their business.

Ethnic Politics

Over the next thirty years, the United States will absorb millions of immigrants, especially immigrants of Hispanic origin. The economic pressure to learn English is overwhelming, and the younger generation always learns to speak it quite well. But the current requirement that English be spoken in order to gain citizenship is very frustrating for today's Hispanic-American political leadership. A huge population has only minute political influence, except in New Mexico and perhaps in Texas. Significant numbers of people, a million or more, have permanent residency; but they will not get the right to vote until they pass English tests. A fight over that requirement looms in the near future.

One argument against immigration is that immigrant laborers keep wages low. But the average voting European-American worker has nothing to worry about. In recent years we've had a two-tier labor market. It's only at the low end of that market that immigration affects wages of American workers. Hispanic immigrants do keep the wages of settled Hispanic workers low—but those workers don't vote.

African-Americans, on the other hand, do vote. They constitute one of the most reliable voting blocs in American politics, because their voting pattern is so uniformly Democratic. African-Americans will grow ever more influential in the Democratic party.

Rise of the Regional Politician

As coalitions change within the parties, new leadership will emerge. By 2000 the situation will be ripe for a new leader who is willing to build political strength from the local level on up.

One implication of more-powerful metropolitan and regional governments is fewer, less-powerful African-American mayors. An odd political coalition will be formed by European-American conservatives, who won't want to give up local veto power, and African-American mayors' political machines, which will want the mayor's job to stay important. Regional governments are less likely than cities to vote in black officials. If there were a Detroit regional government, Coleman Young wouldn't be the head of it. The exception is Atlanta, one of our most-metropolitan areas, which has significant black participation and leadership.

However, it's virtually inevitable there will be an African-American Democratic candidate for president sometime during the next thirty years, preceded by a woman vice-president and a black vice-presidential candidate, probably from the South and possibly from Atlanta, the launching pad of modern black political leadership. The first African-American presidential candidate probably will have been a governor. For much of the next decade or two, governorships will be more important political stepping stones than the Senate. Traditional foreign policy experience is less important now than it used to be. World War IV is about economics, and economic decisions are made by governors, not senators.

Moreover, the federal government will be too broke to afford massive new expenditure programs. The exception, late in the decade or around the turn of the century, will be national health insurance, which will arrive not as some wonderful panacea but as a crisis-mode response to the hash we've made out of our medical-care system. That brutal, divisive fight won't create any handsome princes; each alternative will make a lot of people angry.

The federal government will also be deciding how to cut back Social Security, how to raise taxes, which weapon systems to shut down, and which bases to close. That's a great platform to run on, isn't it?

The New American Religion: Environmentalism

The political movement to watch in the next century is environmentalism. The battle for the soul of the environmental movement is under way. The outcome of this battle will determine not only the shape of the environment but, to no small extent, our political and economic future.

The environmental movement initially sought government help to create national parks and wildlife refuges, and to enforce hunting regulations and migratory bird treaties. They saved the buffalo, the egrets, the ducks, and the geese. They won the first air- and water-pollution control regulations, banned DDT, and brought whooping cranes, bald eagles, and peregrine falcons back from near extinction.

For a while, government became the enemy, as large-scale dam-building programs destroyed more vital wildlife habitat and scenic wonders than the parks had protected. In the 1960s, the Sierra Club, founded by John Muir to oppose San Francisco's Hetch Hetchy dam in Yosemite Park, lost its tax exemption over its opposition to a federal dam-building program on the Colorado River. Now environmentalism has entered the era of big-money politics. The environmentalist constituency has become so large, wealthy, and influential that new, more-radical political groups are fighting for their loyalty. Images are being shaped to meet the political goals of these new allies.

Environmentalism is taking on religious overtones, which give it unusual power. Nothing since the anti-slavery movement of the 1840s has had similar potential for radically reshaping the nation's politics. Religion excuses almost any action, including violence. The environment has all the ingredients of a religion: god, guilt, heaven, and hell. Reaching back to ancient instincts of nature worship, "Life on Earth" has become a new god; a god that asks for protection from the hell of industrial civilization, but promises the heaven of a pristine natural world. To expiate their guilt, its communicants must torture themselves by traveling into savage wildernesses where their god is still omnipotent.

Like any religion, environmentalism faces three problems: money, converts, and heresy. The monetary need is overwhelming in a time of big science, big government, and mass media. Environmentalism needs big money for more research, programs, lobbying, and outreach. Scientific research is the basis for most environmental programs, but Congress has always been stingy with research funding outside of medicine and the military. Only projections of wholesale disaster (preferably the deaths of millions of people) are sufficient to loosen the congressional purse strings. Like some medical researchers, environmental scientists have an unfortunate but compelling incentive to forecast disaster in their particular specialty.

The media can provide the headlines that bring contributions, converts, and congressional votes. But the modern media demand a good script, with clear heroes and villains. Scientific complexity and uncertainty have no place in a 30-second television newsbite. Media needs force environmentalism toward a script so simplified as to resemble a parody:

> "The world faces mass human death and extinction, caused by the evil triumvirate of the White House, big business, and modern technology. All environmental problems will be solved by the heroic Congress spending megabillions, controlling the evil corporations, magically catalyzing the immediate development of cheap solar power, and forcing everyone to abandon their cars, live in apartments, and eat tofu. To save the world, send money to the Heroic People's Environmental Activists."

The need for cash, converts, and congressional clout is leading environmentalism away from its original emphasis on wildlife and toward a stress on dangers to humans. Most viewer-voter-contributors have little concern for birds and bunnies, but they are terrified of cancer and chemicals. As a result, the environmental movement has shifted to fighting toxic chemicals and nuclear power, despite their relatively minor human-health impact.

The need for political coalitions is trapping environmentalism into becoming a quasi-permanent captive of the Democratic party. The Democrats were vital allies in the fight of the 1960s and 1970s for air and water pollution controls. However, this coalition has undergone some strains.

Environmentalists dare not criticize the environmentally destructive subsidy programs of their congressional allies. Yet these pork-barrel programs, forced through by Congress against opposition from both Republican and Democratic presidents, are destroying millions of acres of vital wetlands, forests and prairies. Habitat loss is many times more destructive to wildlife than are widely blamed insecticides and toxic chemicals.

The 1990s will be a watershed if either of two political realignments occurs:

- The Republicans recapture environmental moderates. Since many current wildlife issues can be solved by spending less money, this may not be difficult—except for inevitable conflicts with such strange breeds as Republican Irrigation Socialists (wealthy farmers who vote Republican and thrive on federal subsidies).

- The movement becomes radicalized. The environmentalist religion is not without its challenges from the left. Earth First! and other radical groups have opted for such life-threatening guerrilla tactics as spiking trees. In the June 15, 1987, *New Yorker,* Barry Commoner demanded that environmentalism abandon the "soft political road" and join other "movements" to enforce government control of the "technology of production." Translated from the Marxspeak, this means that environmentalism should abandon traditional democratic politics and join a left-wing activist coalition to seize control of the government and enforce total federal control of what is produced, how it is produced, and who is allowed to consume it.

CHAPTER

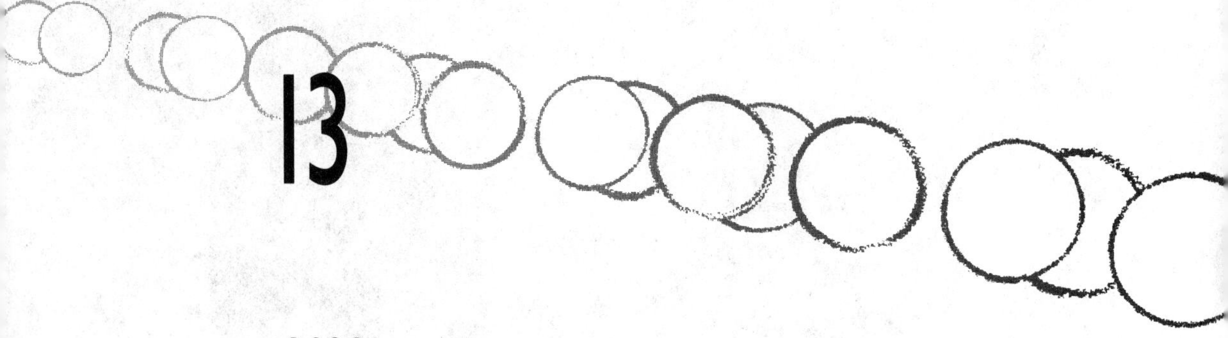

13

2020 Visions

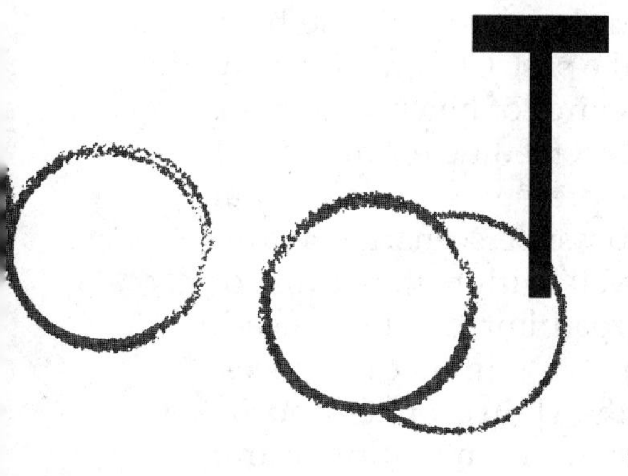

The Cold War is over. The failed Soviet Union is disintegrating, its satellites captured by the gravitational field of the West. No longer need we fear a military challenge from industrial superpowers. Regional conflicts among Third World countries, however, will be rife over the next three decades. The rapid spread of technology makes possible the acquisition of dangerous weapons of destruction by anyone who can pay for them. The industrial megastates will find themselves policing increasingly fierce regional brushfires.

Trade, finance, technology, and the media have spilled over national borders as never before. The developed world is moving remorselessly toward a new political and economic order, probably one in which three blocs led by Europe, Japan, and the United States vie for advantage. The rich, industrialized nations share a common demographic fate: aging populations and shrinking labor forces. Instability, poverty, and overpopulation will be the lot of those countries that have not yet attained political and economic maturity. Waves of Third World immigrants will arrive at the shores of the advanced countries, where they will be both welcomed and feared.

Technology, with its twin corollaries of decentralization and global integration, forces the amalgamation of national cultures into a world culture, for prolonging life and health, for dramatic rises in productivity and personal wealth. But technology also threatens to further separate haves from have-nots, both among countries and within them; to create ethical dilemmas that will make the abortion fight look easy; and to disrupt communities by forcing economic and social change faster than humans can adapt.

Of the three major blocs, a united Europe is in the strongest position politically and socially. A Japan-led Asia is an economic lion but a political coward. The United States has had the most, and the best, experience with absorption of immigrants in the past. Cultural diversity is both America's greatest strength and the source of much weakness.

The United States is unlikely to continue in a mediocre, "muddling along" phase for many more years. The pressures and internal contradictions are too great. Of the many possible scenarios, two—each representing an extreme, but each well within the realm of possibility—serve to depict the fork in the road immediately ahead. One way leads America to turn inward and stew in its own juices; the other leads to expanded ties between the United States and its near neighbors, and to a reckoning with its own multicultural destiny.

Argentina, Here We Come

Political and economic organization, not physical resources, literacy, and European culture, are the keys to the success of a modern society. Of this there is no better demonstration than the case of Argentina, which, through about the 1920s, could best have been compared with Canada and Australia. All three were modest-sized, European-style nations with low population densities and vast natural wealth. All three countries were major agricultural exporters.

Argentina does not fit into the Latin American mold. A country of some 30 million, it has not had a particularly high rate of population growth. Between 1980 and 1990, Argentina's population grew 1.3 percent a year, comparable to 0.9 percent in the United States, 1.3 percent a year in Australia, and 1.0 percent in Canada. For comparison, Guatemala's growth rate was 2.6 percent; Mexico's, 2.1 percent.

Another measure of a country's condition is life expectancy at birth, a measure in which Argentina approaches the leading industrialized countries. In the United States, it's 75 years for the population as a whole; in Argentina, 70 years; in Canada, 77. Life expectancy is only 55 years in Haiti; in Guatemala, 60.4.

In the Western Hemisphere, Argentina, Canada, Costa Rica, Uruguay, and the U.S. have overwhelmingly European populations. Argentina's native populations died out, the victims of imported diseases, while wave upon wave of immigrants, especially from Spain and Italy, arrived between 1857 and 1930. The proportion of Argentina's foreign-born population to its total population in 1914 was 30 percent, twice as high as it has ever been in the U.S.[1]

Until fairly recently, Argentina was a fast-industrializing country. By 1930, it had the seventh-largest railway system in the world.[2] By 1943, Argentina was heavily urbanized and had a large middle class; its industrial economy employed more workers than its agricultural sector. From 1853 to 1949, Argentina operated under a national constitution precisely patterned after that of the United States. The country's literacy rate is 95 percent, comparable to 96 percent in the U.S.

But by the economic measures of success and failure, Argentina has for some time given even the most disastrous Latin American countries a run for their money. Argentina is in a league by itself with respect to inflation. Since 1982, only a single year, 1985, has seen inflation running below 100 percent. In 1983–84, the rate was 626 percent. In 1989 it was 4,923 percent. In March 1990 alone, prices rose by 95.5 percent—which compounds to a meaningless 311,717 percent annually. This was not fate, but a matter of human choice. Every country chooses its own inflation rate through the political process. Prices are most likely to go up and stay up when governments promise the moon to their constituents, then either borrow without limit or coax or coerce central banks into printing more money to pay for it. Either way, the result is more cash in circulation than can be absorbed by available goods and services.

The consequences of that choice can be measured in concrete as well as abstract terms. Argentina—a literate, culturally European, physically healthy, land- and resource-rich nation—is in a tailspin. Social order is breaking down. Movie theaters are closing; begging in the streets is on the rise. Argentina's gross product per capita is declining faster than anywhere in the world; between 1980 and 1987 it dropped from $2930 to $2467, much more similar to the devastated countries of Eastern Europe than to the approximately $15,000 of the United States. Argentina has ten telephones per hundred population, compared to 76 in the U.S.

Why has the Argentinian economy declined so steeply? At the end of World War I, Argentina had per capita income comparable to

Australia, Canada, and the United States. All except the latter were hit especially hard and early by the collapse of farm and resource prices that presaged the worldwide depression of the 1930s. But Argentina's economy performed reasonably well during World War II; by the war's end, its per capita income was comparable to Australia's.

However, starting in the 1930s, Argentina had begun to close itself off from the world economy as the country's citizens grew ever more resentful of the domination of British investors and the encroachment of imported American goods on domestic industries. In 1943, bowing to economic pressures and a variety of internal social factors, Argentina succumbed to a nationalistic, protectionist, populist brand of fascism espoused by Juan Perón, a member of a military coup that overthrew the (corruptly) elected government. In the name of economic independence, Perón railed against foreign investors, nationalized industry, and subordinated all economic activity to government fiat.

It was not long before Perón assumed absolute power, which he held for an unbroken period of over twenty years. At first, Argentina's economic momentum continued, but the dictator's hostility to the productive sector of the economy eventually began to take its toll. Eventually, Perón was overthrown by a military coup. Things only got worse. From 1972 to 1974 alone, the national government's expenditures increased from 36 percent of Argentina's gross national product to 46 percent.[3] The military recalled Perón to power and then, on his death in 1974, installed his second wife, Isabel Perón, as president.

Things got so bad under Isabel Perón that the military seized power again; government spending was financed by borrowing abroad until foreign loan money dried up. The generals tried to get people to stop thinking about their economic problems by invading the Falkland Islands. That didn't work, and the economy got even worse; so the generals turned it back over to the civilians, and things got worse under the civilians, too. Today government expenditures in Argentina are running at almost 60 percent of GNP,[4] and the country is at last launching an experiment: the spinning off of its vast empire of sloppily run companies to private enterprise.

Why did the gobbling up of formerly productive enterprises continue for so long? Because, through nationalization of industries—especially foreign-owned industries—and through government guarantees of jobs in state-owned industries, politicians of all stripes can buy votes. We tend to forget that fascism can be a popular form of government.

Hitler and Mussolini were elected; Franco, who wasn't, had strong popular support. That political concept had great appeal in Latin America.

Populist transfer of wealth can be effected in several ways:

- Direct nationalization; in the nationalized sectors, hire your political supporters at any wages they want.
- Indirect nationalization; order industry to provide free health care, housing allowances, and so forth.
- Deliberate inflation, to subsidize whomever you choose at the expense of savers, primarily the middle class.
- Direct government employment in bureaucracies created to keep track of wildly proliferating regulations.
- Direct transfer payments from one class to another.

The Argentine version of fascist populism has featured nationalization of foreign interests, which happened to be mostly British; guaranteed employment at ever-higher wages in these nationalized industries as well as in the government; and inflation. This kind of system works well at first; you just grab foreign wealth, redistribute it, and assume that the productive side of the economy will keep working.

The problem is that industry's role is not just providing jobs; industry has to produce something. Even nationalized industries require investment and modernization. In Argentina, where since 1972 investment has slid from more than 20 percent of GNP to less than 10 percent,[5] production has collapsed. Argentina has learned that nothing, however redistributed, is still nothing. Cannibalism of the productive sector may assuage hunger pangs in the short run, but the ensuing indigestion is debilitating.

Argentina's demise represents the most serious decline scenario one can consider for the United States. But it is not wholly implausible. The American political system, a compromise between the rigidity of older economic and social orders and the chaos of Argentina, is closer than any other developed country to the brink of destructive populism. Modern economic pragmatism encourages the maintenance of a social and economic safety net. In all developed countries, virtually everybody is accorded an opportunity for education, some kind of minimum-income guarantee, and decent health care.

But there are many instances in the United States where government powers have been used to transfer wealth beyond the bounds of normal social programs. The use of government power simply to reward political constituencies sets a dangerous precedent. A recent textbook example of populism run amok is the case of Proposition 103, passed by referendum in California in 1988. Mandates such as California's Proposition 103 take a giant step beyond ordinary, budgeted government programs, which are limited by a natural skepticism and popular unwillingness to pay taxes.

Proposition 103, a populist proposal if there ever was one, barely carried; yet it was amazing that anyone at all voted against it, as it simply mandated—out of the thin blue air—that insurance rates were to drop by 20 percent, with no control on costs. No doubt about it: Insurance premiums in California—particularly for auto insurance—had been soaring. The insurance companies insisted they were losing money, and this was somewhat correct; they were losing money on basic underwriting, although they were making most of it back through their investments.

Proposition 103 *didn't* mandate that there be 20 percent fewer accidents, or that victims be paid 20 percent less, or that auto-body shops cut wages by 20 percent. It simply ordered a straight transfer of wealth from the insurance companies to purchasers. The proposition's passage, of course, has solved nothing. Rates are still climbing; insurance companies are threatening to yank their operations out of the state; and legal and regulatory entanglements are wrapping themselves around the protagonists like the tentacles of some obnoxious octopus.

Insurance disasters are solved by real solutions: changes in liability laws, changes in the legal system, actual cost savings, not arbitrary transfers of wealth from insurance companies to everybody else. But throughout the continuing ordeal the public's attitude remains cavalier, as expressed in interview upon interview: "This is a democracy. The people rule, and we passed this proposition. Therefore, give us our money."

We are, by design, not that kind of democracy. In ancient Athens, the birthplace of democracy, individuals could be exiled, and their property taken away, just because some majority faction didn't like them. The U.S. Constitution deliberately makes it impossible to do that. But it is tempting.

If voters can simply vote insurance rates down by 20 percent at no cost to themselves, why not vote rates down by 50 percent? If a

Mideast strongman puts a temporary stranglehold on the world's oil supplies, why not vote in propositions that punish local oil industries for raising prices? Why not enact laws that roll back gasoline prices regardless of the costs to producers? For that matter, why not vote that the price of milk be cut in half, or that we should all get free BMWs?

Another example of wealth transfer via direct controls is the movement, mainly by state governments, toward mandatory health-insurance coverage by employers. "The government can't afford it, so why not do it by mandate?" Outright nationalized health care might be more efficient than our current system; but for the government to mandate coverage by employers discards budget constraint in favor of limitless indirect taxation. From minimum health insurance, we will progress naturally to expansive health insurance. With somebody else footing the bill, why shouldn't it include psychiatric counseling, alcohol treatment, drug treatment, and the most expensive treatments the doctors can dream up. If someone invents a $5-million-dollar mechanical heart, why shouldn't everyone have one? Where's the cutoff?

Each populist program splinters the electorate into two groups: those who will benefit and those will lose. Thanks to numerous regulations and government programs, for instance, there's been an enormous transfer of wealth from the young to the old in the United States. Growth control, while a substantive issue, is also a great example of "doing well by doing good"; it tends to benefit not the elderly, but those who bought just before America's great inflation of the 1970s. Another theme now playing in the United States is the spate of new "rights": to higher education, for example, or to a job. The political temptation is for minority groups that have the greatest economic and educational troubles—and, therefore, difficulty fitting into a modern economy—to push affirmative action "guidelines" as de facto quotas in hiring and in the use of contractors and subcontractors.

How does a multi-ethnic society prevent politics from being divided along racial and ethnic lines? By having an economy that produces enough hope and progress so that the populist temptation doesn't triumph. Here lies a challenge to our educational and financial systems. In the 1950s and to an extent in the 1960s, economic progress was widespread; one's level of education made less of a difference. In fact, one of the complaints of the day was that auto workers made more than teachers. Now, with the growing dominance of knowledge industries, education is much more important than it used to be; the pay differential between an average blue-collar worker and a college graduate has more than reversed itself. Wage disparities have widened since the early 1970s, not only between higher-paying and lower-paying job categories, but within those categories themselves. The gap will continue to grow, unless steps are taken. One essential step is to make the educational system really work. Another is to make the financial system work better for small entrepreneurs. A third is to ensure that working parents—especially working couples whose second income now is mostly lost on daycare, extra health insurance, and transportation costs—receive adequate attention from the government.

Unless these improvements come, many slices of America—urban cities with increasing racial gaps; the poor, black, rural South; and Texas and Southern California, with major Hispanic concentrations—will be pushed over the populist edge. It would not be impossible for the rest of the country to follow.

That's what happened to Argentina.

Manifest Destiny Revisited

America's concept of government is unquestionably the world's leading political dream today—even if, at the moment, it has greater power beyond our borders than within them. Another vintage American dream—the doctrine of Manifest Destiny—has resurfaced recently, albeit in a new form. Briefly put, the central tenet of that doctrine, which dates to about 1835, was the inevitability of American territorial expansion throughout North America, followed by the export of American political, social, and economic influences.

The Manifest Destiny concept reached its crest at the end of the 19th century, when the United States conquered its last set of territories, the final remnants of the Spanish Empire. We still own two of those remnants, Puerto Rico and Guam. We kept Puerto Rico, too small to become independent and too poor to become a state, as an experiment. Puerto Rico is quietly turning into a success story; it is already richer than any nation in Latin America. The economic progress being made there, and its desire for statehood, ensure that Puerto Rico will become a state. Guam, a more modest success, is too tiny for full statehood but is moving toward something like it.

Our years of territorial expansion wound down with the absorption of Hawaii in 1898, Samoa in 1899, and the Virgin Islands in 1917.

However, the concept of expansion—not through acquisition, but through merger—has revived in the form of recent agreements to work toward what may become economic union with Canada, Mexico, and the Caribbean.

Table 8 shows the economic and population status of North America and the Caribbean islands. There is great disparity, from the wilderness and wealth of Canada to the tropical squalor of Haiti. However, the region uses only three languages (English, Spanish, and French), has enjoyed nearly a century of internal peace (our gunboat diplomacy in Central America excepted), and benefits from the greatest single economic asset in the world—proximity to the U.S. market. With good economic management, most of the region could catch up to current U.S. levels of wealth within thirty years.

The United States still has much to learn from Canada, the second-richest nation in the world and the best-run nation in the Western Hemisphere. Canada's health-care system, local planning, criminal-

TABLE 8 NATIONAL SUMMARY: NORTH AMERICA

	1987 Population (thousands)	1987 Life expectancy (years)	1985 Literacy rate (%)	1987 Per capita GDP* ($)	1990-2000 Annual Population growth (%)	1980-87 Annual GNP growth (%)
HAITI	6,509	55	38	775	1.6	
HONDURAS	5,286	65	59	1,119	2.6	
EL SALVADOR	5,659	64	72	1,733	2.4	
DOMINICAN REP	7,501	67	78	1,750	2.3	
GUATEMALA	9,249	63	55	1,957	2.1	
NICARAGUA	3,606	64	88	2,209	2.7	
CUBA	10,548	74	96	2,500	0.8	
JAMAICA	2,513	74	82	2,506	1.5	
TRINIDAD/TOBAGO	1,270	71	96	3,664	1.9	
COSTA RICA	3,039	75	93	3,760	2.1	
PANAMA	2,423	72	89	4,009	1.9	
MEXICO	86,888	69	90	4,624	1.8	1.2
CANADA	26,527	77	99	16,375	0.6	2.8
USA	250,372	76	96	17,615	0.7	1.8

*output adjusted to reflect actual purchasing power within each country

Sources: *Statistical Abstract of the United States*, 1989 and 1990; *Economist*, May 26, 1990.

justice system, and immigration policies are exemplary. Literacy is high; crime rates are low; life is civil. There will be no lasting trauma if French-speaking Quebec cuts itself loose politically from English-speaking Canada as long as it retains its economic ties with the other provinces, which enjoy more political autonomy than do the individual states of the U.S.

SUGAR'S BITTER HISTORICAL TASTE

Sugar has probably played a greater role in North American history than any other substance. Slaves were imported to the Caribbean to grow the immensely profitable new crop. The American colonies' commerce developed through the triangle trade: slaves to the Caribbean sugar islands, rum and molasses to the colonies, and cheap manufactures to Africa to trade for more slaves. After the French and Indian War, France traded all of Canada for the sugar islands of Martinique and Guadeloupe. The French evacuation of Canada removed an enemy from the backs of the American colonies and made our revolution possible.

In the 20th century, U.S. sugar quotas have ensured the poverty of the Caribbean, high food prices in the U.S., and the destruction of the U.S. environment. To instantly improve the Caribbean economy, all the United States would have to do is change its sugar-import laws. U.S. sugar-import quotas more than neutralize all the U.S. foreign aid ever given to the region; ending them would be worth several billion dollars per year to Central America and the Caribbean. The quotas not only force Americans to pay about three times the world price for sugar; they also encourage the growth of about 2 million acres of sugar cane and beets—crops that require gigantic subsidies to grow here. Sugar beets are mostly irrigated with scarce western water—enough to serve about 2 million families now forced to ration water and watch their landscapes die. Cane is grown especially in Florida, where water demands, pesticide use, and fertilizer runoff are catalyzing the demise of the Everglades.

To the south, virtually on our doorstep, lie the islands of the Caribbean. These island nations have very real problems. Drug lords, or more accurately their proxies, rule the Bahamas—a situation the United States views with increasing intolerance. Cuba's regime, which survives by Soviet largesse to the tune of $6 billion a year in subsidies, is not long for this world. For a vision of total economic, environmental, and political collapse, look no further than Haiti: economic decline, dictator after dictator, civil war after civil war, complete social breakdown, a near-total absence of stable marriages, an AIDS epidemic, erosion tearing apart the land.

The Caribbean island region is chopped up into economically impossible microstates. Moreover, they suffer from American discrimination against Caribbean exports. But there are bright spots. Jamaica, a democracy that is slowly putting its economy back together after a long romance with socialism, is a promising early candidate for a customs union, especially when Cuba's Castro is no longer around to destabilize the region. The Caribbean states are developing, if slowly; and they are, by and large, English speaking. It would be logical, after Puerto Rico attains statehood, for other parts of the Caribbean and the United States to form a customs union.

While a customs union will encourage trade, the real difficulty is the next step: creating a reliable legal structure, one that will encourage the massive outside investments necessary to build factories in this region, where the blessings of basic legal stability are less than universal. It would not be entirely a joke to claim that American concepts of civil law are the most valuable exports the United States could provide to this region.

Just south of our border lies Mexico, which, far from being a Caribbean microstate, is America's fourth-largest trading partner (after Canada, the European Community, and Japan). With a population of 85 million, and growing at a rate of 2 million people a year, Mexico is already larger than any European nation, even post-unification Germany. By the end of this century, Mexico will have a population of over 100 million.

The economic gap between Mexico and the United States remains huge: Mexican factory workers earn less than $2 an hour, compared with about $14.50 an hour in the U.S.[6] But even wider is the historical divide: a legacy of conflict that has made Mexico justifiably suspicious of its northern neighbor. The United States stole half of Mexico.

The United States still regularly resorts to force to assert itself in the Caribbean and Central America. It is thus understandable if, to the Mexicans, it looks like we're trying to encircle them. But it is also becoming apparent to many Mexicans that only a much closer relationship with the United States will save the country from collapse. Years of single-party rule, with its inevitable corruption and inefficiency, have taken their toll on the country's infrastructure. The roads are a disaster. The postal system barely functions. The telephone system borders on the hopeless.

CULTURES IN COLLISION

While Mexico, under Spanish rule, was expanding north, the United States came from the other direction. First the U.S. gained ownership of all territories on the northern border of Mexico in the Louisiana Purchase of 1806. Then in the 1820s, around the time of the Mexican Revolution, American settlers began to move into the territorial vacuum of Texas, California, and New Mexico. Heavy American settlement in those three areas continued through the 1840s.

American ships were now sailing into California, and the first wagon trains followed the Santa Fe Trail westward. Mexico, under both Spanish and self-rule, tried to impede trade. But the Mexican fringe settlements grew closer to the United States than to the central power in Mexico. It was much easier and much cheaper to ship from nearby Missouri across Kansas into Santa Fe than across the deserts all the way from Mexico. A natural trading relationship flourished.

In 1846, the U.S. cut a deal with the English on the Oregon territories: Oregon, Washington, and Idaho. The Mexicans claimed California and all lands drained by the Colorado. Except for California and Texas, the only Mexican settlements of any consequence were in Tucson and the Santa Fe area, conquered and settled in the 1540s by the Spanish. For trade reasons, the Americans moved in.

Two cultures clashed, and President James Polk engineered the beginning of the Mexican War. The Mexicans tried to counterattack. The American army landed at Veracruz and followed the same invasion route used by the Spaniards almost 300 years earlier, marching from Veracruz to Mexico City. There a ragtag, crazy, sick, and poorly led American army defeated a spit-and-polish Mexican army. With the territories clearly lost, their capital city occupied, and their army defeated, the Mexicans sued for peace.

We wrote the peace treaty, and got what we wanted—affirmation of the absorption of Texas, and the Mexican Cession of 1848: California, Nevada, Utah, western Colorado, all but a piece of western New Mexico, and most of Arizona—and walked away. The following 150 years have been marked by an often-bitter relationship. Although the United States may not feel that bitterness, Mexico still does. It's an important part of that country's history.

Fortunately that country is opening itself up to international commerce and pulling back from government control of the economy. Carlos Salinas de Gortari, Mexico's president, is a Harvard-trained economist who understands modern technology. He also understands the rules of modern politics: Single-party quasi-dictatorships can't survive; ruling elites have to do more than merely use government to protect their privileges. While Mexico's politics in this century have seldom obeyed those rules, 44 percent of the seats in the Mexican Parliament now belong to opposition groups of the left and right, and Baja California's governor is a member of a conservative opposition party.

For a hundred years, Mexican history was all about kicking out the American investors. Now Mexico is finally allowing American investment back in. Salinas has proposed the return of the banking system, nationalized in 1982, to the private sector. And the Mexican and American governments have agreed to negotiate a free-trade pact. The implications of mutual access to one another's markets, workers, capital, and expertise will be phenomenal.

Maquiladoras, factories in special customs zones just south of the Mexico–United States border, have already revitalized Mexico's border cities. An innovation of the late 1960s and early 1970s, the *maquiladora* exploits a loophole in American law whereby, if American components are re-imported in an assembled product, the United States taxes only the value added by the Mexican work force. The combination of American capital and Mexican workers has been able to compete successfully with the once-cheap labor of Korea and Taiwan and the still-cheap labor of Indonesia, Malaysia, and India. Populations along the Mexican side of the border are increasing. Tijuana, a center of the *maquiladora* industry, has been transformed from one of the hellholes of Mexico to one of the most-prosperous cities, demonstrating the power of openness to international investors. If legal stability continues, growth will continue.

Along with the United States, other countries are pouring capital into Mexico to take advantage of the possibility that the U.S., under a so-called Caribbean Basin initiative, might grant preferential treatment to Mexican and other Caribbean imports—the first step toward economic unity.

A North American Common Market

Raise the temperature of water at 211° by just one more degree, and the water boils. Quantitative change gives way to qualitative change. In the Western Hemisphere, economic integration is an idea whose time has come.

The United States is moving toward economic and ultimately political union that will extend at least throughout North America and the Caribbean. This integration will proceed in the following stages:

- Free trade
- Open investment policies
- Uniform currency

- Free movement of people
- Uniform commercial laws
- Coordinated foreign policy
- Full political integration

Asia's success and the lingering U.S.-Asia trade imbalance are the economic parents of the North American Common Market. Asian success has demonstrated for all the world the importance of trade, technology, and the private sector. Once-impoverished nations like Korea and Taiwan caught up to Mexico and South America in a few decades—showcasing the relative failure of Mexican-style, insular, nationalized development. (Cuba's continuing poverty is also exemplary.)

The U.S., meanwhile, has learned a different lesson: Trade with Asia is one-way. Imports from Japan, Taiwan, and Korea are not reciprocated, while North America is our best market—although a few of our most-willing North American customers have run out of money.

Throughout North America, limitations on trade and investment are disappearing. The United States has already negotiated nearly full free trade with Canada. The Caribbean possesses limited privileged access to U.S. markets. Mexico is opening up to U.S. products and investments. Thus, economic integration is already proceeding. Further steps toward a political union—a single currency, unified commercial rules, and foreign-policy coordination—will be so attractive that they should be well advanced by 2010.

The political impetus to integration stems from the long-term potential threat to U.S. security from an unstable, impoverished, radicalized Mexico and Central America. Bloody, anti-U.S. revolutions have occurred in Cuba, Guatemala, Panama, El Salvador, Puerto Rico, Nicaragua, and the Dominican Republic. Furthermore, illegal immigration to the U.S. is proving almost impossible to stop. This immigration disrupts U.S. politics, but only economic development south of the border can slow it to manageable levels.

The stickiest issue of integration will be that of free movement of people, as U.S. voters fear a jump in immigration from the poor nations of Central America and the Caribbean. By 2010, however, economic and demographic change will have diluted this fear. U.S. population growth will have slowed sharply; our labor shortage will be acute. American voters will have a stark choice: Allow more immigration, or declare the Social Security system bankrupt.

American industry will also be able to draw on inexpensive Mexican labor by building factories south of the border. As Mexican workers thus employed find decent work, migration to the United States will slow and disruption of communities on each side of the border will diminish.

Furthermore, population growth is slowing in Mexico, the Caribbean, and Central America. Since 1960, the region's growth rate has slid from nearly 3 percent to less than 2 percent. Economic development and the education of women are by far the most effective birth-control mechanisms in the world. With full economic integration, the entire region's population growth rate should be below 1 percent by 2010.

As the population issue disappears and the region's economies converge toward equality, political integration will proceed with surprising speed. The Canadian provinces, with the possible exception of Quebec, will merge with the American states. Admission of a Caribbean, Central American, or Canadian state to union with the U.S., around the year 2010, will create a bandwagon effect; everyone will want to gain commercial advantage by beating their neighbor to joining. As a political trade-off with the increasingly black-led Democratic party, the English-speaking Caribbean—Jamaica, Bahamas, Barbados, and possibly Trinidad and Belize—will be admitted at about the same time as a single, nearly all-black state, with a population of between 5 and 7 million.

The integration of the Spanish- and French-speaking nations into a predominantly English-speaking confederation will not be as difficult as it appears. By 2000, the European Community will have demonstrated how to structure a multilingual megastate confederation. Puerto Rico's admission as a Spanish-speaking state around 2000 will give the U.S. direct experience with multilingualism. Quebec's posturing vis-à-vis Canada's English provinces will ultimately be resolved amicably. By 2020 automatic translation will be a widespread technology.

The smaller Spanish-speaking Central American nations are likely to apply for Puerto Rico's present commonwealth-type status even before 2000. This will both solve their economic problems and stabilize them politically. History entitles Mexico to move slowly into political integration with its old predator, the U.S. Yet if Mexico, falling once again into the protectionist hands of a recalcitrant oligarchy, resists economic integration and its economy deteriorates, the country will face an ironic fate: the possibility of its richest, ever-more-Americanized northern states—Baja California, Chihuahua, and Sonora—seceding and joining the United States (just as Slovenia and Croatia are likely to spin off from Yugoslavia to join the European megastate confederation). It is even remotely possible that these states would be traded to the U.S. in a straight commercial exchange, in which Mexico's debt to the United States is wiped out.

The Handwriting on the Wall

The handwriting—the megastate concept demonstrated by the European Economic Community—is on the wall. France and Germany have put down their ancient enmity; we in the Western Hemisphere must do the same. The North American community will, like the European version, be multicultural.

After its economy began to outstrip population growth, West Germany brought in *gastarbeiters*, or guest workers—initially Portuguese, Spaniards, Italians, and Greeks and, later on, Bulgarians and Turks. The countries supplying those early guest workers have mostly ended up becoming incorporated into the larger European Community.

As the world—especially Europe—congeals into regional megastates, the United States can ill afford to ignore the Spanish-speaking cultures of the Western Hemisphere. North America's Hispanic population will outnumber the European population before the middle of the next century. Nor can we ignore the mostly black Caribbean microstates. If we cut ourselves off, much of the region to the south of us will follow Haiti into desperate poverty, environmental degradation, and political chaos. Our southern neighbors can't get along without us. But we need them, too. The United States in the 1990s—and, even more so, in the next century—cannot fend for itself, let alone match its competition, without new workers. And they're not going to come from Canada or Europe.

To put the choice starkly, if the economy fails to grow strongly enough to *require* immigrant workers—or if older, white Americans planning to retire after the turn of the century are unwilling to allow young foreign workers, who will be mostly brown and black, into the United States—Social Security will collapse. Without allowing more immigration, nothing like current (much less "promised") levels of real benefits can be paid, because only domestic employees pay into the Social Security Trust Fund.

The United States is thus going to become more multicultural than we've ever imagined. Hispanic-Americans will become the largest U.S. minority by early in the next century. That's why Puerto Rico, that tiny little experiment out there in the Caribbean, is so interesting: It is our first attempt at a true bilingual relationship, with the entire Caribbean, Mexico, and possibly Central America hanging in the balance.

For over 370 years, the United States has been torn by racial tension—its Achilles' heel. As a European society and culture the U.S. has been immensely successful, but its non-European populations were, until quite recently, separate and unequal, even under the law. The rising economic strength of America's non-European populations began to sap racism's potency well before these groups manifested their political muscle in the civil-rights struggle of the 1960s. America's residual race problem is now, at bottom, a cultural problem.

Mere economic poverty is easy to deal with—you simply hand out money—but social and cultural collapse is not. It is easy to tell individuals: "Go to school. Don't do drugs. If you're going to have kids, get married and *stay* married at least for a reasonable period of time, and everybody will be happy." But what do you do when whole populations don't follow these rules, or even *want* to?

The rapid ascent of a relatively new ethnic group, Asian-Americans, up the economic ladder despite racist resentment is a reaffirmation of those cultural traditions that have served this group so well: reverence for family, education, and bootstrap-entrepreneurship. It remains for this country's political system to guide the members of its self-sustaining inner-city underclass into the mainstream with pro-family government policies; a revitalized K–12 education system freed from its current bondage to geography; and strict law enforcement that places priority on safe streets, shops, and infants over headline-grabbing, Constitution-breaking busts of victimless drug users.

With respect to America's failed War on Powders of Pleasure, keeping our powder dry will also reap great financial savings, and we will need those as much as we will need immigrant labor. With a little help from our friends, the United States has proved itself the world speed champion at piling up a mountain of debt. The descent, however, will be a solo affair. Western European capital is earmarked for Eastern Europe for the foreseeable future. The aging of Japan's population, and the popping of its financial bubble, will curtail that country's underwriting of America's growing debt. We must now become a nation of savers—which is to say, when we spend money we had better spend it wisely.

The drama of Iraq and Kuwait which has seized the world's attention, in combination with fears about global warming, has reawakened American concern about energy production and consumption. The industrialized countries—the U.S. included—have become much more efficient on the consumption end since the first oil price hike in 1973. But America has yet to make full use of formidable new nuclear-power technologies and modern energy-conservation approaches.

The world has changed. America's strongest hope for competing in the new world order lies in maintaining a vibrant, mobile economy that permits skilled individuals of both genders and all races and ages to contribute and be rewarded for their contributions. The rise in the U.S. of single-issue politics, rule by referendum, and veto by litigation is undermining the republican form of government, substituting mediocrity for merit, and reinforcing political tensions instead of dissipating them.

Within the new global context, our continental nation is a small country. To remain a power, the U.S. must solve a number of economic and social problems at home. This calls for fundamentally rethinking our policies on health care, the environment, housing, education, the rights of communities vs. the rights of individuals, and, finally, the political process itself. To adopt the politics of the enclave—to shut the nation's doors to immigrants, to shut communities' doors to the workers supporting those communities, to pit the old against the young and pander to ethnic constituencies—is to travel the road that leads to Argentina.

Far better to embrace the diverse peoples across our borders and within them, to create zones of stability in which the young can be educated and the weak protected, to let technology bridge borders and cultures—to play the song of the 21st century. Performed with sufficient diligence and passion, that tune will sound quite familiar to our ears; it is, after all, an American classic.

Notes

(Far from an exhaustive list of references, these notes are intended as a guide for curious readers.)

Chapter 2

1. James D. Robinson III, "U.S. Financial Services in the Global Economy: International Competitiveness and Safety and Soundness," *Vital Speeches of the Day*, January 1, 1990.
2. Robert B. Reich, "As the World Turns," *The New Republic*, May 1, 1989.

Chapter 3

1. Martin Peretz, "Visionaries and Fantasists," *The New Republic*, May 4, 1990.
2. Richard J. Barnet, "But What About Africa?" *Harper's*, May 1990.

Chapter 4

1. Werner Faros, President, The Population Institute, "Gaining People, Losing Ground," speech to Commonwealth Club, San Francisco, California, January 26, 1990.
2. Barbara Doyle Torrey and W. Ward Kingkade, "Population Dynamics of the United States and the Soviet Union," *Science*, March 30, 1990.
3. William Pfaff, "Europe Uneasy Over Immigration," *San Francisco Chronicle*, May 29, 1990.
4. Diane Crispell, "Workers in 2000," *American Demographics*, March 1990.
5. Torrey and Kingkade, loc. cit.
6. Crispell, loc. cit.
7. Louis Menard, "Don't Think Twice," *The New Republic*, October 9, 1989.
8. Jagdish Bhagwati, "Behind the Green Card," *The New Republic*, May 14, 1990.
9. Julian L. Simon, *The Economic Consequences of Immigration* (New York: Basil Blackwell/ Cato Institute, 1989.)
10. Crispell, loc. cit.

Chapter 5

1. Joseph S. Nye Jr., "The Misleading Metaphor of Decline," *Atlantic Monthly*, March 1990.
2. Ibid.
3. Ibid.
4. Herbert Stein, "A Little S&L Budget Honesty, Please," *Wall Street Journal*, June 25, 1990.
5. Leonard Silk, "Why a Recession Should Be Feared," *San Francisco Chronicle*, August 25, 1989.
6. Alfred L. Malabre Jr., "Is the Bill Arriving for the Free Lunch?" *Wall Street Journal*, January 9, 1989.

7. Leonard Silk, "Total Cost of S&L Bailout Could Exceed $1 Trillion," *San Francisco Chronicle*, June 21, 1990.

8. Leonard Silk, "Rich-Poor Gap Gets Wider in U.S.," *San Francisco Chronicle*, May 12, 1989.

Chapter 6

1. H. M. Hubbard, "Photovoltaics Today and Tomorrow," *Science*, April 21, 1989.

2. John J. Taylor, "Improved and Safer Nuclear Power," *Science*, April 21, 1989.

3. Thomas Levenson, "Computers: At the Speed Limit," *Atlantic Monthly*, March 1990.

4. Karen Wright, "The Shape of Things to Go," *Scientific American*, May 1990.

5. Ibid.

6. Robert Wright, "Achilles' Helix," *The New Republic*, July 9 and 16, 1990.

Chapter 7

1. Joel W. Hay, Senior Fellow, Hoover Institution, "American Medicine: Should We Save Lives or Dollars?" speech to Commonwealth Club, San Francisco, March 8, 1990.

2. Harmeet K.D. Singh, "To Lower Infant Mortality Rate, Get Mothers Off Drugs," *Wall Street Journal*, May 1, 1990.

3. U.S. Department of Commerce, Bureau of the Census, *Statistical Abstract of the United States, 1990*, Washington, D.C., p. 310 and p. 314. Health care costs include direct expenses (4.5 percent), Medicare (7.5 percent), veterans (1.7 percent), tax deductions (3 percent), and others (1 percent).

Chapter 8

1. Gregg Easterbrook, "Everything You Know About the Environment Is Wrong," *The New Republic*, April 30, 1990.

2. Ibid.

3. Ibid.

4. Bruce N. Ames and Lois Swirsky Gold, "Too Many Rodent Carcinogens: Mitogenesis Increases Mutagenesis," *Science*, August 31, 1990.

Chapter 9

1. N. Gregory Mankiw and David N. Weil, "The Baby Boom, the Baby Bust, and the Housing Market," *Regional Science and Urban Economics*, No. 19, 1989.

Chapter 10

1. U.S. Department of Commerce, Bureau of the Census, *Statistical Abstract of the United States, 1990*, Washington, D.C., p. 839. The U.S. spent 6.7 percent of GNP on education vs. West Germany's 4.4 percent. The U.S. has a 20 percent higher per capita GNP and 40 percent more children per capita than West Germany.

2. Karl Zinsmeister, "Growing Up Scared," *Atlantic Monthly*, June 1990.

3. Ibid.
4. Lewis J. Perelman, *The 'Acanemia' Deception*, (Indianapolis: Hudson Institute, 1990).

Chapter 11

1. Zinsmeister, loc. cit.
2. Benjamin K. Hunnicutt, "No Time for God or Family," *Wall Street Journal*, January 4, 1990.
3. Editorial, *The New Republic*, June 4, 1990.
4. Zinsmeister, loc. cit.
5. Ibid.
6. Charles Murray, "How to Win the War on Drugs," *The New Republic*, May 21, 1990.
7. Ethan Nadelmann, "Drug Prohibition in the United States: Costs, Consequences, and Alternatives," *Science*, September 1, 1989.
8. Ibid.
9. Ibid.
10. Ibid.
11. Peter Reuter et al., Money From Crime: The Economics of Drug Dealing (Santa Monica, California: Rand Corporation Drug Policy Research Center, July 1990).

Chapter 13

1. Arthur P. Whitaker, *The United States and Argentina*, (Cambridge, Massachusetts: Harvard University Press, 1954).
2. Ibid.
3. Armando P. Ribas, "Argentina's Monetary Tango," *Wall Street Journal*, February 16, 1990.
4. Ibid.
5. Ibid.
6. Rudiger Dornbusch, "Why U.S., Mexico Need a Trade Pact," *San Francisco Chronicle*, June 20, 1990.

Richard Carlson is a business economist, futurist, and president of Spectrum Economics Inc., headquartered in Mountain View, California. His 25-year career has spanned the public and private sectors. His list of clients includes Shell Oil, ARCO, Hitachi, Applied Materials, Time-Warner, Edison Electric Institute, Blue Shield of California, the French Ministry of Industry and Research, the Chinese Office of Science and Technology, and numerous government agencies.

Carlson received his undergraduate degree in economics at Harvard College and did graduate work in economics at the University of Maryland and Stanford. He worked as a policy analyst on education issues in the Executive Office of the President in the Johnson and Nixon administrations, and was a member of the 1968 Interagency Task Force on Early Childhood Education. From 1973 through 1975 he was assistant director of the Illinois Bureau of the Budget. In 1976, Carlson became senior regional economist at Stanford Research Institute (SRI International), where he authored *Solar Energy in America's Future; The West: Harbinger of Change*; and *Managing the Changing Workforce*. Between 1984 and 1988 he led a team of consulting economists in the multi-billion dollar Washington Public Power Supply System litigation. In 1988 he formed Spectrum Economics.

Carlson's current projects include analyzing the economic impacts of proposed air quality rules, forecasting Bay Area housing prices, forecasting demographic and economic change in California's Central Valley, and reviewing the impacts of California's proposed Environmental Initiative. He is often asked to speak on strategic planning, marketing, and forecasting to business and government groups. He frequently appears as an expert witness.

Carlson lives with his family in Palo Alto, and canoes, skis, backpacks, and windsurfs in his spare time.

Kathryn J. MacDonald

Bruce Goldman is editor and manager of the Portable Stanford Book Series. His articles on subjects ranging from medicine to real estate, literature, and biotechnology have appeared in the *Miami Herald, San Francisco Examiner, San Francisco Chronicle, San Jose Mercury News, San Francisco Focus, In Health* (formerly *Hippocrates*), *Harvard Medical School Health Letter*, and *Genetic Engineering News*. He has written about poetry, education, drug addiction, superconductors, the Iran-Contra scandal, novelist Ken Kesey, and UFOs for *Stanford Magazine*.

After graduating with a bachelor's degree in philosophy from the University of Wisconsin in 1969, Goldman taught inner-city students in the Milwaukee Public School System, then wrote advertising copy for a department store chain in Boston. In early 1972 he left to travel extensively throughout Europe and Asia, managing to drive a car from Athens to Kabul, Afghanistan, and continue his overland journey as far as Nepal before returning at the year's end. For most of the next four years he was a letter carrier for the U.S. Postal Service in Boulder, Colorado. In 1977, Goldman enrolled at the University of Colorado; he graduated in 1981 with top honors in engineering physics. From then through 1984 he was a National Science Foundation graduate fellow at Harvard University, where in 1983 he received a master's degree in cell biology and won an award for excellence in his teaching of undergraduates.

Goldman's career with the Stanford Alumni Association dates to early 1985, when he joined the staff of *Stanford Magazine* as assistant editor. He was promoted to associate editor in late 1986. In early 1988 he became editor of the flagship magazine of the Bechtel Group, a San Francisco-based engineering firm. In late 1989 he returned to the SAA to assume his present post.

Goldman, who lives in San Francisco, is married and has a baby daughter. His hobbies include songwriting, travel, and moviegoing (lately curtailed).

Series Editor and Manager: Bruce Goldman
Production Manager: Amy Pilkington
Cover Illustrator: Andrzej Dudzinski

The Portable Stanford Book Series

This is a volume of the Portable Stanford Book Series, published by the Stanford Alumni Association. Subscribers receive each new Portable Stanford volume on approval. The following books may also be ordered, by number, on the adjoining card:

$10.95 titles

- *2020 Visions: Long View of a Changing World* by Richard Carlson and Bruce Goldman (#4055)
- *"What Is to Be Done?" Soviets at the Edge* by John G. Gurley (#4056)
- *Notable or Notorious? A Gallery of Parisians* by Gordon Wright (#4052)
- *This Boy's Life* by Tobias Wolff (#4050)
- *Ride the Tiger to the Mountain: T'ai Chi for Health* by Martin and Emily Lee and JoAn Johnstone (#4047)
- *Alpha and Omega: Ethics at the Frontiers of Life and Death* by Ernlé W.D. Young (#4046)
- *Conceptual Blockbusting* (3rd edition) by James L. Adams (#4007)

$9.95 titles

- *In My Father's House: Tales of an Unconformable Man* by Nancy Huddleston Packer (#4040)
- *The Imperfect Art: Reflections on Jazz and Modern Culture* by Ted Gioia (#4048)
- *Yangtze: Nature, History, and the River* by Lyman P. Van Slyke (#4043)
- *The Eagle and the Rising Sun: America and Japan in the Twentieth Century* by John K. Emmerson and Harrison M. Holland (#4044)
- *The Care and Feeding of Ideas* by James L. Adams (#4042)
- *The American Way of Life Need Not Be Hazardous to Your Health* (Revised Edition) by John W. Farquhar, M.D. (#4018)
- *Cory Aquino and the People of the Philippines* by Claude A. Buss (#4041)
- *50: Midlife in Perspective* by Herant Katchadourian, M.D. (#4038)
- *Under the Gun: Nuclear Weapons and the Superpowers* by Coit D. Blacker (#4039)
- *Wide Awake at 3:00 A.M.: By Choice or By Chance?* by Richard M. Coleman (#4036)
- *Hormones: The Messengers of Life* by Lawrence Crapo, M.D. (#4035)
- *Panic: Facing Fears, Phobias, and Anxiety* by Stewart Agras, M.D. (#4034)
- *Who Controls Our Schools? American Values in Conflict* by Michael W. Kirst (#4033)
- *Matters of Life and Death: Risks vs. Benefits of Medical Care* by Eugene D. Robin, M.D. (#4032)

$8.95 titles

- *Terra Non Firma: Understanding and Preparing for Earthquakes* by James M. Gere and Haresh C. Shah (#4030)
- *On Nineteen Eighty-Four* edited by Peter Stansky (#4031)
- *The Musical Experience: Sound, Movement, and Arrival* by Leonard G. Ratner (#4029)
- *Challenges to Communism* by John G. Gurley (#4028)
- *Cosmic Horizons: Understanding the Universe* by Robert V. Wagoner and Donald W. Goldsmith (#4027)
- *Beyond the Turning Point: The U.S. Economy in the 1980s* by Ezra Solomon (#4026)
- *The Age of Television* by Martin Esslin (#4025)
- *Insiders and Outliers: A Procession of Frenchmen* by Gordon Wright (#4024)
- *Mirror and Mirage: Fiction by Nineteen* by Albert J. Guerard (#4023)
- *The Touch of Time: Myth, Memory, and the Self* by Albert J. Guerard (#4022)
- *The Politics of Contraception* by Carl Djerassi (#4020)
- *Economic Policy Beyond the Headlines* by George P. Shultz and Kenneth W. Dam (#4017)
- *Tales of an Old Ocean* by Tjeerd van Andel (#4016)
- *Law Without Lawyers: A Comparative View of Law in China and the United States* by Victor H. Li (#4015)
- *The World That Could Be* by Robert C. North (#4014)
- *America: The View from Europe* by J. Martin Evans (#4013)
- *An Incomplete Guide to the Future* by Willis W. Harman (#4012)
- *Murder and Madness* by Donald T. Lunde, M.D. (#4010)
- *The Anxious Economy* by Ezra Solomon (#4009)
- *The Galactic Club: Intelligent Life in Outer Space* by Ronald Bracewell (#4008)
- *Is Man Incomprehensible to Man?* by Philip H. Rhinelander (#4005)
- *Some Must Watch While Some Must Sleep* by William E. Dement, M.D. (#4003)
- *Human Sexuality: Sense and Nonsense* by Herant Katchadourian, M.D. (#4002)